D1279036

KEEPERS

ALSO BY BOBBY JACK NELSON

The Last Station

Brothers

The Pull

KEEPERS

A Memoir

BOBBY JACK NELSON

W. W. Norton & Company

New York   London

To protect their privacy, the names and identities of some
individuals in this memoir have been changed.

Copyright © 1998 by Bobby Jack Nelson

A slightly different version of the first chapter of *Keepers*
originally appeared in *Harper's* magazine

For information about permission to reproduce selections
from this book, write to Permissions, W. W. Norton &
Company, Inc., 500 Fifth Avenue, New York, NY 10110.

The text and the display of this book are composed in
Centaur.
Composition by Justine Burkat Trubey
Manufacturing by the Haddon Craftsmen, Inc.
Book design by Judith Stagnitto Abbate

Library of Congress Cataloging-in-Publication Data
  Nelson, Bobby Jack.
  Keepers : a memoir / by Bobby Jack Nelson.
     p. cm.
  ISBN 0-393-04597-8
  I. Nelson, Bobby Jack—Biography. 2. Authors,
American—20th century—Biography. I. Title.
PS3564.E45Z465 1998
813'.54—dc21
[B]   97-26817
                                                  CIP

W. W. Norton & Company, Inc., 500 Fifth Avenue,
New York, N.Y. 10110
http://www.wwnorton.com

W. W. Norton & Company Ltd., 10 Coptic Street,
London WC1A 1PU

In the general waste of living, a few things are lasting—the first love, the lost child, the turning point—those are keepers.

—BJN

KEEPERS

MARIE WANTED TO DIE. She'd been wanting to most of her life, I think, and wasn't it time? She was asking me. She'd been thinking about how to kill herself for months, years, especially the last few weeks. Or, rather, she knew how she was going to kill herself, she was simply focusing more on when. She was eighty and a couple of her teeth had recently fallen out, her stomach was swollen, food made her sick, and she was in pain all over, the worst pain she'd ever had, she said, though every pain her whole life was always the worst. Over the years, the hundreds of times she was sick, each time she was "deathly sick." Each pain for decades had been "the most horrible pain" she'd ever felt. You never knew. She'd turn the least matter into melodrama, managing her life neurotically, even from the beginning I've come to believe, by pretending, by living the world of pretense. If she told you the truth of a certain situation, you would find out later little really happened the way she said.

Anyway, she might as well just go on and get it over with, didn't I think so, too? I told her that sort of thing had to be up to her. But didn't I think she might as well? What did she have to live for? She had terrible noise in her ears and couldn't hear, she'd disconnected her phone, no one called anyway, she had no friends. She had lived for fifteen years as an almost total recluse, and other than a son she hadn't heard from in thirty years and a sister she hated, there was only me. She couldn't see her soap operas except as a blur, she was shaky, trembly, she got out of breath walking from her room to the front of the house, so before becoming too helpless, while she could still manage, wasn't it time?

She hadn't bathed or showered in a couple of years, I think. She couldn't lift her legs enough to step in and out of the tub. She sponged off, she said, but she was still able to go to the toilet on her own, she was still feeding herself, only lately oatmeal, buttered bread, a little yogurt was all, anything else in the past weeks made her vomit, and she was weak and getting weaker. "No, I'm not going to the doctor," she said. "I know what he'd do, he'd put me in the hospital and I'd be kept alive for no reason or left in a nursing home and I don't want that. I want to lay down right here in my own bed and go to sleep and not wake up. You don't know how many times I've prayed I wouldn't wake up, every night I go to sleep praying, dear God, please just let me die and not wake up. If I was needed, but I'm not and you wouldn't be stuck here if it wasn't for me, so I'm going to do it. But I can't by myself, you'll have to help me."

This was Wednesday noon. She was going to take pills. Years before she'd saved a stash of pills for the purpose, but when she couldn't afford new medicine one year, she'd used the stash instead. Recently, though, she'd gotten a prescription for a hundred Xanax, a sedative. I called in the order for her and picked it up from the drugstore an hour later, a regular brownish cylinder of pills with a white cap. Marie said she was going to take them that night about eleven or eleven-thirty, when it was her usual bedtime and it was quiet and peaceful. I didn't know whether she would or not. She had talked suicide too often. But the pills would put her right to sleep. All I'd have to do then was slip a bag over her head and wrap it airtight around her neck with a scarf. Not rubber bands. They might leave telltale lines. She showed me the small plastic trash bag and the blue silky scarf she had. She'd already tried the bag on to be sure it wasn't too big. She said it wasn't. A large bag would retain too much air and take longer. She'd read that in a book from the Hemlock Society. She gave me the bag and scarf. "Now you just go on about your business," she said. "Tonight when I'm ready I'll call you."

I went to my room and tried to think. If this was for real, if this time she was actually going to do it, was there anything I needed to consider? Feelings, emotions? No. My feelings for Marie were fairly reconciled. She was my mother, I came into this world out of her body, or the physical me did, so there was that kind of blood bond, but I didn't like her as a person, I was ashamed of her as a mother, I wouldn't miss her. How about details? Maybe I should check the bag. In a kind of gruesome test I slipped the bag over my head for size. Okay. But it covered my head only barely to my neck. I could see the scarf not quite wrapping enough of the bag to completely cut off air and the final act getting messy. Marie would struggle, even zonked on Xanax, she would be clawing the thing to get free, to breathe. The Hemlock book said that normally happened and I could see myself trying to hold her hands down, or maybe frozen, just standing there watching. If she scratched herself or I bruised her somehow trying to keep her suffocated, that might look bad to a coroner. It might look like murder. And to some degree, it would be. The word hung in my mind. Murder. The vague image had no depth. The word itself, pronounced, had no resonance. Just the same, no matter how sick and sad and miserable a person is, you're helping to kill a human life. A sharper word, kill. And in this instance, if it came about, I would be helping to kill my own mother. Could I do it? More precisely, at the last moment, would I do it?

I drove to town and got a box of slightly larger plastic bags. If it was going to be done, the bag should be the right size, not too small. The last act should go smoothly and not with a struggle, not with my hands fighting hers, the meanness of that. But it'll be okay, I thought. I stopped at a liquor store and got a bottle of vodka. Might need something to fuzz the edges, I thought. Afterwards, it would be my first drink in months.

It was now about three in the afternoon. I tapped at Marie's door and went in. A rare visit. I'd been in her room perhaps three times in two years. She was sitting in her chair watching TV, her daily soap operas. For the past two and a half years I'd provided this place for her in my house, a largish room perhaps 20 × 20, also a sort of efficiency setup with cooking facilities, a refrigerator, an adjoining bath. In this one room she stayed alone and kept to herself and never left the house. She'd leave a list for groceries and medicine along with a signed check on the kitchen table and I would shop for her. Her social security was just enough to pay for what she needed. She'd show me her bank statement at the end of every month with only five or ten dollars left in her account. When we talked it was usually for less than a minute when she was in the kitchen and I also happened to go there. But it wouldn't be a conversation. She might ask my opinion on the weather or some TV news item. Typically she'd say, "Do you think it's going to rain today?" I'd start to answer, "Well, no, I think—" She'd immediately interrupt to disagree. And invariably it was to disagree, to disparage, to give air to unhappiness. "That's what the weatherman says, but they don't know. They said it was going to rain yesterday, there wasn't a cloud in the sky. I don't think they have any idea what the weather's going to be. I was going to make a salad but I don't want to, I just don't have the interest. Nothing I fix tastes good anyway. I made a stew yesterday, it was like slop, I had to throw it all out. The arthritis in my hand is so bad, I took four of those pain pills, they didn't help a bit, I don't know what I'm going to do. I was going to make some macaroni and cheese but I don't even want that now. Those ratty kids next door were playing so loud, hollering and carrying on, I couldn't hear myself think. I wish that family'd move away, they're nothing but white trash. I saw the woman out in her yard yesterday wearing shorts, with big ol' fat legs, I'd be ashamed. . . ." She would talk like that forever if I would listen. I'd pretend to for about a minute, then simply walk away. She would still be complaining, mouthing negatives. If she began with a good word, her next word would qualify it and she'd end up carping. She didn't like herself, or more, she hated herself, and the way it showed was depressing.

Now I stood in her room. "How 'bout a visit?" I said. She got up from her chair. "Here, sit down." "That's all right," I said. She only had the one chair. "No, no, you sit here, I'll sit on the bed, I need to move anyway." She sat on the edge of her bed and I sat in the chair facing her. The room was dirty and cluttered. I'd offered to vacuum her carpet but she said the noise drove her crazy. She didn't want me moving things around in her room either. I told her she didn't have to hear the noise, she could wait in the living room, but it was too bothersome. Just leave it, I'll do it, she said. And never did. The carpet was spotted and matted where she'd spilled food. "Well," I said, and that was all. She started talking. "It's going to be all right," she said, "don't you worry." She was decided. It was time. She was sick and it was probably a consumptive heart condition, that's what her father died of, and with that you don't get better, you just get worse. She'd read up on the symptoms in her medical book where it starts with a shortness of breath and your stomach, you can't keep food down, and that's what was happening to her. Then it affected your kidneys and liver, they turned to mush, you became bedridden and couldn't go to the bathroom or feed yourself, you couldn't eat anything anyway and you'd just lay there in agony and finally die. So she was ready. "Now, one thing I want you to do," she said, "I don't want you to tell Frances, or wait till you've gotten rid of all my stuff, 'cause she'll just be over here in a minute picking through all my clothes and taking everything and I don't want her to have anything. Promise you won't tell her. Or I don't care, do what you want, but I'm telling you, I know how she'll do, you don't know how selfish she is." And so on, how Frances, her sister, had always taken and not given and had plenty of money and could afford to buy a new car every year and everything else she wanted. Marie went on with her resentments against her sister, with no forgiveness. About my brother and me she said she wished she'd made a home for us, that she knew she'd messed us up, especially Billy, she knew he'd been the most hurt, but it was too late now, she couldn't go back and change what happened, and she'd already cried herself out, she hadn't cried tears now in years. She'd made a mess of her life, too, but she couldn't change that either.

I'd heard it all before many times, the regrets, the bad times. I kept hoping she would finally declare some peace of mind or settled spirit. She didn't. I tried to remember some good moments we'd had together, some fun times I could mention and we could end with easier feelings. I couldn't think of one specific time. She probably loved me the best she could, but if there was a time when I was small that she hugged me, that I felt the warmth of a mother's embrace, I couldn't remember that either. So I sat while she talked. She had lived a lifetime. I was seeing her span of time before me. But at the ending of a life, after eighty years of awareness, hopes, desires, after only one chance at this world as we know it, shouldn't there be a final comprehension, a summing-up, a point at least for having been? You live, what for? I wanted her to say what living had meant to her, but she was talking incidentals. Her extra glasses, they were good prescription glasses someone might could use, don't throw those away. She had put a clean cover on the bed and she was going to dress in a nice clean gown. Should she wash her hair? No, she didn't need to. I could donate her clothes to charity or just burn them but don't let her sister have any. Marie had already thrown away a bunch of junk and straightened the room all she could. Straightening tired her out. She said to tell Billy she was sorry but she couldn't go back and make things different, and me, well, I could handle this, couldn't I? I told her truthfully I didn't know. But she knew, she said, because I was always able to handle whatever came along, I never let problems bother me, did I? Except problems are problems, I said. But she knew, I could help her die, I wouldn't let it bother me. She was sorry she didn't stick with my father but she just couldn't, she'd wanted to have fun, and then her life became such a mess, she never intended to leave us kids, she married other men so she could have a home for us but it never worked out, she never got what she wanted, which was just to be happy and for us kids to be happy, but she couldn't help any of that now, she couldn't go back, she was just sorry about this and that and so on. She spoke as usual remorsefully, self-pityingly, but not exactly bitterly. It was as if she recited by rote and she talked as she always had. Things happened, she could have done differently, but it wasn't always her fault either, but then it was always too late. After the fact, it was always too late. She voiced no new insight, no particular understanding. I felt depressed, and after about an hour I got up. I'd be back later, I said, we could talk more then. Well, don't worry about me, she said, I'll call you when I'm ready, about eleven o'clock.

I went to my room and tried to read. It was five o'clock and I began to feel it was going to be a long night. She wouldn't do it, or she would fake it. She was involving me once again in another one of her emotional dramas. I might have to call the EMS. She was only going to become more disoriented, more helpless. I should probably start thinking about placing her in a nursing home.

At six-thirty she was at my door. "I can't think about it anymore," she said. "I want to just go on and do it, is that all right with you?" "If you're ready," I said. "Well, I'm ready, I keep sitting back there thinking about it. Now you've got the bag? And the scarf, don't forget the scarf." "They're right here," I said. "All right, let's get it over with."

We walked through the kitchen, she was hobbling feebly. I asked her if she'd eaten. "Not since this morning, I'm afraid I'll throw up." "But shouldn't you have something on your stomach, to keep the pills down? How about a little buttered toast?" "I don't know, not buttered, maybe just a piece of dry toast." I put a slice of bread in the toaster and followed her into her room. She sat on the edge of her bed. "Now here's what I'm going to take," she said. A couple of pill bottles on her bedside table. "This one's fifty Wygesic, they're my pain pills, they might help. These are Xanax, the ones you got today, and I had some more. There's a hundred and thirty-eight altogether. That ought to do it if I don't get too drowsy and fall asleep before I can take them all." "You're going to take a hundred and thirty-eight pills?" "If I can get them down. And the Wygesic, too, if I can swallow enough water. I've got a pitcherful over there. You'll have to get that for me." She was opening the pill bottles. I felt numb. "Wait a minute," I said. I brought the toast from the kitchen on a napkin. "Get this on your stomach first." She forced herself to chew several bites slowly, sipping also at a glass of water. She ate about half the toast, then immediately poured a few pills into her hand and swallowed them with water. She took another handful and another, one after the other as if on automatic. She was concentrating solely on what she was doing and not looking beyond her hands. Then her glass was empty. "More water, more water!" Almost panicky. I got the pitcher and poured her a glass. "Hey, go slower," I said, "take your time." "I don't want to fall asleep before I get them down." "It's okay—okay? Take it easy." She drew a breath and downed several more pills. She took off her glasses and laid them on the table. "Don't throw those away, they're good prescriptions, somebody can use them." She swallowed more pills. I was only sitting in front of her, watching, and a terrible feeling came over me, a weight of darkness. Here was this old lonely woman actually going to die, killing herself. This was the last moment she would ever know, a worthless measly last moment in a dismal cluttered room. She would never again see the two squirrels in the tree outside her window. Or the sky, the sun, the rain. This earth, this great beautiful earth around her would be no more. She was going to die, and I had no words for what I felt except pity. Poor old woman. "Marie," I said, "let me hug you." I stood and leaned down to put my arms around her shoulders, my cheek against hers. I think she sort of patted my arm. "I love you," I said. "I love you, too," she said. I sat back in the chair. It was the first time I'd hugged her in years, and even in those years a quick hug was a mere politeness. This time was almost the same. It had not been exactly awkward but neither had it felt natural. My words, I love you, had been what, perfunctory? Hers to me had sounded the same. There had been no clutch of emotion. She immediately went back to taking her pills, hurriedly, several at a time, one swallow after another, downing them with water. I filled her glass three times. She never looked up. We didn't speak.

Then she did. "Well, that's it." She had swallowed 138 Xanax and twenty or so Wygesic. She started to lie back on her pillow and stopped. "Turn your back. I'm going to put a towel between my legs. The book said people lose their bowels when they're going and I don't want to make a mess." I turned my head. When I looked again, she was lying on her back, the end of a towel showed at her knees. She had folded her hands on her stomach. "Now I'm going to count," she said. "That's what I do to put myself to sleep. I read that once and it works. I start at a hundred and count backwards, I never get to one. I can get to twenty, fifteen sometimes, then I'm always asleep." She closed her eyes and started counting in a normal voice, "Ninety-nine . . . ninety-eight . . . ninety-seven . . ." She counted as if by seconds, steadily, correctly. At eighty-five, her count had slowed. She was several seconds between numbers. After eighty, she said seventy-eight, paused at length, picked up the skipped seventy-nine and continued with seventy-eight, but more slowly. Her words were slurring. At sixty-six I thought she was asleep. She'd stopped counting. Finally she managed to repeat sixty-six and that was it. She was breathing deeply and snoring intermittently with her mouth slightly open.

It was seven o'clock and beginning to get dark outside. I closed the curtains, feeling guilty that I hadn't closed them earlier. Then I didn't know how long to wait or if I should wait at all. I watched Marie breathing. If I touched her, or shook her, would it rouse her? The Xanax might not have worked. She might suddenly wake. Or how long would it take before she was so absolutely doped there would be no chance she could be awakened? I imagined the moment I started to put the bag over her head, she would open her eyes. I waited perhaps fifteen minutes, went to my room for the bag and scarf, and came back. She had not moved. Her mouth was still slightly open, she was breathing the same and softly snoring, her hands at rest on her stomach. I lifted one of her hands and it fell back. I nudged her shoulder. No reaction. I called her name, then louder, and shook her. She showed no response. I walked through the house to shut the blinds and lock the doors. I took the phone off the receiver. If anyone knocked or called, I wouldn't be home. Did I need to think of anything else? I couldn't think.

The bag was not a difficulty. I lifted her head from the pillow and slipped the plastic easily over in a single movement. I did it as gently as I could and felt no weight in her head at all. Her neck was limber, entirely relaxed. Lifting her head again, I overlapped the loose ends of the bag and wrapped the scarf evenly twice around. But not tightly. I felt an odd tenderness and sadness. Poor Marie, I thought, your whole life so damned unhappy. I felt sorry for her. I snugged at the scarf to be sure it was trapping the air.

I stood over her and watched the bag filling and being drawn back against the outlines of her face, and for a time there was nothing else. Her breathing appeared easy but soon it was slightly harder and the bag was being sucked tighter at her mouth. Her hands barely started to lift and I stopped them. She didn't struggle. Her hands didn't resist mine and she didn't strain or move otherwise. There was no strength or force in her. She was only breathing harder and lying completely still. Then she quietly stopped breathing. I waited. In another moment, her chin tucked, she almost drew a half breath, that was all. The bag was collapsed and molded against her face. Her body had not convulsed or shuddered. There was no sudden absence in the room. It seemed only that she was no longer entirely present. She might have still been alive. I felt a faint pulse at her wrist and under my palm on her chest a bare tremor of heartbeat. I wasn't sure. I know now it was my own blood pulsing at the end of my fingers. But I needed to be sure so I waited. Perhaps five minutes. She remained absolutely inert. I loosed the scarf and pulled the bag from her head. She had died at seven twenty-five in the evening, April 19, 1995. The big news that day was the bombing of the Federal Building in Oklahoma City.

I sat beside her another hour. The lines in her face were gone. It was a smoothed face and didn't look quite like the Marie I remembered. Her mouth was still ajar. She had been a dirt-poor country girl, her parents sharecroppers from Alabama, moved to Texas. She claimed she graduated from high school, I think maybe she got to the tenth grade. She was a big girl, five-ten, a little hefty. Not a bad face. Her face had been attractive. She had nice teeth, an appealing feature. Growing up, she'd worked in the fields like a man. When she was seventeen, she met my father, who was twenty. He'd quit school and had a job shining shoes at a barbershop. This was during the depression. Marie would walk by the barbershop going home from school and flirt with Charlie, the twenty-year-old shineboy. They went to the movies together and kissed. She'd never had a boyfriend. Charlie had never had a girlfriend. He was shorter than Marie and an introvert, a repressed soul. She was more outgoing, at least a girl who wanted to have fun. So they got married, each having no other choice. Charlie's mother had been domineering, and guess what, Marie was too. She married Charlie, she said, to get away from home. She had my brother and me by the time she was nineteen. Charlie worked as a farmhand, at a service station, a canning factory, and finally as a postal clerk, a lasting better job than he'd ever hoped to expect. It offered security, a steady income. They made a down payment on a $1,400 house and bought furniture on credit from a mail-order catalog. When the war came along the world was turned upside down and soldierboys were everywhere. It was an exciting time. The world might end tomorrow. That's when Marie decided to join the war effort, so to speak. She left her husband and kids and went off to frolic with the soldiers. She became a waitress in small-town cafes. She married six times, well, seven, if you count the one she married twice, the one who regularly beat her. Billy and I lived mostly with grandparents. We would see Marie in the summers or she would appear occasionally with small meaningless presents and play like everybody was happy.

It's probably not possible but I've tried to understand Marie beyond my personal resentments. What kind of person was she? The word unfortunate comes to mind. Not tragic. To rise to that level, you'd think a person needs first to aspire to something worthwhile. Marie's most articulate aspiration was "just to be happy, that's all I ever wanted." That was her litany. She never learned happiness is a matter of degree, not a permanent condition. Or she may have pretended to happiness because she knew it was nowhere, an impossibility for her, and by never finding it, she essentially confirmed her self-image that she didn't deserve to be happy. She didn't like herself for whatever reason and that predetermined every relationship, every dead-end path she took. It may well be that simple. She never understood herself, or if she did, some truths were too hard to face. We all know this. We all bury some truth about ourself so deeply it can never be seen again.

Anyway, early on, Marie began to live in a world of pretense. Maybe we all do. The void all around is so immense, and we're so tiny, if we're scared, if we're not gritty enough to stand against defeat, maybe pretense is a way to survive. It's also a way to get lost. And I believe that's what happened to Marie. She pretended, she rationalized, she assumed a protective lie and became lost in a life that never happened. Except for the fall-out.

To hear her tell it, most of her life was occupied with "getting a man." "I always had to have a man," she said. If she could attract a man, if she could get a man to want her, that had to mean she had some value, didn't it? On the other hand, by being so easy any man could screw her and did—screwing is what she called it—didn't that really prove she was of the least value, a throwaway? Being little more than a fuck is being little more than faceless. Not surprisingly, when a man married her, she was immediately contemptuous of him. No doubt in her mind any man who would marry the likes of her had to be worthless, too. Of course, she only married men she could dominate, my father first, then the others. I was present at times when she browbeat three different husbands and they took it. But Marie would also pretend her husbands were other than they were. She said her third husband was an air force pilot. He wasn't. He was an enlisted man. Her fourth husband worked in a paint and body shop but she said he was going to inherit a fortune, that his parents owned thousands of acres of prime wheatland. They didn't. They farmed about two hundred acres of which each of their five sons and daughters might one day be allowed a portion. Marie said her sixth husband was part owner, a partner, in a big construction firm. He was an employee. Her seventh she said was a doctor, he knew a lot of medical terms. He turned out to be a nurse's aide. When Marie was no longer a waitress but a frycook, she claimed to be a dietitian. She told each husband she'd only been married once, to my father, and that he'd died, he hadn't, but that made her a widow, not a multiple divorcée. She also told each husband she was a few years younger than she really was.

Was she smart? She never learned, she kept repeating the same mistakes, which may have been compulsive, but I believe she was at least averagely intelligent, not much more. She didn't read books, even trashy ones. Or I take that back. She read my novels and said she liked them, but she wished I would write a happy book, my stories were so sad. She had no idea what I was about. She read magazines, the *Ladies' Home Journal* type, and the tabloids. She read five of those every week. She watched soap operas and game shows on TV. She worked simple crossword puzzles and played solitaire. She never had a friend, never another woman as a friend, and men were never friends, only men she screwed. So what kind of person is it who never, never once in their life, has a real friend? Marie started out to befriend two nieces once, then abruptly and maliciously alienated them. She alienated her sister, her two sons, every husband, and in the end, at sixty-five, when her last husband died and she could no longer "get a man," she became a recluse. And it wasn't so much she didn't want to see people, she didn't want people to see her. She hated seeing herself.

In her last years her flesh was globs of shapeless clabbered fat. She was no longer five-ten but about five-seven and half blind and deaf. She had no outside interests. She had no property, no money. One house she had after a divorce, she simply lived in without making the mortgage payments until the bank foreclosed, and she could've made the monthly payment, it was less than rent would have been. She had a clear title to her last house when she was sixty-five. She simply gave it away to a thirty-six-year-old Cuban who "promised to take care of her." She also gave him $12,000 cash, the sum from her late husband's life insurance, and signed over the title to her car. Why? I think it wasn't so much the man conned her as she very calculatingly tried to buy him. She couldn't and probably knew she couldn't but it was her last chance "to get a man." It was typically self-defeating and she was left with nothing, the one thing she must have felt she deserved.

So she'd finally come to the end. She didn't have a religious faith or a belief in God. She pretended she did, she talked a lot about praying, but what she said she really believed was in nothing beyond this life. When it was over, that was it, a complete stop. Now she was lying on her back in a casket position, her eyes closed, her hands folded on her stomach. She had dressed in a thin velvety black robe. Black. She'd chosen that color for her corpse, and I tried to figure it. It seemed to me she was most likely determined from birth, born with an unfortunate mix of conflicted traits that gave her mold a negative cast. Her nature was not a positive one. Unhappiness was her primary fix and she caused unhappiness. She'd tried suicide several times before. A psychiatrist might say her attempts were cries for help. I felt compelled to help a time or two, which sounds self-righteous, but each time I only caused a kind of scorn in return. It was like Marie considered help an interference, she didn't want the way she was interfered with. Like: Get away, leave me alone! At the same time an offered kindness might make her cry. She'd be grateful. Then she'd immediately distrust the kindness, what was it for? Her suicide attempts in all likelihood were added ways to pull others more into her miasma of sorrow. Finally, if we can say it just happens some people are fated to live miserable lives, then Marie, unfortunately, was one of those. I felt sorry for her. I felt pity for her. It's almost sure she never knew what it was to love or be loved wholeheartedly.

She said she never meant to leave us kids. But she did. After all, when you have children of your own, you find out, you don't just up and leave them after a few years and make an X for them in your life, not if you care, you don't leave your kids with a hole in their hearts.

I pulled the towel from between her legs. It was not soiled. I stuffed it and the plastic bag and scarf and pill bottles under a wad in the trash. There was nothing else to clear away. She'd been wanting to die a long time. When she realized she was at a point she might be hospitalized or put in a nursing home, I think that decided her. She knew then others would see her, she would be exposed and no longer able to hide, and that did the trick. She would make it another fantasy escape, and in her mind probably, if she could count on me to do the hard part, her part was merely a matter of going to sleep. She'd had nightmares all her life. She may have believed in this sleep she wouldn't.

I opened the blinds and unlocked the doors and put the phone back on the receiver, then mixed a vodka drink and sat in my room. It was eight-thirty. I would wait a while to call the police. Needed to get it set in my mind what I would tell them and how I would act. Anyway, it was over. I didn't feel easy. It seemed an oppressive weight might soon lift, but mostly what I felt was depressed. I was still tensed. The drink made me lighter. A friend called from Austin. I didn't mention Marie. We talked of nothing in particular and joked. After hanging up, I realized I had laughed too loudly. I would need to control myself better later. I mixed another drink.

About nine-thirty I called the police, said I didn't know if I should call them, but I thought my mother had died in her sleep. The police arrived within minutes and called in the coroner, a local justice of the peace. I told the coroner my mother had deteriorated rapidly in the last weeks, she'd had a consumptive heart condition, shortness of breath, stomach problems. He took a cursory look at her, pronounced her dead from natural causes, and called the mortuary. They arrived and Marie's body was taken away. I gave the mortuary man her birth certificate and social security number and told him cremation. He asked about embalming. I said, no. How about a service? No, none of that, I said, just the simplest quickest way.

They were soon gone, Marie was gone, and the whole last business was finished. The house was suddenly stone quiet and I felt an odd distant loss. I need to get drunk, I thought. I poured my drink out instead. The one woman I'd known my whole life, I thought, she'd given me life. But I'd known her only as Marie. I never called her mother and she never called me son.

THE BIG QUESTION THEN, WHAT FOR?

I return first to Dallas, 1970, to a time my life would change and never be the same. Call it a turning point.

I went home late one night. It wasn't particularly the place I wanted to go but the bars had closed. I'd been married a year for a second time. Who was in the White House? What were the hit songs? Who cares, I went home that night full of voices, my usual condition at the time and probably my best way of socializing. I had a mental circle of phantoms I liked to commune with. They were nearly always agreeable conversationalists. I was also drunk, another usual condition.

Tracy was sitting cross-legged on the bed in her sexy nightie pretending to file her nails, a succulent beautiful woman, an instantly desirable woman. Every man I knew wanted Tracy. In fact every man Tracy knew wanted her and she loved being wanted. She loved sex and was so good at it, with the right man she could go for hours every whichaway and never run out of inspiration. The only problem was that most men could never last long enough and she misunderstood that. Fucking was so wonderful, why couldn't they last? It was a failure of parts.

I stopped at the bedroom door and grinned, "Hi." She didn't look up. "I'm here," I said. She gave me an icy glance, "You know what time it is?" "It's night." "It's two o'clock." "It is?"

She went back to filing her nails. She had perfectly shaped blood-red fingernails. I staggered into the bathroom. It was going to be another one of those nights. We'd both spoken fairly casually but with the tension barely held in check. A stupid scene was going to repeat itself and I dreaded it.

I gotta do something, I thought. I splashed my face with water and looked in the mirror. My face was dripping, my hair a regular rat's nest. My eyes were hollows of madness, a voice was telling me. The "hollows of madness" was from some poem I knew as a kid, some of it I could still recite, ". . . Where Tim the ostler listened . . . His eyes were hollows of madness, his hair like moldy hay . . . Dumb as a dog he listened, and he heard the robber say—'. . . Then look for me by moonlight, watch for me by moonlight, I'll come to thee by moonlight, though hell should bar the way.'" Imagine, moonlight repeated three times. But it worked. Snippets like that were coming back to me more and more lately. All the same, my eyes in the mirror did look pretty screwy. They were bloodshot and bleary.

I spoke to my reflection, "You know something, you're one miserable sonofabitch, aren't you?"

The image nodded back, "Yeh, I really am."

"Then do something, okay? Either live this life halfway brightly or put a bullet through your head."

"Yeh, that's what I oughta do."

"Then make up your mind, one way or the other."

"Right, make up my mind, I need to."

"So do it."

"I can't, I'm depressed."

Which is the way it goes, you're depressed, you can't make a decision and talking to a mirror is no help. I gripped the sides of the lavatory. I gotta do something, I'm not making it, I'm dying. The voice was babbling in my head, the sorriness of the babbling a kind of self-pitying rage against myself and everything else including Tracy. She wasn't to blame. It was my fault she married me. Beautiful luscious Tracy sawing at her nails with the emery.

I dried my face and started brushing my teeth. It was like I was frothing at the mouth. My teeth felt like they were falling out. I held the toothbrush in a fist the way I had as a kid. I sank to my knees and finished brushing with my chin lopped over the rim of the lavatory. A goner, a melted pitiful sight. Look, this is how I'm ending, I thought. The tile on the bathroom floor was little black and white squares. Public rest rooms in Greyhound bus stations had the same kind of tile on their floors. But this is a wonderful house, I thought, two-story Victorian with arched doorways, scrolled paneling, thick walls, fireplace, veranda, sunroom, swimming pool, the works. I'd bought it the year before for a song, before the real estate boom. It was luck. Half my life was luck. The interest on the mortgage was six percent. Those were the days. Tracy would soon sell the house for $200,000, five times the lien against it. I had new cars in the garage, a closet hung with tailored suits. I was making money producing sales films and stupid TV commercials. For the first time in my life I had money. I didn't count pennies, I didn't count $20 bills. I had a table reserved in the space for big spenders at the Chateau Club. So what was my problem? I had failed. I had somehow become only another ordinary person and being seated, say, in an upper row of the middle class was no distinction. Let's face it, in this world the privileged are on top, the rest are on bottom. The middle is a false space, a feeding slot for bankers and mortgagees, and that's where I was living a lie, in that false space. My soul was in pain. I could prattle on. You get the idea. The fact was, I was thirty-five and that's a bad age for men. It may not be a good age for anyone. You can't be excused for inexperience. You've used up your credits for potential. The kiddy clock in your brain stopped at twenty-five but you suddenly see you're older and getting more so. You're the old saggy body on the beach you once deplored. You're a prediction that didn't happen and if you don't make your mark now, you never will. But what mark? You're suspended in midair. It's like a point of no return. You can't go back, you have to go forward, but there's nothing forward. A blank. You have yet to admit your artistic nature, that you might actually be a writer. You suspect it's there but where you grew up "arties" were called sissies and the only thing worse was called a quitter. So that's out. The suspicion anyhow only hovers in the cellar where you keep the rest of your secret rats. You're at the crucial watershed age, that's the informed way of saying it. More simply put, you're messed up, you don't have a clue.

I finally got up from my knees at the lavatory and opened the door. Tracy was still on the bed filing her nails. How long can a woman do that? Her tawny legs and the lovely tops of her breasts were bared apart from her sheer teddy. The business with the nails aside, she was the picture of pure sex idling under the golden folds of the tented Arabian canopy. She'd designed the canopy herself and it really was a neat overhang. You could lose your mind beneath that tent in all kinds of harem fantasies. But I was stopped. I imagined the energy it would take to crawl the sand into that tent and perform.

"I'm going to shower," I said. I retreated back into the bathroom. But she had looked up as I turned. Expectantly? I'd said shower, the wrong word. Now she was going to anticipate my body returning freshly laundered, my cock clean as a whistle. She probably was. I knew her. I was soggy, limp, not an ounce of carnal desire in me, but she wouldn't care. You can do it, she'd say, c'mon, gimme that, I'll make you hard. She'd try, she'd suck my poor paltry weenie till I passed out, or I'd plead occupational necessity, that I had to get some sleep, I had work to do the next day, which I did, but she'd get more frustrated and argue. She wouldn't let it go, I wouldn't get my sleep, then it would be dawn and I'd have to go through the motions of the day a walking zombie. How many days more could I keep doing that? Actually, it wasn't that hard, producing sappy TV commercials didn't take a lot of brains, but every day it seemed I was only going through the motions, sopheaded, sleep-deprived, dispirited. I'd have to start my nipping by midmorning to brace me through. What I dreaded most, though, was the coming harangue. Not again. I was a man in my own house, I deserved sympathy.

Now I liked Tracy. I've felt since that I liked her a lot more than I knew and I miss her. She was wonderful in many ways, truly sensual, fun, warmhearted, honest, all those good things, but with a bone to pick, she couldn't help picking it to death. You had to be there. She was also, I sorta surmised, not very deep. All she had to do was understand me, she couldn't, so that narrowed it. The fact that I couldn't understand myself was irrelevant. You have a partner who's legally contracted to you for the rest of their life, the contract is good in court for half your worldly goods, it's also sanctified by the Higher Authority, you expect something in return. You expect them to at least fill in a few blanks. I probably needed Tracy to *perceive* I was in trouble. She only perceived she wasn't the center of my world. So she was in trouble. She was an only child. Never marry an only child. They expect the universe to revolve around them, especially when they're beautiful and sexy and attract men like a magnet. I was in ruins. She was on fire. I wanted peace, a place to hide. She wanted excitement, explosions. My body was sick, I didn't want it touched. Her body wanted touching, licking, fucking. It thrived on orgasms. And dancing. Tracy was a great dancer. The way she moved—well, because of Tracy I'm convinced the best dancers are also the best in bed. That's my experience, too. Dancers like the feel of their own bodies.

I fumbled with my clothes and finally got them off, hung them on the hook, and turned on the shower. First cold, then hot, then cold again. I couldn't feel the difference. I guessed it was hot when it was steam and cold when the steam disappeared. But which to use? I decided to stay with the cold. Maybe it would revive my senses. It didn't much but I stood under the cold water a long time. A safe place to be, I thought. In water, you're out of the weather, the seasons don't change. What you feel is the isostasy. In water, too, you can save your soul, you can be born again an amphibian, a more mindless simpler creature. And that's what I wanted to be, simpler, less complexed. Like Red Stulislavsky, the most popular boy in high school. Red was an athlete with miraculous reflexes. He was All-State and you watched him play ball, you could tell he didn't have to think, he simply reacted without thinking, and that's how I wanted to be. Red was also modestly monosyllabic, not a big talker. In fact, he was smarter when he didn't talk. He didn't have a brain in his head and the girls still loved him.

Anyway, I was standing in the shower under the cold water thinking about Red. Because Red was the ideal hominoid, a healthy physical specimen entirely devoid of messy mental matter, a simple two-stroke engine operated by fuel-efficient reflex. That was how to be. So why couldn't I be that way? It was like I had a prisoner down in a dungeon inside me and he didn't like it down there. He'd become deranged and was running around banging on the walls trying to get out. But there was no door, no way out except up through my mind where it was a labyrinth of spaghetti tunnels and dead ends. If I could help him, if I could mark the no-exit turns, and he could remember what the marks meant, he wouldn't repeat them, he might find the eventual convolution that led to daylight. He'd leap to freedom, I'd be rid of him. Except I couldn't find the way either. My thinking led nowhere. So we were both trapped, him down there, me up here, but we were both in the same boat. He was banging on the walls to get out. Me, too. He was clanging his tin cup against the bars, I didn't have a tin cup, but I could identify, I knew how he felt.

The cold water was finally numbing. Time to turn it off, step out, face the music. Tracy was waiting. It wasn't going to be easy. She was pissed and whatever I did would be wrong. I'd try to cuddle her, she'd shove me away. "Don't touch me! Where've you been?" I'd tell her, she'd accuse me of lying. "You don't think I know when you're lying?" That would be the start. Anything I said would be a lie. She'd been left alone to twiddle her thumbs, which meant I didn't care, I didn't love her. Most men would give their eyeteeth to have a woman like her, didn't I know that? Yes, I knew. Then why don't you care? Well, I do care. You don't love me. No, I do. Then where were you? At the

Chateau with a client. No, you weren't, I called, they said you weren't there. Then I drove around awhile. For six hours by yourself! Who were you with? No one. Then where were you? Tracy, sweetheart. Don't sweetheart me, you bastard, you were with some slut model you called in to audition. I know you, and she got the part, didn't she? All she had to do was bat her eyes and sit back on your desk with her heels behind her ears so you could stick your dick in and do it standing up, that's why you showered so I wouldn't smell her sex, you bastard!

And so on—and on and on. Jesus. I could write the script. Except I didn't know where her jealousy came from. She was thirty but passed for twenty-five, easy. Even in a room full of other beautiful women, she was the one who caught your eye, and it wasn't only her face and body, she also had a bright ineffable quality of freshness and bloom. She had no reason to be jealous of anyone. So why did she show her claws with me? Because she knew she wasn't my all-and-all. Something stupid about me excluded her and she felt that as a rejection of sorts. As an only child it was a new experience for her and somehow threatening. After all, her father and every other man she'd known had been crazy about her. Of course there hadn't been that many. She'd married right after high school. The guy was a beginning engineer. He was a good dancer and she'd been faithful. A few years later however she was twenty-three and bored with practical bedroom engineering. She felt her looks were being wasted. She wanted to be in showbiz. Someone saw her, he said he was a Las Vegas talent scout and she was offered the chance to be in a chorus line in Vegas. Her husband said no. He didn't like the idea of his wife's body parading seminude in front of other men. So she divorced him. It turned out the chance to be in the chorus line had to be approved by the casino manager on his couch. The manager was a short cigar smoker. Tracy could've closed her eyes, it would've been a quickie, over in a minute. To her credit, she declined the approval interview. Which left her still living in Dallas but that was okay. Dallas had a lot of low-budget film stuff going on and the world-famous Trade Mart. She became an instant model. Not the fashion kind, she wasn't that skinny and cadaverous. She became a model for bikinis and sexy lingerie and trade shows. Incidentally, it was interesting to me to learn that at the new car exhibits, the models related their worth to the cars they posed beside. I hadn't known. If you were the model for a Ford or Plymouth, that's about where you placed on the modeling scale. The classiest models were the ones who showed the Cadillacs and Lincolns. Tracy was always a Cadillac girl. So she modeled, she became a star feature in the trade show and advertising circles and in six years slept with ten, fifteen men. She didn't count. She was a small-town girl from Arkansas cashing in on her looks and it was a heady time. She had a ball buying spiffy clothes and living the free spirit. She had men chasing after her like slathering dogs.

Then we met. I auditioned her for a TV spot along with a gal named Patsy who later became known as Morgan Fairchild. I gave the job to Tracy. She had that extra something. Not that the future Morgan Fairchild didn't, but it wasn't exactly a toss-up. We finished the TV shoot, a dumb household appliance thing, and I broke my rule of never hitting on talent. I asked Tracy out. Maybe because I hadn't gooned her during filming, that was a change for her. We had dinner at the Fairmont, a supper club in those days, and despite the supposedly chic but dull entertainment, ol' Vic Damone singing in a tux, we had a good time. The waiters wore white gloves. The maître d' spoke with a French Texas accent. Then it was still early and a warm evening. I drove to the lake. The moon was out and we strolled the shore not far from the H. L. Hunt house, his replica of Mount Vernon. Tracy was bumping me with her hips and being flirty with her body, showing it off. She hadn't been in the spotlight in a few hours so she was taking the stage. Old lechery H.L. might've been peeking from his window. I made sure Tracy saw my appraisal was appreciative and in no time she slipped her clothes and stepped into the lake. I wasn't surprised. In another era it would've been daring. I stripped my clothes as well and we played at splashing in the water. But with no feelies, no hanky-panky. You're an experienced man, you know to keep your hands off. A woman's naked in the water, that intrigues 'em every time. I took Tracy back to her apartment and left her at the door with a peck on the cheek. The hands off, the peck, well, a little too pat, I suppose, but as usual it worked. I had exuded masculine confidence and left her dazzled.

Now that's the way I tell it and still the way I remember it happened. Or it might've happened a shade differently. I have to admit it had taken me years to perfect my technique. Every so often I have to be careful to keep my moves updated, but you're a boy raised in the sticks, you learn early one proven rule: treat a whore like a lady, treat a lady like a whore. That way you cover the spectrum and score from top to bottom. In your heart you know you can't really pigeonhole women that way, you know it's poolroom bullshit for no-hopers, but that's your daily society, you're an oversexed adolescent, so it's the beginner rule you start with. From that springboard you're launched into research. After a while your information changes, if it does, and you find out women are people, too, only different. How? The question occurs. It's a good question. You conduct more research. You discover women are different because they're not like men. You're a genius. Your experiments show women's minds cogitate without facts, their emotions flow from ethereal sources. Your discovery is a personal revelation. It's also confusing. And you don't know it, but the confusion now and then is going to last a lifetime. Marie was perhaps a bigger influence than you suspected. You didn't like her but she was your mother. It's a perspective with pieces that don't mesh. You try to write it out, to understand. Feelings and thoughts go into words, the words become stories. It's an oblique approach. Eventually you're going to depict women in your novels in one of two places, on a pedestal or on their backs. You won't be able to write about them fairly. So you don't write about them much at all. The main characters in your stories will always be men. You'll be a writer all right, but a limited one. No one will consider you a Tolstoy. You'll have to reckon with that, that your talent is merely middling, that you really are only ordinary after all and you should've stayed with the filming game and Tracy. It was the best you could do. In fact, you were doing just fine. At the breezy level, at the cocktail hour, Tracy was an asset. The word was used. From the business angle, in the jargon, you were considered well positioned with the window of opportunity open before you. Intelligent people with analytical minds talked like that. You could've stayed with the game and made bunches more money. You might've become filthy rich. The only possible drawback, and in your mind a creeping certainty, you would've ended up really crazy.

That's what Tracy couldn't understand. Moneywise you were comfy, the future looked like a cakewalk. You were known to be "creative," a misnomer. You were gimmicky, not creative, but let that pass. The client came to you with a product he wanted to advertise. He wanted a TV commercial. The product had features or benefits, so called. You'd tell him, okay, that's *what* you want to say, now here's *how* you say it. That's the "creative." This is lesson one in elementary advertising. The client wants to have input. He calls it that. He has his own ideas and personal tastes, he wants these included in the how-you-say-it part. He doesn't exactly demand it, his title is Advertising Manager or Marketing Director, he's not that secure. So you have meetings and five-martini lunches to assure him his thinking is brilliant. The martini lunches are perks of the trade. In the end you use your idea originally presented but by now the client assumes it's his. He signs off on the package with the tacit understanding if the commercial fails to sell, he's not responsible, it wasn't his idea, but if it succeeds, naturally he gets the credit. With some variations, it's about that simple. You relate the product to sex and success, to mythical freedom, the consumer can have it all. Or if it's a homey product, you bring in the kids and dogs. A consumer is not who he is, but what the product makes of him. You stick with what has always worked, only hyping the visuals with jazzier shots, faster cuts. People are distracted, you've gotta grab their attention and hold it. You're in the business of manipulation.

By 1970 I began to see the kind of business I was in and it wasn't me. Being manipulative was not being straight-arrow, the way a man's supposed to be. A man's supposed to say what he means and mean what he says. You're only as good as your word. You're also what you do. But what I was doing was TV stuff. I was given the subject, the client's product, I didn't have to like it, and I was given what to say: look, here's the product, it's blue, it's cheap. Feature. Benefit. The feature is appealing, the benefit saves money. I only had to invent the how-to-say-it part and relate it to sex and success. Or to dogs and kids. Even with dogs, you tried to pick the sexiest ones. But you invent the how-to for a TV spot, it's like saying whatever it takes. Not exactly a proud profession, the filming business, and not one that takes particular expertise. Anybody can get into it. Ask anybody. At the same time it's known as a glamour industry. Pretty faces harken to the call and flock to the studios. Look, actors, actresses! Lights, action, camera! You're a director, you can have a field day. The lowly grips can have the leftovers behind the scenery. The talent's eager and waiting to be discovered. You're a cameraman, though, you're out of luck. Your eye is stuck to the viewfinder like a repressed voyeur, you see the talent but they don't see you. That's your fate. And as a cameraman, you're also always fiddling with lenses, focuses, light meters. You can't help it. You're obsessed with adjusting the gadgets of your trade. Which drives the producer nuts. I know, I was the producer watching the clock. The shoot's costing $1,000 a minute for studio time, equipment rental, wardrobe, makeup, every cost you can name. The clock's ticking. But what's happening? You look around, spiders are weaving cobwebs. The cameraman's bent over in the corner fondling his f-stop. Gotta get it right, he says. And like for hours, he keeps doing it. You're the producer, the cameraman's imperturbable, you need to have patience.

That's why I started drinking. Or I take that back. I didn't just start. To put it quaintly, I'd always imbibed. What I started was drinking more and too much. Most people couldn't tell. I was handling it. But I was also occasionally blanking. I'd find myself somewhere, I couldn't remember where I'd been. I might be told later and have to call back and apologize. Let's face it, you're a good steady drinker for fifteen years, your liver quits filtering, it becomes a lump of pasteboard. Count on it. And without the filter, your blood checks out ninety percent apple juice. You go where there's people, you have to gear up for the crowd, a couple of quick ones. Then you're sipping away, you think you're still a happy-go-lucky wit, you're a brain-dead dribbling drunk.

Anyway, I was out of the shower. The harangue was coming for sure. It had been waiting, filing its nails. What to do? It wasn't my nature to meekly endure a storm until it passed. A storm came, I railed against it. A man's gotta stand up for himself. That's why Tracy's harangues lasted all night. She attacked, I chipped back. She wouldn't concede a pebble of disputed territory, neither would I. But not tonight, I wasn't up to it.

I stood dripping in the bathroom, my mouth hanging open, my eyes hollows of madness. Voices in my head were conspiring. So promise, they said. Okay, I said, but what? Promise yourself no matter what, you won't say a word. Okay. But you gotta promise to stick with it. Okay, but it's going to be hard. You can do it, play like you're too drunk to talk. I might be. And think of sleep. Yeah, sleep, a good idea. So make it a promise, not a word. Okay, I promise. And, remember, think sleep. Right, sleep, boy, do I need sleep.

That's how I decided. This time, no matter what, no arguing. Tracy could blast away, I'd simply ignore her. It would be a new tactic.

It would also be a new mistake. I should've known. Because after being ignored a while, Tracy disappeared and returned with a fully loaded pistol. She cocked the hammer and pointed the thing between my eyes. Where did she get it? I didn't know she even had a pistol but it was a .38 and the big bullets in the cylinder were staring me straight in the face.

It WAS THE UNMISTAKABLE cold metallic *klic-klac* of the hammer being cocked that first penetrated my stupor, then froze my scalp. Coming out of the bathroom I did what I promised my parliamentary advisers, I ignored Tracy, I didn't say a word. I was going to control the situation with inner strength. She was still sitting on her side of the bed. Or I don't know why I say "her side." A bed to her had no boundaries. It was open hunting ground she sinuously prowled when she was in it. If there was prey to be had, she took it in her jaws and between the paws of her thighs and hungrily devoured it. Anyway, I eased past her, slid under the covers, and pretended to fall asleep. She was following me with her eyes but I wouldn't look at her.

She was obviously dumbfounded. "Now what are you doing?"

I didn't reply. She was also saying more I didn't bother to register. She was trying to goad me into the usual arguing that would end with the usual tempestuous sexual arousal on her part that we would have to reconcile with the usual frenzied fucking after which we'd wonder why we ever argued in the first place, we'd be so depleted. I would be. Tracy of course would still be ready for more at the slightest excuse, even if I only turned and accidentally brushed a pip of her erogenous zone, which apparently swathed her entire body, she would read the touch as an instant alert, that the man's body beside her was still breathing, still usable. I'd think, God help me, this woman is going to be the death of me yet.

Now it appeared she really would be. And I mean really. The moment remains indelibly imprinted in my brain. I had stayed under the covers with my back turned. She was ranting. I didn't care. Then she was suddenly quiet. What now? I felt her ease off the bed. Her movements after that were noiseless, the carpet was plush and deep, but I pictured her bare feet lightly impressing the plush, her hand opening the bedroom door and her abject defeated body leaving. I might have heard a drawer opening. I didn't. I only thought, whataya know, it works, she's gone off to pout. I could get some sleep now. And boy, did I need sleep. A weight lifted, a soft fluffy cloud began to settle around me and I felt grateful.

Then the *klic-klac* sounded behind my ear. My heart stopped. I knew that sound. I had been shot before. So I couldn't just lay there. I forced my head to turn—but slowly, carefully.

Tracy was pointing the pistol straight between my eyes. I

wasn't exactly surprised but absolutely galvanized. Her beautiful face was demonic, her lip curled. "You sonofabitch," she hissed.

"Now, honey—" I said. I had the covers clutched under my chin. The hammer cocked in the air behind the pistol had me fixed. It would only take a slight squeeze at the trigger, a slip, a spastic tic, that would be it. Her finger already appeared to wrap the trigger too tightly. Her finger with its blood-red claw. That's what I saw. At the same time, strategies swirled in my mind. You're in trouble it's only natural to want to figure a way out. Call it an instinct for self-preservation. Whatever, I was in trouble so my brain was racing. Maybe I should try to smile and act unconcerned. My voices told me to call her bluff: "Go ahead, shoot, you wanna pull the trigger, do it." The voices had seen that in the movies. She'd break down and start crying and weakly lower the gun. I could take it from her hand then and console her helplessness with my gentle strength. But that wasn't happening. Her eyes were blank and she was fronting me with mindless intent. Try reasoning with a foregone conclusion. You can be diplomatic: "Yes, of course, dear, I understand, but whataya say we take a moment to review the facts, just to be sure?" That's brilliant. You're conversing with blind fate. Blind fate has the empathy of a dried cow chip. So you're dead. But you're going to die someday anyway, why not now? Even if you're surprised and it's unexpected, never mind, it's inescapable.

Now, pause. We should try to understand what's really happening here, otherwise we're wasting our time.

Put yourself in the situation described. You're lying there with a gun pointed to your head. It's two-thirty in the morning, you're drunk but also scared sober. Your spouse is going to put a lousy bullet through your brain and kill you. It's the kind of thing that happens to others, not you. But now it *is* you. It's a defining moment.

In comparison, everything else in your life to this point has been impressionistic. No experience, no person, was ever remembered but reimagined, reinvented. Even you. Look, you're a reflection in other people's eyes, yet ten different people describe you in ten different ways. Well, to thine own self be true, you think, the truth shall set you free. It's easy to recite the proud shibboleths, it's a mark of intelligence, but we deal in cheap philosophy and we know there is no such thing as truth absolutely, there are only degrees of truth, and everything is eventually abstract.

Except right now the gun at your head is a reality and not abstract and your first thought in personal historical terms is a revelation, that what you do in the next second is going to be terribly important. It's a thought steeped in blood from the dawn of time. You move, you're dead. Whatever dead means. Certainly it's staring you in the face. Meanwhile, your mind is a quagmire. You are stuck in the vortex of the human condition.

Which is the old story of man and woman. And if you're the average guy you probably won't see the whole or specifically the predicament of the tender murderer before you. She's distraught. Okay, you see that much. But deep down what you really think is that she's a she, a woman, and everything that implies. Which means in your mind she is also the locus classicus of every godawful emotional fit possible and in the throes of one of those fits, like right now, forget the eons of cerebral evolution, the final larger brain. The mind is defeated. Feelings rule. That's all. Which puts you in a bind, you're a man, you believe the issue should be clearly stated, the answer is this or that and you move on. It's like taking care of business, you're handling logistics and proper managerial skills are required, otherwise there's no modern progress. So you stay away from feelings. You fool with personal feelings, it gets messy. Except in this case there's no other game in town. The feelings before you are how come you're presently about to be snuffed. You have to face them.

Tracy had hissed, "You sonofabitch." My reply, "Now, honey."

It was a moment fraught with suspense. If you're an optimist, you can hope. But if you've been shot before, as I had, you can't. You know absolutely it's going to happen again. The finger moves, that's it, the bullet is instant. You feel it going in, that it already went in. It doesn't hurt. The shock comes later. You simply see immediately a complete picture of your entire life, and not unexpectedly, you've been told it happens. What's startling is the peripheral, the sudden solid frame looming around the picture. Your mind has retrieved the whole of your life but restaged it somehow inside an enclosure. You view all at once your minor saga pictured in whorling time yet stopped cold in space. The enclosure, the frame all around, is like an outside wall and you see plainly you were always only within, that this was your single place, and that's the startler, the abrupt awareness of your tiny fixed territory. Your existence was unimaginatively merely this bare barricaded spot and nowhere else. You can guess the wall stands for the boundary of mortality. What's beyond is not shown, it's no-man's-land, a free-fire zone, it's off limits. But it's the picture itself that holds, your passing life strewing the surface of days and years with unimportance, scraps of incidentals, almost nothing. You might have done more, been more. You might have created something larger than life but your being was so limited. You might've looked beyond the wall, at least chiseled a peephole to see through. You had your chance.

So what happened? The picture crosses your mind in a

nanosecond, and offhand, you see also how inexplicably fortunate you were. For no reason except a mindless happenstance of barnyard genes you were gifted with a certain amount of regular looks, an engaging manner, a disarming smile, all the natural attributes of a future part-time actor. Maybe that's what happened. You didn't have to try for much. Things came your way. Without purpose, you didn't want much anyway. You made money, you spent it. Living was easy. Women were attracted to you, that was nice. Some people thought you were intelligent, you let that stand. In an ordinary room, you were a presence. It wasn't your fault. With a different shuffle of cards you might've been someone else in another time and place. But you weren't, you were lucky, and for a long time it seemed enough. Until now. Until recently.

I heard my words before I knew they were mine. I didn't know I was going to speak, even cautiously. My lips barely moved. "I forgot to tell you," I said. "Harry called. He wants you in his next Six Flags spot." I was lying. I wasn't proud. It was a weasel gambit to appeal to her weakness.

Tracy's eyes stayed blank but appeared to halt. I held my breath. Gradually her look thinned. "He does?" She was still pointing the gun.

"He wants me to feature you all the way through."

"But you don't want to."

"No, I do. It's his call, though, he's the client."

"You never use me." Flatly. The old resentment. I didn't use my wife in commercials so she wouldn't get the jealous criticism that she was being cast because her husband was the producer. And I didn't use her because I didn't want to be blamed for nepotism if the commercial turned out wormy. I was being sensible. Tracy didn't understand that.

"You don't," she said, "never, not even for Northpark, not

once, and they wanted me, they told me."

"Sweetheart—"

"Don't sweetheart me, you sonofabitch!" A screech, the gun jabbed at my head, but at least she was talking.

"You don't love me," she said.

"Tracy—"

"You don't. Why can't you?" A good question. I couldn't answer. "Tell me!" Her teeth bared, her eyes suddenly glistening. "What's wrong with you?!"

Clearly, she'd imagined a different sort of life with me, which had started out fine but within the year had somehow petered out. Literally. She'd imagined a partnership with exciting prospects for herself. We were both, in her mind, in "showbiz." With that main interest between us, no doubt we'd become a dynamic duo. I was TV producer, she was beautiful. It was the perfect one-two punch. I would make her a star. But it wasn't happening. I wasn't using her in my TV spots. Worse, we'd started out fucking every day, now it was only a time or two a week and at no time for very long. She was frustrated. Her infinitely desirable body was being needlessly neglected. She'd designed the Arabian canopy and specially installed the mirrors in its folds. They were turning opaque with disuse. At bedside, the exotic oils and scents, all the salubrious sidebar condiments, were being left to waste. In another house, flies might have swarmed.

A year before I'd awakened with a woman's body in the bed beside me. I didn't have the foggiest notion who it was. It had been another one of those nights. Then she woke, snuggled against me. It was Tracy. She murmured dreamily, "Did you mean it last night when you said you were going to marry me?" I had known her maybe a week. "Did I say I was going to?" She nodded. "Then I'm going to. If I said it, I meant it." A man is only as good as his word. I was still drunk but we drove to Oklahoma that afternoon and got married. In Oklahoma in those days there was no blood test required, no waiting period. It's probably the same today. A ten-minute stop at the court-house for the license, a drive down the street to the first church, it's done. Once you start to get married in Oklahoma, you can't have second thoughts. Your stomach feels queasy, too late, you're already married. In our case, the first church down the street turned out to be a Servants of the Paraclete Pentacostal and the preacher went on so about the sanctity of vows, the holiness of matrimony, what God joins together and so forth, I had a fifty ready, but I finally only gave him a ten for the tedium. He took the ten with a greasy smile and eyes glinting pure hate. Tracy and I then flew to Acapulco for a honeymoon week spent almost continuously in every position possible in bed. And on the floor, in the shower, on the table, under it, against the wall, you name it. We saw the beach maybe once. We had our meals in our room and ate naked. At the end of the week Tracy was radiant. I had lost ten pounds.

That was then. Now, a year later, it had come to this. After all the gossamer frills and sexy spiked heels, the dressy cocktail parties, being envied by women, ogled by men, the daily gym and massage—in short, after all the days and nights of simply being beautiful, Tracy was going to murder me. She might. It was a dangerous time yet and I wasn't moving.

"Why?" she repeated. "Why can't you love me, what is wrong with you?!"

Now it just happened at that moment I experienced what might be described as a flash of extrasensory perception, one of those things everyone has now and then and can't explain. It's a mouthful to pronounce. The two words together are eight syllables. Anyway, what happened was, in a flicker, I saw her twilight. It seems now the whole was clearly shown and I was looking straight at it. And more, I was seeing within the light a specter of pain. Certainly an aura of pain was glimmering the edges. And deeper, more centered, I saw her shadow of dread. I felt amazed, I hadn't known, or cared to look, but a dark dread had plainly taken hold of her. It was spooky. She had seen her future. She was thirty, if she didn't look it, she would. Doomsday was just around the corner and approaching on grinding wheels. It wouldn't be long, age would arrive, her taut smooth skin would wrinkle, she'd grow baggy knees and saggy breasts. Her ticket had been punched. And my thoughtless uninterest had been the final straw. She'd depended on her looks for love. She'd compelled infatuation instead, almost the same thing in the short run but not quite. Infatuation has a bad habit of burning itself out. You stir the ashes afterward to see what was there, it's cold and dead. The point being, her looks were not going to last, what they inspired had never lasted, and Tracy was having to face that. Not a pretty picture.

But there's probably no simple explanation. It may be I never actually saw her twilight at the time, that I'm only imagining it now to make some sense out of craziness. Which is really a problem of history. The past is like an accident. We would be enlightened to know what happened, especially whose fault it was. But in history, what's missing is the warm body at the time, the actual mind thinking. What did Cleopatra's word sound like in Antony's ear? She was Greek. Antony was Roman, he may not have understood a word she said. And he was alcoholic, he may have only seen her as a blur of kohl and wispy veils. Any midafternoon he was probably passed out on the couch, the goblet dribbled from his hand. We can imagine what his drunken performance as a lover was like. It was probably like mine.

I think that now. I wouldn't have at the time. I wasn't performing very well with Tracy and hadn't for months. Didn't have the energy, much less the desire. Drinking was a big part of it but more was also involved, you could say the image of myself as a man. It had somehow faded. I didn't know why but any idea of a lessening of my ability to perform, to take a woman and leave her gratefully subdued, well, no way was I about to face that. It might hint that I was becoming impotent. I might have to admit I was no longer a real man. You shake your head. It was 1970 and I was really that simple-minded? The dumb thing is most men still are. The basic male is one thing, the role he assumes he's supposed to play is another. And in this role, to have any decent self-respect, the natural man usually turns cunning, a basic maneuver most women are quick to perceive, though not all. Some are still surprised that what they see is not what they get.

Which is what happened to Tracy, I think. She didn't get what she had seen in me. Or had imagined. From a man who had cunningly zeroed in on her charms and lusted over them, I'd become someone only occasionally and somehow indifferently lured by her tantalizing thighs and breasts, her succulent mouth, her slick snug pussy. Actually, a tight snapping pussy. So I had surprised her, then depressed her. She'd never conceived of the Acapulco honeymoon not lasting. Why wouldn't it? Sex was love. And love was endlessly wonderful, morning, noon, and night. She was a romantic.

She was also thirty and needed to adjust. But she was caught. Most of her confidence came with the effect she had on men, and she could see that effect disappearing all too soon. Thus the dread, the insecurity. I'm sorry I didn't sympathize. Tracy was a good person. I didn't think she had a lot of intellect. I may have thought that was important, and in a way it is and isn't. The heart counts more and normally Tracy was warmhearted and caring and fun and I miss her. I liked her more than I knew, and when I think of great sex, I still think of Tracy. But it was bad timing, too. She was trapped in her body and I was trapped in my psyche. She was a woman in turmoil. I was a man in crisis. We might've tried to talk plainly and honestly but we had no understanding. Love might've helped but for love Tracy looked to me and I failed her. She wanted to know, "Why can't you love me, what's wrong with you?"

Well, one thing I'd never told her. Or anyone. But there's been time, it's been a while, maybe I can return to that stop in my life almost four years before Tracy. The day and place in another town in Texas.

THAT DAY, KATHERINE CALLED and said Jimmy was missing. I got to the location as soon as I could. A police car was stopped in the middle of the street and I pulled up behind it.

This was Argyle Street, a good area, and not yet dark. The neighborhood was patrolled and supposedly secure. Fine old houses lined the street and lawn after lawn was green and neat. The green as far as you could see was calm and deep. Cars passed without a sound and the avenue itself was a long tunnel of shade canopied with oaks and walnuts a hundred years old. The feeling in the air was of a wide settlement of ease. Only decent citizens, you'd think, could live in those fine houses. A person would need to look respectable to belong in this area.

Jimmy's bicycle was leaning on its kickstand on the sidewalk and two policemen were going from house to house ringing doorbells. Katherine was standing at the curb looking pleasantly cool and poised, the way she always looked, smooth as marble, her permanent smile fixed in place on her precise lips. Her name was never Kathy or Kate, but the whole thing with three syllables.

I got out of the car and she faced me. "This is your fault," she said, "your fault entirely." She spoke politely, she always spoke politely, but her eyes were flat.

We'd divorced two years before and I'd fought for custody. I lost. Maybe I was bitter. In the past month I'd found out Katherine was still taking Jimmy to school and I latched onto that. It became a sore point with me. You're too protective, I told her, you need to let go, a boy needs to learn independence. But he's still just a baby, she said. I got loud. Just a baby! Katherine, he's seven years old, you're treating him like he's two, dammit, you're smothering him. He wants to ride his bike to school, let him. The school, Katherine, is only six damn blocks away.

I kept after her until she gave in and Jimmy was allowed to go to school on his own. I imagined the bright look on his face riding off into those six blocks of freedom every day, his eyes shining, his hair flying, a regular little towheaded kid. I could see him testing his wings and growing up confident and independent. Given half a chance the boy would find his own way and become his own man someday. I felt proud.

Now, a block from school, the bicycle was left waiting. Cars were gliding by, the lawns were plains of green, and Katherine was calm, she was serene and smiling. The air was still. And the bicycle was leaning as if forever, its front wheel canted, its seat slightly crooked, and that's what held me. That seat. I'd promised to fix it.

The police were still asking at the nearby houses but no one had seen anything. One of the policemen told us, "Don't worry, we usually find 'em hiding or playing around somewhere, they turn up." Katherine nodded agreeably. The police were the proper authorities after all and this was Argyle Street with its oaks and walnuts a hundred years old, a world in order. You could feel an abiding permanence surrounding. Katherine said, "He didn't know his directions." I was thinking, two minutes. That's all it would've taken. The bolt for the seat was stripped, and when Jimmy pedaled, the seat swiveled, he showed me, and I told him, next time, okay? I'll fix it for you next time. "He got that from you," Katherine said. "You didn't know your directions either."

The next moment something in me stopped and I felt chilled. My hands were suddenly cold and I knew.

A week later Jimmy's body was found in the dump on the west side and the search ended. They call it a landfill now. It was a dump. The coroner told me I shouldn't look, I didn't need to see it. The body had been mutilated and was decomposing.

So. A space.

Jimmy, I think.

I write this now in an old house in northern New Mexico. It seems like yesterday. It was nearly thirty years ago. Two or three days are still missing. A blank. I was crazy. I was filled with pain. I was filled with hate. The worst finally was the weight of helplessness, of being weak and helpless. I couldn't change what happened and neither could I accept it.

Trees were passing. I could see daylight through the limbs. Then it was dawn and I was walking in a street but without the feeling of walking. It was like some instinct was carrying me and I was drowning and trying to surface. I was trying to breathe again and afraid I couldn't.

I knocked. It was Molly's door and she was opening it, standing back, her eyes startled at the sight of me. I felt ashamed. "I'm sorry," I said, "I think I need somebody." Her arms opened and enfolded me.

The next day, or the next, I was in the bath with the water up to my chin. I'd slept a long time, a deep sleep, and a soreness in my body was soaking away. Molly was sitting on the side of the tub lathering my face. A nice girl, not quite pretty, you couldn't call what we'd had a relationship. I'd usually show up at her apartment late at night and sleep with her when there was no one else. Now she was going to shave me. "I can do that," I said. She shushed me. I told her I could shave myself. She made me hold still and I kept quiet. The shaving was soothing. It felt nice being cared for. The magic of a woman's hands, I thought. But I was also undeserving. "I'm imposing," I said. "Will you hold still?" "No, I'm putting you out." "Listen, you—" She abruptly sat in the bath with me, in her robe. "In case you didn't know, there's room around here for two—see?" She flicked a splash of water at my face.

So I stayed with Molly perhaps a week. It was a place to be and for that time, the time I needed. Not to heal. That's not the word. I ate and slept, I was present, but away from Molly and on my own, I wasn't healed. I was still crazy.

Walters kept telling me, "Now you stay out of it, we'll handle it." But no one was arrested, no one was charged. They started picking me up instead. They said I was scaring kids the way I was hanging around the school. I was stopping cars that didn't look right and threatening people. "And you can't keep doing that," Walters said. "You're going to end up hurting someone and making things worse." They were picking me up for carrying a concealed weapon, for being a public nuisance. Walters said they were doing me a favor.

Al Walters, a plain man with brown hair and big hands, he was in charge of homicide. He said it was usually somebody known, a friend or relative, or some nice uncle type Jimmy wouldn't trusted. He asked for names, I gave him every name I knew. He asked for friends, I gave him Grady Walsh. My mind was seeing a psychopath in every face, even Grady's, my best friend. But it wasn't Grady and it wasn't anyone known. All the names were checked and cleared.

It was another day in Walters' office. The police had hauled me in again. I'd gone by Katherine's house and Derek Trammer had answered the door, her latest boyfriend. But he'd only opened the door a crack and stood guarding it, a thin-lipped small-time bar owner. I could smell his stale air, his sawdust floor. I told him I wanted some of the album pictures of my son. He said Katherine didn't want to see me. I told him Katherine didn't have to see me, I just wanted the pictures, that's all. I didn't like him blocking my way, standing against me. You better leave, he said. I told him not until I got my pictures. A tic twitched in his cheek, he slammed the door shut and locked it. When the police arrived, I was breaking the door down. It was the kind of door they used to make, an old heavy solid thing, but I was kicking in the panels.

It was the door, I said. Walters gave me a look, the door? It was nothing, I said. I had sounded screwy. Walters was patient, he wanted me to go back to work, to stay busy. I told him I was staying busy enough. He said I should try to stay with a friend awhile, I was living alone. I told him I'd rather be alone. He sat back. Okay, he was through talking. That was fine with me. He shook his head and turned to pour a cup of coffee from a setup behind his desk. It was a Joe Dimaggio Mr. CoffeeMaker and I felt strangely touched. He must like baseball, I thought, when he was young, when he was somebody's little boy. My brain was twisted trying to make connections. All grown-ups were once only small innocent children and I needed to see them that way before they became misshaped into adults, to see the distorting process, to find out who. A warped mind was once a child's mind full of wonder until—Derek Trammer's face loomed before me, his tight lips and marble eyes.

"It was Trammer," I said.

"You told me, at the door." Walters was turning back with his coffee.

"No, it was him." I was excited, it was a certainty. "You said it'd be somebody we knew, a friend, a relative, some nice uncle type, that's Trammer, he was always acting nice, giving Jimmy candy."

"He was also in Houston at the time, I told you."

"He could've flown back, switched planes—"

"Bob." Walters stopped me. "You gotta clear your head. It wasn't Trammer, we checked him out, believe me, he's clear."

I think that's how we talked. Trammer's face faded and the certainty was gone. I felt small and again an overwhelming helplessness descended.

"Then who?" I said.

"That's what we're trying to find out." Walters was speaking kindly. "But you gotta leave that to us, okay?"

It was so futile. I wanted to cry. I was so damned pitiful and helpless. I may have cried. Walters was patting my shoulder, hey, now, c'mon. I didn't like his hand patting. He kept saying, it's gonna be all right, now, c'mon. I finally straightened. Walters handed me his coffee and watched me sip, to see that I was going to make it. The police car would take me home. If I still wanted my son's pictures, Walters said he'd get them for me. I told him I didn't want the pictures anymore. He walked me to the police car. Now you just take it easy, leave things alone, he said.

I'd become so miserable and hopeless, I'd felt myself sinking, which was a way out, to sink on down into some kind of oblivion and never return. I wanted escape. I was hurting. But just there, it was like at bottom, in the dark, I felt a choice. It wasn't conscious. Call it a choice with despair. The alternative was given and I saw my body rising. I could rise above the hurt. Walters was patting my shoulder and I straightened.

The next day it was as if a sickness had passed and I was clear. Not whole. A part of me was gone. And maybe I'd never get things just right but I was continuing and Jimmy would still live with me, in me. In that case, the boy would need his father to set an example, to show him the way. Look, this is how you live, you experience the worst, your heart breaks, it happens, so go on, quit feeling sorry for yourself, show some pride. That's the way. And lighten up, have some fun. Look, I'll show you.

But it wasn't overnight. I couldn't walk through the next door, just like that. I still wanted to know who, why? And not that it was simply chance, or if it came to that, I needed to see the workings of that chance, to understand. What brought that moment? What confluence or mutation of circumstances? What made my son that victim?

Walters was concerned that I was keeping it in too much. He thought I needed to talk it out, to let go. There was a group that met, people in the same boat. He could give me the number to call, I could meet with them and find out I wasn't alone. He was talking about a victims' survivors group, and I imagined it, a meeting in someone's living room with everyone seated in a circle. They tell their stories, each in turn, each one until then a stranger to the other. A psychiatrist is there to encourage them. He says, that's right, let yourself feel it, you need to share it. So they do, they recite the horrors, they cry, they break down and comfort each other. There's a lot of hugging and sympathy, their pain in common a solidarity, and I could join a roomful of people like that, I could tell my story and get hugged and comforted, too. They'd have coffee and a plate of cookies to nibble. Did I need to go? I didn't think so. Out in the open was never exactly my place to hang feelings. In a group like that I'd probably end up play-acting to show how bad I felt. What I really felt was not in me to show.

The coroner's report said a broad blade, not overly sharp, perhaps an ordinary kitchen knife. The hands and feet and genitals were missing. Death had resulted from the loss of blood, from the mutilations, and not before. Bits of cotton material were found in the teeth, the material from a gag maybe, and a trace of semen was identified. So it was a man and probably alone. In this type case it was nearly always a lone individual. That was the guess and the west side was the last place the man might have been seen. The dump was on the west side.

But Walters decided the man was nowhere. After a month the investigation had only cleared names. He said, "You see, the problem is, it's not happening again. If the guy was still around, we'd be turning up another kid or two. This kind of thing is compulsive, sexual stuff, mutilation, it doesn't stop with one, they keep on. But we're not finding any more, so the guy hits and runs, he's a mover. He's probably outta state now."

I couldn't accept that. I moved to a room on the west side where the man might have been seen. The room was in what had once been a motel, a fifty-unit three-sided affair with a courtyard of sorts in the middle, a trash heap in one corner. The sign in front was shot full of holes. An old swimming pool in the courtyard had been filled in and covered over with cement. But as soon as I moved in, I had a feeling of home, that I'd returned home. It seemed I'd grown up in the same kind of places, and by going back, by reverting back like that, I could regain an original energy.

The room was an efficiency, a square maybe 15×15 but large enough. It contained a fridge and hot plate, a sink and cabinets. The walls were plaster, the rug a worn shag, black in spots and matted flat. What had been left to molder in the shag I could imagine. Smothered lives had passed in that room and spoiled the air. Their hands had turned the fridge door brown at the corner, the hot plate still smoked from their old grease, the progeny of their roaches still roamed the cabinet. Even new the motel was never a good one and it had become a worse tenement, the people in it what you find on the fringe of circumstance, their chances played out. They appear close-eyed like scavengers prowling the alleyways. That's the impression. But I felt comfortable there. The smells were familiar, the wasted lives a given. In a similar place when I was fourteen, I'd first imagined myself, that I was smart and tough and I could do anything. I wanted that same mindset again.

I began with the one known fact: it was a man. Semen had been found. I write in a notebook: a male. How old? For sure old enough to drive. Jimmy might have been taken without a car but the man had to drive to get the body to the dump unnoticed. I write: a male old enough to drive. How big? Well, big enough to carry and handle a seven-year-old. I write: a male old enough to drive, at least 5', 100 pounds. But that looks too specific. I think instead, medium-size. That's still not it. The man could be a midget and strong enough. It can be almost any size man. I cross out the numbers and write again: a male old enough to drive. Color? To pass in that neighborhood, probably white. But what about yardmen, garbage pickup people, delivery drivers? I don't have a color. Alone? I can say yes. It's an assumption but in this type thing it's nearly always one person alone. Therefore: a lone male old enough to drive. That's the description, the way I begin, and it's plainly nothing. It's fifty million suspects.

But that's taking the country as a whole, everybody in it, and I don't have to do that. I can stick with the city, within a population of 400,000, divide that in half to eliminate the ones too young and too old to drive, and the figure gets down to 200,000. I can halve that number again to count only males and reduce the possibilities to 100,000. That's not all. I can estimate how many of those would actually commit that particular type crime. The guess is that twenty percent could steal, ten percent could do worse, but how many would be sexual deviates capable of molestation, murder, and mutilation? The official figures say less than one percent. Now we're getting somewhere. We're down to 1,000 realistic possibilities, and that's not an unmanageable number, especially when you consider how many of those 1,000 had the opportunity on that particular day at that specific time in that singular location with that one little boy. Not many. Perhaps a few. But ultimately only one. So it's possible. That one can be found.

My next problem is the mental profile. I read the jargon on criminal and abnormal psychology until it's senseless. So little seems known for sure. Reasons for certain acts are given after the fact, selected to prove a thesis. Then every exception proves a rule. Child molesters were molested as children themselves. Or usually. But not always. The exceptions multiply. A single act is a beehive of motivations. Violence is someone's anger finally exploding, given certain conditions. The pressure builds, which you only see later, then something, maybe some incidental thing comes along, and the pressure explodes. But not always. The trick is to predict and you look for a pattern. You predict the pattern will repeat itself until it doesn't, then you look for the reason it didn't to prove another pattern. That's the stuff I read. Murderers are made, not born, but the reasons they're made depend on the person, certain influences, causes. Only some people are born murderers because no other reason makes sense. They're simply that way. But not evil. The act can be called that but not the murderer himself. That would be getting into religion and we need to stay with the legal. The murderer is called a felon.

It was depressing. I had looked for answers. I'd read a stack of smart books and ended up knowing almost nothing more than I might have known before. But a mutilator, you'd think that would be a special type, a special sickness. Yet the history of man is littered with pieces of human beings purposely tortured and maimed. The history of humanity is an ocean of blood floated with bodily debris. Down through the centuries, millions of mutilations. So who are the mutilators? You'd think maddened animals, but there have been so many, you'd think ordinary people, too, with ordinary sensibilities. So many, it would seem cool minds at work. And cool hands. Thousands of surgically trained hands daily slice into living flesh without a qualm. They do it regularly and with such detached emotion, it's an artistry with them. They eat lunch and go back to it normally. It's a thought. I write in my notebook a final profile: a normal-acting lone male old enough to drive. It's moronic. I'm nowhere. But I've learned. The journey of a thousand miles begins with the first five million steps.

I'd sit in that room with time to myself. The old swimming pool in the courtyard had been long gone and filled, its surface an uneven layering of cement, its edges broken and crumbling.

At night, especially at night, lying awake, I'd see the pool full of water and cool in the sun. I'd hear Jimmy splashing in it. He loved to play in water and run splattering through rain puddles. Sometimes he'd come into the room with his hair still wet and dripping. He'd still be running and playing and I'd have to tell him, now, settle down, son, not in the house.

I'd never imagined myself a father or a family man. Maybe because I'd never known a regular family life. Who knows. When Jimmy was born I'd waited at the hospital most of the day. It wouldn't be long, I thought, I'd be leaving, Katherine could have her life, I'd have mine. I was in the corridor when the nurse wheeled the cart from delivery to show me. Her mask was down at her chin and she was smiling. It's a boy, she said, and he's fine, just fine. I looked down and saw a small squinting face, a streak of blood they'd missed wiping at the neck and a metal clamp at the middle where the navel should have been. The feet were wrinkled and red. And your wife's fine, too, the nurse said. Oh, good, that's good, I said. I should've asked. Then the nurse wheeled the cart away and I was left standing. It seemed a baby had come from nowhere and for no reason I was supposed to be a father.

I stepped into the room to see Katherine but she was dopey and bleary-eyed. I don't think she knew me. They were keeping her sedated. Her labor had lasted too long and her blood pressure was staying too high. They closed the curtain around her bed saying she needed to sleep and I left. I called Katherine's friends that night and told them the baby had arrived. They all said, oh, that's wonderful, congratulations, you must be excited. I said, yes, it's great, just great, thank you. What I really felt was depressed. Katherine was pregnant when I married her. I'd done the honorable thing, I thought, she'd wanted to get married, but we soon found we didn't much like each other. And with me, what was a baby? I'd been planning to leave, I still would. I wanted to be free and roam the world. I wanted to at least feel honest. Anyway, the night of Jimmy's birth I sat in our house and got morbidly drunk. It had all been so much pretense the way I was living and it went round and round in my head the way it should have been, the way I'd once imagined myself. I'd wanted to be somebody and I wasn't. I was an ordinary nobody.

The next day Katherine said, James. She wanted to name the baby after her father. I didn't care. I was still leaving. But Katherine was in the hospital another two weeks and the baby was left to me, the day and night feeding, the diapering, bathing, all of it. At the same time, Katherine was indifferent. She'd wanted a baby but now it was like she didn't. I'd take the baby to her in the hospital and she'd hold it coolly, her affection never spontaneous or instinctive. I tried to think it was just her way, her remote and aloof manner. Or that she was still too ill. Maybe she'd never received affection from her own mother. I didn't know. But Katherine should have cared. I should have. It wasn't the baby's fault. It was a bad roll of the dice and with nobody caring the kid would have to grow up inside himself to make it. I could see that and empathize.

Then it happened. I was holding him. His head was resting on my shoulder and he was sleeping. He was soft and peaceful and breathing very gently. I liked the new sweet smell of him. I liked the tiny sleeping life in him. It was a new closeness and all at once that pure innocence was an astonishing thing to hold in my arms.

It was a magical moment and I still see Jimmy that way. Or sleeping facedown swimming with his arms. Sometimes he's lying so still I don't think he's breathing. I rush to see but each time he's fine and my alarm fades. My son is only small and helpless and that helplessness about him is a compelling need.

He grows quickly and becomes fascinating to watch. He gurgles when he's tickled, and learning to crawl, he's a wonder at scampering, one second there, gone the next. I find him absorbed in new discoveries, in the cavern inside a shoe, in the endless story of a string. He's seeing things in ways I've forgotten. And he's funny. He likes being tossed in the air and swung around. He likes the outdoors, the feel of the breeze in his face, and riding on my shoulders he likes holding at my hair. He thinks it's a special treat to gallop through the sprinklers like that and he makes me think so, too. He's so wonderfully simple, we have good times just horsing around. I think, my son. I could never have imagined. My son/me. Like a new being. I felt changed, opened, blessed, all those corny words, and I no longer thought of leaving. I started hoping in some way, for Jimmy's sake, to have a mother and father together in one place, Katherine and I would make it.

We didn't, of course. In a bleak, loveless sort of fashion, we lasted another five years. Then Katherine divorced me, she said she'd found someone else, and the judge ruled I could have my son on weekends. With that pronouncement I felt the loss coming and a spark of fear. It was going to happen again. The source of what again I couldn't articulate, only that the middle was going to be gouged away and left a hollow of pain and that's what you get when you love and care and can't help it, you get hurt again.

I started having the weekends as my allotted time with Jimmy and I thought of it bitterly that way, that I'd been apportioned only an allotment with my son. But on each of those weekends when I arrived and Jimmy acted surprised, even after waiting, it's the light I remember now. I'd get there at nine. Jimmy had a place by the window and would've been waiting since waking. Driving up, I'd see the curtain move. I'd have to hurry. The next instant Jimmy would come bursting through the door—Daddy! Daddy!

It's an old story. A child, your own, is running to be lifted and hugged and swung around, but it's the light you see, the small shining brightness that comes rushing up to you and into you with eagerness and warmth. You feel the rush of love. You feel lifted and swirled, too, but it's the light you see no less, and incredibly, the light is happy, noisy, every time.

And I think, Saturday. We went to movies and ball games, the zoo, you name it. We took in the circus and carnivals. Jimmy loved the tilt-a-whirl. Sometimes we'd have one of his little friends along to share the same-age excitements and I wouldn't try to keep up. We threw Frisbees and flew kites and ate a thousand hamburgers, and those were the days, I think, the fun days. We had good times, great times. Driving back Sunday evening, the weekend over, nearly always Jimmy would get quiet sitting beside me. I would sense a small sadness of parting in him and we'd ride the last few blocks in silence. At the house, he'd jump from the car with a happy face, "Okay, Dad, see ya!" He'd never say the word goodbye and neither would I.

Then the first of May. Jimmy played with some of the other kids after school that day. They fooled around the swings and kicked a soccer ball. No one later remembered seeing a stranger. The other kids left when their parents picked them up and when the school buses arrived. I picture it. Jimmy starts riding his bicycle home. It's two blocks north on Oleander, then four blocks east on Argyle. He crosses Lytle Lane, the first street. The time is approximately three-fifteen. He turns at Argyle after another block and a car pulls quietly to the curb beside him. Jimmy stops and gets off his bike. He puts the kickstand down and goes to the car. The man inside is smiling, acting nice. But what does he say? His hand reaches across and opens the car door. Jimmy gets in. Would he do that? There's no sign of struggle, no marks on the soft lawn at the curb. And no one hears a cry. The car drives away with Jimmy inside. It drives slowly and moves without a sound like all cars in that neighborhood and no one spots it. The street is quiet. A moment later, Mrs. Ida Kromer comes out of her house. She remembers it was during a break in her soap opera, a cosmetic commercial she doesn't like. The TV station later places that break at three-sixteen. Mrs. Kromer notices the bicycle on the sidewalk across the street, but that's all. She sets her sprinkler and goes back inside. In another few minutes Marion Dunn comes home from his office. His head is hurting again. His secretary confirms the time he left his office, and the time he takes to drive home is always the same. He pulls into his drive and thinks he recalls seeing a bicycle parked in front but he's not really thinking. He has a migraine and goes to bed. A little sooner either person might have seen what happened but the moment has passed. The paperboy remembers swerving his moped around a bicycle and throwing Mr. Dunn's paper wide, but he's later also. The log of the security patrol shows its car was cruising several blocks west at the time. In another week the security man on duty will admit he was in a different area, parked and asleep. But it's the same result. No one saw. I return in my mind to that spot in front of the Dunn house and I still see the front wheel canted, the seat slightly crooked, and just so, as if forever, the bicycle is waiting.

A broad blade, the report said, perhaps an ordinary kitchen knife, not overly sharp. Did the man carry it purposely? Blades in pocketknives are not called broad. A switchblade is a keen instrument. A butcher would keep his knives sharpened. It could have been a hunting knife. There were other possibilities. But it seemed to me a dullish knife was an afterthought. The man saw he needed to dispose of a body and decided it would be easier to get rid of in pieces. He looked for something or a knife at hand decided him and he started using it. But bones are hard. He cut away the genitals, they were infantile and impotent, suggestive of his perversion maybe, so he did away with that first, then the hands and feet. Except the knife was dull. He had to hack. Did he see the body was still alive? Death resulted from the loss of blood, not before, that was in the report. So blood was spurting, the heart was still pumping. And while he hacked, was the body conscious, screaming? I couldn't think it. Even with it frozen in me to figure it, I couldn't, my mind wouldn't. But what else? The clothes, the jeans and T-shirt, the satchel of school books. Those were never found. And the blood, the stains. Washed down a drain or still in the trunk of some car? And the dump on the west side. The man knew the way in and out. He knew how to go there and not be seen. But why didn't he hide or bury the body instead of simply throwing it away? He must have thought he'd never be traced. Or did he leave the body like that in order to be found himself? I felt the man knew what he was doing, that he was deliberate and thinking in a conscious manner. He'd somehow planned what he did and he's likely walking around today like any normal human being.

Katherine said once, "You didn't grieve, did you?" I didn't answer. She'd suffered but she had her feelings and I had mine. The way she said "grieve," though, made it sound too simple, as if you could define grieving by the looks it had, the sounds it made. The word itself had no value. Still, we can say grieving has an assigned place and that it comes so regularly with death, we can assume it must. We can make a rule that we're supposed to pass through the grieving stage to accept death, to let the dead die, and that's the process. But grief is such a withered thing and I had been crazy, maybe I hadn't grieved properly. Jimmy was still with me.

Like one day in my room on the west side—I was standing at my window looking out. A smoldering mattress was down in the courtyard to one side. It had been tossed from one of the rooms and left to burn itself out. The building manager took a look but didn't bother otherwise. So the mattress remained the night. The next morning it was still smoking and charring from within. It rained and the thing became a sodden heap. And that's the way it is, I thought. It was a bad day. Daddy, Jimmy said. He had come into the room and taken my hand. I looked down and saw my hand through his fingers. I saw the rug and table corner through his face and I could tell he thought I was sad. I squeezed his hand. It's all right, I said, it's going to be all right.

Time was passing. When Walters no longer returned my calls, I went to see him. The investigation had apparently stalled and I wanted to find out. If you're dropping the case, I said, just tell me. Walters claimed the case was still open, I should leave it alone. But I pushed, I needed to know. Walters finally rubbed his face with his big hands. He was tired. "Look," he said, "look at that." He waved his hand across his desk, across piles of folders. "It's all there, you name it, shootings, stabbings, stompings, the whole roller derby. Okay? I get two, three a week, a hundred and fifty last year. You're asking, I'm telling you. Look at 'em, hundreds of cases, and with most of 'em we're pissing in the wind, they don't get solved. Okay? It ain't like TV. Most of 'em, forget it. The ones you read about—" He dismissed the rest with a hopeless gesture and turned to the window. I was left with the stacks of folders before me. There would be others in archives, in other rooms. Over the years, a mountain of folders. "The thing is," he spoke with his back turned, "you can't take 'em all personally." I hadn't thought of Walters as a bureaucrat, but now I did, even if the description didn't specifically apply. The man worked within a system. His function determined him. And the folders, too, were in a system, full of details and names and printed matter, but no longer living concerns. They were statistics for the analysts, to justify budgets, to continue the system. The subjects in the folders were abstractions for accounting and you could figure them in different ways, the numbers of bodies as so many pounds of dead meat. You could calculate the carcasses by the tonnage. You couldn't take 'em all personally. The folders went into the daily, yearly work flow and you had to be concerned with the plural, not the singular. In multiples the singular becomes a blur anyway and I needed to understand. What mattered, what went on, was that flow, that blur.

But Walters had leveled, he wasn't a bad guy. He'd wanted to be sympathetic. I felt that. It was just that he had his job to do and it was too much. There were plenty others where I came from. I stood to leave. Walters turned from the window. He said he was sorry. I said I understood. He said if anything turned up. I said, right, if anything turned up. We shook hands and I left.

A month later on my way out of town to rebuild my life in another place, I paid a last visit to Argyle Street and stopped in front of the Dunns' house. At the same spot the ghost of the bicycle was still waiting. The trees were bare but as always I saw them green and filled with leaves. The lawns were neat. If you didn't know, the long avenue really was a beautiful street. I sat in my car a long time. Mrs. Ida Kromer came out of her house to check her mail. A few months previously, coming out of her house the same way, she had noticed a bicycle leaning on its kickstand across the street, but that was all. The moment had passed.

S o I w e n t o n and now I'm trying to go back.

I have to remember it's been a few moments but Tracy is still aiming the pistol point-blank between my eyes and I'm still fixed in place.

Now, looking at the situation clinically, you could say for what she intended her best timing had passed. Her next-best timing, however, was still hanging. She had committed herself to simply doing away with me because I'd turned my back and ignored her, I didn't love her. She was an only child. So something had clicked behind her eyes. She'd eased from the bed, pulled the gun from wherever, returned, and cocked the hammer behind my head. Her finger would squeeze, the explosion would resound in the room, but in her mind in the distance probably, she wouldn't really hear it. The deed would be done, that's all. But she'd hesitated. A blip had crossed her screen.

Now I was thinking. The fact she had a gun was new to me but she'd obviously gotten the thing and hidden it some days or weeks before. She'd purposely gone somewhere and obtained it, so it couldn't have been a mere impulse. She'd prepared for this moment. Or more precisely, this eventuality. In some circles that's known as premeditation. A chilling thought suddenly. Just behind that beautiful face, in a darkness beneath that lovely skin molding that perfect body, she had mindfully conceived and planned what she would do. Who would've guessed? Well, she was a fiery woman. Women like that can do things. Like Jennifer Jones in *Duel in the Sun*. But now there was a lull in the action, a piece of business she hadn't rehearsed maybe. The surprise, a Six Flags commercial had popped up. I'd lied but she didn't know that yet. She was seeing the image of herself in front of the camera, her beauty receiving its due. The arrival of the Six Flags spot was probably also inspiring a continuing series of images of more spots to come and the reward of eternal illusion on film. All would finally be as it should have been. But with Tracy, it had to be a problem, too. She was an honest person with the honest person's special sense of personal honor. She'd most likely sat down and stared at the wall awhile, then decided definitely she was going to shoot me. Now, the problem was, if she didn't, and she hadn't yet, would she have to think less of herself for not following through? She was perhaps having to mull that over. She'd been raised in a small town where once you're declared and committed to something, you have to go ahead with it. In a small town after all that's how you get taken for granted. By the time you're six, if you're tabbed a goofy, you're going to still be a goofy when you're forty. It's taken for granted the way you start out is the way you end up. In that way human nature is discernibly simplistic, no need to figure it like quantum mechanics. If you're skinny, you're Skinny. You grow old and fat, you're still Skinny.

In other words, I was lying there struck with the sudden thought, My God, she *planned* this, she's going to do it, and not emotionally, not crazed out of her mind, but coldly, purposely. I thought I knew Tracy, but not this new streak in her. Where did the homicidal trait come from? I'd never harmed her. Well, I slapped her once but that was after she slapped me first. She'd thrown herself into a jealous fit when some good-looking woman cozied up to me at a party and I didn't mind. But that was the end of it. We never slapped each other again. We might have been surprised that such impulses in each of us had so quickly lashed out. Or actually, with me, I must've thought it was pretty natural. You're a man, you don't just stand there and take getting slapped. With Tracy, the old answer would be that another woman had tried to move in on her territory. In that case, she should've slapped the woman. She slapped me instead, like it was supposed to be my fault other women can't keep their hands off me.

Anyway, the woman at the party meant nothing and I was only a little drunk, having fun. Then Tracy stepped between us dripping sugar. She said a few bitchy sweetly smiled words to the woman and I laughed to smooth it. That's when she slapped me. I might have been surprised but it wasn't like my face was stung and I stood there thinking about it. I slapped her right back, whap!, that quick. Tracy was stunned, then only looked at me. A splotch of red spread her cheek. But she didn't react. She still held her drink unspilled. She would hold a single drink like that at every party a whole evening and maybe take two sips.

But now she was only facing me. We didn't speak. I felt what? I want to say sorry. Cheap is a better word. In the next beat, Tracy raised her chin, smiled brilliantly, and calmly walked away. I was left definitely low-rent. The thing is, lying with the gun to my head, I remembered that incident. We'd made love later more desperately than ever and the slapping was never mentioned again, but with Tracy a breath away about to kill me, the party episode seemed a connection. She'd slapped me in a fit of jealousy. Normal enough. We expect people to strike out in sudden fits. I'd reacted. But then Tracy had turned completely controlled. How could she? She was a fiery passionate woman. Her emotions reigned free. That's the way she was. Then she'd sleep with a clear conscience. Her beauty sleep, she called it, a nice name, but it was for twelve hours straight sometimes. Whatever, to the naked eye she was simply a natural human being.

I thought. But now there was obviously a dark streak in her as well. Some kind of cold impersonal thing that would have its own dead reckoning. Or maybe what I sensed in Tracy that night was plainly the reptilian brain we all have though it's usually smothered in humanistic sentiment that began with the Age of Enlightenment when intelligent men in knee stockings honestly believed we would someday discover the reason for everything. It was a hopeful era but we know now the answers are not coming tomorrow. We have to find our own reasons for the moment. And for the moment what I saw in Tracy was a real reason for getting away, and I mean out of the whole legal twosome deal entirely.

Of course, I'd been raised in small towns, too, I'd taken her for granted. From the beginning she'd been sexy, beautiful, little more. At the cocktail hour, an asset. She increased a man's invisible net worth, but what did she know, what could she talk about? Not Hobbes. Not Hume. Well, to be fair, who could? I didn't know about those old guys either. She could talk about cartoons. She liked the Roadrunner on Saturday mornings. She would lie in bed watching Wile E. Coyote run SPLAT! into a highway painted on the side of a cliff. BEEP!BEEP!—the Roadrunner would zip by in a cloud of dust. That was funny. But Tracy was supposed to be grown. How deep can you go with a mangy coyote prone to cartoon disaster every four seconds?

I mentioned the Six Flags spot again. "You'll like it," I said. Tracy's eyes changed as if returning from a trance and it was like her craziness vanished in thin air.

"What will I wear?" she asked, meaning during the filming, her expression brightening. She was also now sitting cross-legged on the bed with both hands absently hugging the pistol to her stomach. The hammer was still cocked. One good huggy squeeze, she'd blow a hole in her leg. "Well, I dunno," I said. I scooted my butt up and adjusted the pillow until I was sitting upright. "Harry said he was going to send the script over tomorrow." Harry, the nice guy advertising director for Six Flags. If he'd ever initiated a script before, I couldn't remember. The way it worked, Harry and I would have lunch. He'd call it a creative session. I'd put it down as a business expense. We'd toss around a few ideas with the martinis. Then he'd decide on one, "Now that's great! Terrific! Let's go with it!" The usual dumb fun-for-the-whole-family thing, nothing new. I'd take the idea scrawled on a cocktail napkin and farm out the script to be written along with a storyboard. So the script development was always up to me, not Harry, but Tracy wasn't privy to that sort of top-level corporate decision-making. I eased the gun from her lap and neither of us pretended to notice it. Tracy in fact appeared oblivious to her whole previous murderous threat.

I said, "I'm going to put Jack onto the storyboard, see what

he comes up with." Jack, my ol' standby artist who'd only wanted to be a great painter but found he had kids to support. I
uncocked the hammer and laid the pistol on the floor, at the
same time nudging it under the bed. My fingers had trembled
uncocking the hammer. But Tracy was only focused now on the
Six Flags spot and wanted to know the theme, her role in it.
"Oh, it's good," I said, "you're gonna be terrific in it." "Tell
me!" Her eyes alive waiting to hear, she was almost bouncing on
the bed she was so eager. It was too easy. So I started telling her,
making it up as I went along, which I was good at. ". . . like
'California or Bust,'" I said, "only it's going to be 'Six Flags or
Bust' and you're going to be the person trying to get there any
way you can. Lots of action stuff. Maybe the camera opens on
a long shot of a desert, all we can see are sand dunes, then we
zoom in on this tiny figure in the middle of this huge desert
and it's you riding a camel. A sign tacked to the camel's hump
says, 'Six Flags or Bust.' It's hot, the sun's blazing down, and
you're perishing but you're not giving up. You see in a mirage up
ahead a shimmering vision of Six Flags. Cut to a raft in the
rapids of a roaring river somewhere and there you are on the
raft fighting the waves in a clingy dress getting all wet. A sign
waving on the raft mast signals, 'Six Flags or Bust.' In a spum-
ing spray of white water we see the splashing image of the Six
Flags log slide, lots of people laughing and having fun. Then we
cut to you riding a horse hell bent for leather. You're a Pony
Express rider and Indians are chasing you shooting arrows, an
arrow gets plugged through your hat. A sign on your saddlebag
says, 'Six Flags or Bust.'" Etc., etc.
   I went on with endless scenes of Tracy determined to get to
her final destination, hang-gliding, skiing an avalanche, whatever popped into my head. The scenes all together would've lasted thirty minutes. And all of it, of course, too offbeat for the

traditional Six Flags image. The wet clingy dress would never make it. What I was describing in fact was better suited for General Transportation. The point was, I was saving my life. And not then, but now, I can see I was doing the saving in the way easiest for me, the way I made money, and in a way that made me at the mortal age of thirty-five a pretty unhappy guy.

If I can explain. In my work, I was known as "creative," I could come up with ideas. You'd think, well, who couldn't? I thought that, too. People have brains, they think, it naturally follows they also have ideas, right? Apparently not. Take a look. The average brain is Silly Putty. You can knead it and mush it around but left alone a brain is pretty inert matter. Which is not nice to say but being realistic you gotta admit when you finally find a singular mind in action it's almost a discovery.

My reputation was for coming up with "creative" ideas, one after another. I could toss 'em out as long as anyone wanted to listen and swill martinis. And I could do that, I think, because I didn't care, it wasn't important. So my problem in part was what did having a bunch of ideas for advertising amount to? You can argue it helps progress. Advertising sells products to make people's lives easier and the world a better place. That may be. I don't have any quarrel with easier living and a better world. Although greed sneaks in. A product is sold essentially to make money. Greed however is forever and beyond righteousness. No, the main problem with my part in advertising was with the "creative" qualifier attached to the idea label. I didn't believe it but I went along with it. So I was deceitful. Now, to be really honest, I can't define "creative" but I feel it needs to have something to do with originality, with what seemingly emerges on its own. My ideas didn't do that. Look at the spot I imagined for Tracy, the camel and Pony Express stuff. I was simply taking the tired old "California or Bust" pioneer slogan and applying it flippantly to Six Flags. You can't say that's creative. It's gimmicky. The slogan is apocryphal anyway, mythologized first in the old-timey eastern press, then in the movies. So I was only reimagining a cliché that had already been imagined to death. I did that in advertising and got paid for being good at it. And in my mind, for being phony. You see the conflict. My work was a false front. I wasn't "creative." But when I tried to say so a few times, it was thought I was only being modestly self-deprecating. My reputation had already been accepted by word of mouth. Which probably goes back to the power of suggestion. You drop a hint, that's all it takes. You suggest such-and-such is so-and-so and pretty soon it is.

So there I was getting credited for something I wasn't, and it was a personal moral issue I didn't know I had except I knew I was somehow messed up and drinking myself into stupors. At the same time, when you consider what really happens on this earth, the actual horrors, the slaughters and starvations taking place every minute somewhere in the world, it goes without saying my small selfish concern was nothing. And maybe that was part of my predicament, too, that my plight was so tiny. It should've been more important. Some kind of personal worth was at stake.

That was one thing. Now, my situation with Tracy. Based on sex. Not a bad base. Try having a life without it. But when you're a man and it's always the same woman, I don't care how many variations you try, if it's not a fresh new conquest now and then, pretty soon it's routine. Sex counselors talk about intimacy like it's a learning skill for making passing grades. Forget that. Sex is real and an end in itself. It's also a natural resource with depletion allowances. That's why two people living together, sleeping in the same bed night after night and facing each other in the mornings, need a little extra capital in common, a small bond in love and respect maybe, some stocks of mutual interest to talk about. You might hope finally for a meeting of the minds if only at the lower level of the cranium. Perhaps then, if it wasn't only sex, two people might be able to live together halfway naturally.

But I didn't feel my life with Tracy was very natural. Even if you could say it was naturally uninhibited, it was also physically concentrated. By that I mean the body was always the focus, to dress and undress, to display, to use erotically in all its sensual forms to extrude sex. As I said, not a bad base. But unless you're sixteen when even a bus ride is amorous, sex alone is not enough. The inevitable flow of day-to-day living continues and a feeling of loss accumulates. Or that's what happened to me. I felt weighted with a sense of loss. And it wasn't Jimmy. That was different. So how to figure it? In most ways it appeared I was doing all right, enough money, enough creature comforts. Still, I was weighted. When we were younger, my old friend Grady once asked if I thought we were "driving" or "driven." The first having to do with courage, the second with fear. I told him I didn't think it was the right question. He said that was because I was ignorant, it was the perfect question. Then the perfect answer is one or the other. And maybe it should be. Driving/driven. Either/or. The trick, to keep it simple.

But back to the bedroom. Tracy was excited, searching her closet for different outfits. I was lying there watching her try on clothes. She pulled out a Grecian toga gown, loose and clingy, for getting wet on the raft. What did I think? Fine, I said, but I would rent the wardrobe. She didn't care, she was into modeling her roles. And this? she asked. A big floppy hat for the Pony Express. She looked cute in it. That's fine, I said. I was sinking. Tracy jumped next to the camel ride and what she should wear for the desert. It would have to look Arabian Nightish, a skimpy harem thing to show her navel. Fine, I said. And tomorrow, I thought, I could put off the Six Flags spot, tell her Harry was holding the script for further corporate approval. Harry was a master at corporate politics. Tracy would be disappointed. Then I would have to lie again to finally cancel the commercial entirely. I'd make it Harry's fault. He had failed at corporate politics, he might be on his way out. There'd never been a Six Flags spot to begin with but right now Tracy was having fun dressing her roles and killing me was no longer in the picture.

Which was good because I was falling to sleep, I was so damned tired. I'd hide the pistol in the garage in the morning. Tracy wouldn't find it but the following week she'd have another one, a larger .357 Magnum. She'd have to hold it in both hands to aim.

But that was the future. At the moment she was dressing for her camel ride in the desert and I was sinking into oblivion thinking desert. And all around, sand and heat, a blowing wind. I was fading and vaguely dreaming I could draw a line in the sand.

Now, at this point, my mind returns to the desert around the town of Dalton and my last year there. I was sixteen. I'd like to forget that place, I'd thought to escape it, but in many ways those days still determine me.

So I think Dalton, my first line in the sand and my first encounter with a real live nemesis named Myrtle.

YOU COULD GIVE DALTON a nice homey sound and call it a farming community. The town itself was a courthouse square surrounded by a few flat miles of irrigated farms, plots of dull greenery in the spring, but beyond and otherwise, the distance was barren landscape, sand and wind, a wide emptiness. The wind always blew.

The usual businesses lined the square, Dalton Drugs, Wimpy's Cafe, Moore Hardware, the State Bank, and so on. Cars parked into the curb, not parallel. The courthouse was three-story with the barred windows of the jail on top. Once or twice a year you could look up and see a prisoner looking down. Most of the storefronts had porticos. Glenda's Fashions had a blue awning she rolled out in the morning and back at night. The post office faced from the west, a red brick affair built by the WPA during the depression and next to the bank the most solid-looking building in town. The Texaco station was north of the square, the Sinclair with its green dinosaur sign was south. I worked at the Sinclair after school and weekends. The drive-in movie was west, the school east. A tall water tower stood like a lone sentinel at the edge of town. The only trees to speak of shaded the courthouse, then the rest of the scene as far as you could see was plain and level. The farms were plain and level. Here and there, an old salt flat, sand dunes, nothing more. Billy the Kid out of his known territory once supposedly hid for a night in one of the salt flats. This was Dalton's one claim to fame. The salt flat however remained unredeemed.

At the turn of the century the area was opened for home-steading. The lure was sixty free acres, so people came out and lived in dugout holes in the ground and tried to dryland-farm. But with no rain, with only a few sprinkles a year, the wheat didn't make it, the cotton blew away. Old photos show haggard women, ragged kids. Whole families starved. Then irrigation was brought in and the crops became peanuts and sugar beets, beans and broomcorn. The first farms with irrigation pumps made money and expanded with more pumps, more money. A few became the haves, the rest the have-nots, the usual story. During the fall people worked in the fields, the peanut mill, the sugar beet plant. The rest of the year they picked up odd jobs or sat around. Idle men played dominoes and whittled sticks. It didn't cost much to live. The population in town leveled off at three thousand, the county overall at about five. The Chamber of Commerce had a sign at the city limits:

WELC ME TO DALTON
WHERE FRIENDS ARE F IENDS

Now, the time I'm going to talk about, my brother and I lived with my dad, Charlie. We didn't call ourselves a single-parent family. We didn't know we were that complicated. Marie had been gone eleven years. I was sixteen and you could say I was doing all right. I did well in school, I was first-string line-backer, I worked at the Sinclair. The town, well, for sure the place needed to be livelier. You could go nuts waiting for something to happen. The movie was over by ten, the City Cafe closed at eleven. Only the Sinclair stayed open all night. Nobody knew why. You wanted to chase girls, you had to ask yourself where. Darlene was the most beautiful girl in town and my secret obsession but not yet quite in my life. Still, I had hopes and dreams every day that the future was just around the corner.

Then the corner turned and the future appeared.

"This is Myrtle," Charlie said. It was Saturday. He was wearing his old blue double-breasted suit from before the war and she was standing there trying to smile, a total stranger dressed in pink taffeta and white pillbox hat, white gloves, and white patent-leather shoes—flat-heeled, so as not to be taller than Charlie—but *white* in that daily blowing dirty wind. Walking from the car to the house, the stitches in her gloves had turned brown. The gauzy veil around her pillbox had filled with sand. She stood wide and bald-faced as if slightly addled but also with a mad victorious gleam in her eye, the instant ugly step-mother.

Until that morning I hadn't known they were getting married. And I hadn't known about this woman or any woman with Charlie. When did he go out? Or where? Not to bars, he didn't drink. Besides, the county was dry, there were no bars, only three cafes and two movies, and if he'd gone to those places, I prowled the town, I would've seen his car parked. He might've met her in church, the known spot for women, but he never went to church either. A friend might've introduced them but I couldn't guess who. Charlie didn't have friends.

But it had come about. Charlie had found this woman, dug her up somewhere, and there she was. "I hope we can get along," she said. Then pointedly, "I know we will." Her eyes leveled. She was stepping in, you could tell. She was going to muscle her way in and lay traps. She had already planted her flag on the hill. If I'd had any experience I would've walked straight past her on out the door and never looked back. But right then I wasn't experienced. I hadn't been arrested or thrown in jail yet and I was still only good-hearted. I wanted to show I could at least act civil. I stuck out my hand to shake and she pulled hers back. Her white gloves. My hand was still greasy from work. "Sorry," I said. "Oh, that's all right," like she was being nice and forgiving me, but with a prissy cutesy mouth.

They'd just come from being married in the First Church of Christ. I don't know who stood up for them, probably the preacher's brother and his wife. The preacher's brother was a secret pervert. His wife would eventually commit suicide. But whoever, it was Saturday, the rest of the church would've been empty. Charlie and Myrtle had stood in front of the pulpit and exchanged vows. Then what, kissed? I couldn't imagine it. Charlie was thirty-eight and Myrtle was thirty-three, which might not have been too old, but in my mind at the time neither in any way looked like kissing material. Charlie was small and scrawny, a skeletal body with spindly legs. He never filled a chair and he was so repressed and withdrawn you could hang him on a wall and never notice him. Myrtle was lumpy and misshaped. Above the waist kinda normal, but from the waist down a big blob of hips with heavy legs and bowlegged calves. You could've tossed a firelog between her calves. Her skin was pale and clammy-looking.

Still, they had married. What they wanted with each other was hard to figure but it was probably practical. Charlie had a steady job at the post office with a government pension at the end and Myrtle had a whole brood of kids she needed someone to help feed. She'd bring her kids in later that day, and I say a whole brood, I want to be accurate, it was actually only four, but four of the whiniest most awful little brats you ever saw, ranging from twelve to six years old, they were spaced in age at regular two-year intervals as if timed by some monotonous routine. It was going to be on me to play like a big brother to give them someone to look up to, and Charlie, the pointless way he was, was going to be their brand-new stepdaddy. It crossed my mind, poor kids, they didn't stand a chance. As obnoxious as they were, I felt sorry for them. I should've felt sorry for myself. In the same situation the dogs of fate were about to eat my lunch, too.

It was the middle of the day. The kids and my older brother, Billy, would show up later. Meanwhile, Charlie, Myrtle, and I were standing in this house where we're all going to start living together and become a sudden family without warning. It was an old rent house on a caliche road at the edge of town. The outside was tacked with tarpaper, the roof was warped. Tumbleweeds had stacked up against the westerly side and trash was blowing in the dirt yard. A toolshed stood in back. I thought it looked all right. I wouldn't think so now. In fact, when I returned to Dalton twenty years later, I drove by to see that house and I couldn't believe we'd actually lived there. It looked smaller than I remembered and although the tarpaper had been stuccoed, the dirt yard, the tumbleweeds, the whole ratty rest of the place was still the same. Maybe at the time, because Billy and I had been living with Charlie the past year in a revamped garage, the house seemed better. It came complete with two bedrooms and a bath, living room, kitchen, and back porch. It also came with saggy ceilings and permanent rings in the bathtub, but the doors closed, the windows had screens, the rooms had nozzles in the floor for gas heaters. In short, the place had indoor plumbing, modern conveniences, what more could you ask?

"Well, I know one thing," Myrtle said, "we're going to need a new linoleum in that kitchen." She'd pulled off her white gloves and walked through the house. "And I like yellow," she said. "I saw a pattern at Sears that had little yellow and white squares. I think that'd look pretty in there, don't you?" She was asking Charlie and he sort of shrugged, if that's what she wanted. "We could paint the cabinets to match, yellow doors with white handles. Now that would look good, don't you think?" Another question, another shrug. She could ask Charlie all day and get the same back, I could've told her. Charlie wasn't conversational. "And a clothesline," she said. "I'm going to need a clothesline first thing right out there in back." She was still speaking to Charlie and again when he didn't exactly commit, she turned to me. "I bet you could put one up for me—couldn't you?" It wasn't a question. She had bared her teeth and lowered her chin to fix me with the tops of her eyes. I knew right then it was going to be her or me and the following, if not verbatim, is the way I remember we talked.

"Well, I dunno," I said, "if I had some wire or something."

"Oh, I bet you could find some wire around, just go to the hardware store."

"I'd have to find some poles, too, to stick up."

"Some poles are probably out there in that ol' shed, something you could use, I'm sure."

"And something to dig the postholes with, that ground's pretty hard."

"If it is—oh, I know, you can just stretch the clothesline from the back of the house to the shed, that'll work just as well and you won't have to put up no poles."

"Except right now I have to go back to work."

"Then tomorrow morning."

"But not on a Sunday, tomorrow's Sunday."

"That's right, I forgot. Then it'll just have to be Monday morning."

"Except I go to school Monday morning."

"Right after school then."

"If I could, but I work after school, too."

She was still smiling, or showing her teeth, but she was beginning to see me now. A jellied look had come into her eye. Charlie had eased back out of the way. Being introverted, he didn't like being in between anything.

"All right," Myrtle said, "then I guess you'll just have to do it when you get off work."

"Except I don't get off till ten."

She appeared stopped.

"Y'know, ten's after dark," I said.

"Now don't tell me you're afraid of the dark, putting up a little ol' clothesline."

"If I knew what was out there, I mean, if I knew where I was sticking my hands. I got bit by a black widow spider once and I still got the scar on my finger." I tried to show her.

She couldn't see it. "So one little spider bite. One time."

"Yeah, but you never know what's been living in an ol' shed like that and still hanging around, 'specially snakes."

"Not snakes."

"Might be. Supposed to be a whole new influx of snakes this year. They killed a sidewinder on the square last week right in town."

"You saw it?"

"A big one, about eight feet long. They brought it over to the Sinclair and we hung it out on the gas pump to show."

She turned to Charlie. "Charlie, did you know about that?"

He shrugged.

Myrtle squared her shoulders. "Well, I'll tell you, one thing's for sure, I better not find no snake in this house. I hate snakes." She was marching through the house checking the closets and behind doors, a regular mean-eyed snake hunter. Charlie was following, patting the air with his hand, "Now Myrtle—" Any snake with any sense was crawling back in its hole.

I took the opportunity to head back to my job at the Sinclair, about a mile's walk. The wind had picked up, the sand was blowing, and I had time to consider. I was resentful. I'd gone out of my way to be a good guy and I should've known better. I'd used up my noon hour and missed my regular hamburger at Wimpy's. Well, okay, I could miss a meal, I could shake up a few peanuts in a Coke, I liked doing that, but, dammit, I'd gone out there with the best intentions to act decent, to see the new house and meet the new stepmother, and look what happened. She'd started right off telling me what to do. And not asking but telling, like she had the say-so and could order me around. I could put up the clothesline for her, couldn't I? Like hell. She wanted a stringy damned clothesline up, she could put up the rinkydink damned thing herself. I should've told her, hey, now let's just hold it right there, I don't take orders from nobody, understand? Especially some bigass new stepmother. I make my own way and I'm my own boss, so get that straight, you mess with me, you're meat, I'll flatten you like a pancake. You come at me, you better bring an army with you because nobody, and I mean nobody, tells me what to do. They never have and they never will.

I should've told her. And I should've known. I was walking back to the Sinclair. Imagine, an old dirt road and a lone ignorant kid stomping along ranting to himself. Up ahead, the dusty town. All around, the eternal sand blowing. And that's it. Yet all the ingredients are here for the mixing of Destiny, a time and place, a resentful hostile kid with a rebellious spirit, not yet a man, but with a dangerous mind for that time and place, and the one thing that caused everything, a fluke, a transcendency— a simple dumbass clothesline.

You want to believe in the battle between Good and Evil, in some kind of great Cosmic Confrontation, but what happens, the world turns on a dime.

So, the new step-deal with the new step-snivelings. Four of them. The first time I saw them all together, it looked like forty. They'd swarmed the house like an invasion of termites. We were going to need the exterminators out to save the furniture. But they were only four and they were only kids so they weren't really coming out of the woodwork and eating the furniture. What furniture? We were poor. It was just that I wasn't used to living with a crowd where I had to share the space, especially the one bathroom in the mornings before school. There were eight of us, my brother and me and four of them, and Charlie and Myrtle. Actually, Charlie got up early and disappeared and Myrtle never used the bathroom, I don't know what she did, so they didn't have to compete. Still, with the six of us, you had to wait in line and bang on the door to get in. Then you were sitting in there yourself trying to be calm, but with the doorknob twisting and turning, with the knocking and scratching and whiny pathetic pleading—"let me in, let me in, you're taking too long"—it wasn't easy. They'd start throwing their weight against the door to break in. You'd hear them backing up to get a run at it, then you'd hear the running footsteps coming. It's a sound you never forget.

Their names. Now get this—three girls and a boy, the girls, aged twelve, ten, and eight, the boy, six—their names were April, May, June, and August. And they weren't even born in those months. Or May was, the ten-year-old, she was born in May, and because her older sister had already been named April, although April had been born in November, Myrtle must've thought, Well, May comes after April, and that's how she came up with May. The other two were born in October and February but by then Myrtle was on a roll and tabbed them June and August. She'd been inspired by the annual lumber company calendar that pictured the months with the moose in January and the grizzly in July. Since I could never keep their names straight, I started calling the four calendar kids more simply, Eenie, Meenie, Minie, Mouse. The boy, August, being the Mouse the way he kept hiding in corners behind doors. When you couldn't find him, you knew he'd crawled under the house with the lizards. He liked it under there. He was also a pretty sneaky little night creature. I'd catch him trying to steal my shoes from under my bed at night. I'd tell Myrtle and she'd defend him, "Oh, he was just sleepwalking, that's the way he does." He was her "baby" but I knew, the little creep was a born thief and future convict. His sisters were not much better. I thought they were all retarded.

We moved into the rent house, the three girls were given one bedroom, Charlie and Myrtle took the other. My brother and I and Mouse were left to the screened-in back porch. My brother and I had our army cots at one end, the Mouse had his at the other. A burlap curtain was hung across the middle to divide the space, you might say, into two rooms. In the winter we covered the screen with plywood to keep out the cold, and of course the year-round blowing sand. We had what we needed, a box for socks and underwear, and nails in the wall and a broom handle across one corner for hang-up clothes. I can't recall sticking up posters or fixing the space with personal touches. It was a place to sleep out of the weather. Or almost. The roof leaked between the cots and the sand sifted through the splices in the plywood. We'd wake up with the sand settled solid on our pillows except where our heads had lain and there'd be another layering of sand on the quilts. In the winter on the coldest mornings, we'd hit that icy board floor with our bare feet and turn blue scrambling into our clothes frozen stiff in the night. Then it was on to the siege-and-besieged at the bathroom.

Personally I would've preferred taking my morning leak in the backyard but the dog wouldn't let me. And here I'm talking about the pet four-legger that came with the new step-setup. The thing looked like a bad cross between a canine cyclops and some kind of mangy alley scavenger. It was blind in one eye with only a white mucky orb in that socket, while the other eye, the good one, was like a bulging red marble that never blinked. Picture the ugliest meanest-looking dog you can, this is what I'm talking about. It had hair like bristles on a wild boar. Its head was scarred and war-torn. One ear was half missing, chewed off somewhere. Its teeth were yellow and jagged, and it had huge muscles in its chest and shoulders that kept knotting and unknotting. It had sinewy legs and lean shanks and broken ragged claws. The thing was a regular motorcycle gang on paws. But he was a good watchdog, Myrtle said, and every house needed one, so she kept him chained to a corner of the shed with just enough slack in his chain he could run the length to within a few inches of the back door. If you didn't know—well, you can see what's coming. The first morning I thought to step out to take a leak, he saw me with his one good peeper flaring and immediately charged. It was like a dark blur hurtling toward me. He was coming with his full weight full speed and leaping. I felt death at my throat. Fortunately, at the last instant he hit the end of the line and the chain held. He was yanked backwards and left stretched in midair with his hind end forward, his legs clawing at empty space. Then he was on the ground straining his chain a fraction from my life, snarling and frothing, his terrible feet tearing the earth, his lips curled back showing his dripping fangs.

Now think. It's early morning. You decide to take a leak, so you go outside. You're standing on the back steps not hurting anyone. Suddenly there's this insane canine psychopath about four inches away, straining its chain, snapping its jaws, slathering to get at you—and right there you're going to unzip, you're going to pull out the most prized precious part of your anatomy and go ahead? Excuse me, I don't think so.

Myrtle called the dog Sybil. "Here, Sybil, that's a good boy, nice boy." Which didn't figure. It was a male dog, right? It had two big oblong balls hanging down between its hind legs and she gives it a girl's name. Where's the logic? The function of the human brain is to place the known objects of this world in proper perspective so we can see how things fit and know where we stand. We're supposed to use our brains to perceive what's real and what's not so we don't end up in the funny farm doing therapy with plastic arts and crafts. You call a tree a tree because that's what a tree is and everybody knows it. But not Myrtle. She called her fully male killing machine Sybil.

The two of them also had what can only be called an affectionate relationship. She'd pat his old scarred head and rub his little pointy mangled ear and coo at him, "Oh, you're a good boy, Sybil, a sweet boy, yes, you are." She'd scratch up the dandruff in his leathery ol' hide, he'd get a sappy look on his ugly mug and waggle his tail. His tongue would loll and his one good eye would close wistfully, leaving only the white blind one to stare out at nothing. You could believe the two together had some kind of lower-IQ alliance. She would feed him. But not in a bowl. Because Sybil, she said, chewed up all his bowls, even the metal ones. She said this laughingly one day. So what she'd do, she'd throw a bone to him on the ground, say a big ham bone. He'd snap it from the dirt snarling and crunch the thing instantly into splinters. He'd grind up rib bones like they were saltine crackers.

And he was always pacing. I would watch him from the back porch pacing the length of his chain, making low throttling sounds in his throat, the hair raised on his heck. It was like he just couldn't wait for something harmless to come within range. When nothing did, he might've learned, but he was obsessed and every day I'd watch him in his solitary track pacing back and forth, back and forth. He had me fascinated, and I think the reason was, I identified. Not in looks, of course. I could see in the mirror, I was better-looking. And that's a thought, how did I see myself? It's vague. Girls told me I looked like James Dean, meaning the comparison as a compliment, I suppose, but I couldn't see it. Dean was smaller and squirrely-looking. He had shifty eyes. I really believed at the time I looked more like Sonny Tufts. Now there was a guy. He'd get knocked down and kicked in the head, he'd struggle to his feet and keep on fighting. It's a shame he's no longer remembered. He played in Hollywood B movies and almost became a star. If he didn't quite make it, at least he tried. A handsome devil, a man's man, he always took up for the underdog. Actually, he *was* the underdog. So maybe it wasn't so much a physical look we had in common but the hopeful moralist's outlook from the bottom of the barrel. We could fight for causes and risk our lives because we had nothing to lose. In any case, I must've figured Sonny and I were twins in essential ways. Then he vanished from the screen and I understand he ended up in Akron or somewhere selling insurance. Ol' Sonny Tufts. The name still has a ring to it.

But I'm talking about identifying with Sybil. Here was this poor animal chained and restrained to a very small world and I felt that was me, too. The animal didn't know why. Me either. Then, too, the thing was mean and mad at everything and I could picture myself the same. I figured I could get mean enough when I had to, and if I wasn't exactly mad at everything, I might've been. Anyway, in some primordial way a creature inside me was a lot like Sybil and deep down I could feel it pacing, always pacing. It was like a wildness or sheer craziness or I didn't know what. I was afraid if the thing got loose, no telling what it would make me do.

As it turned out, I eventually made friends with Sybil. I think I felt I needed a friend in the new step-deal and Sybil was my best bet. Besides, I liked dogs and I wanted to like this one, too, if he wouldn't eat me first. Anyway, the first time Sybil and I reached a truce, I'd been approaching him for weeks. Then I was mincing my steps toward him again, but closer. He flashed me a look with his one good eye and I halted. He was standing rigid with his muscles trembling, they were knotted so hard. I reached my hand out gradually until I could feel his breath on my fingers. Then he wasn't breathing. He was waiting. A string of drool hung from his jaw. One false move I could see my hand getting snatched away in a meat grinder. So I was taking a chance. But I was also sixteen. At that age, you're a guy, you have to prove yourself. Which is why you do stupid things. You face fear even when you're afraid, or especially when you're afraid because that's how you can tell it's fear.

Whatever, Sybil was waiting. A breathless moment. Suddenly his mouth opened. I thought I was a goner. But his tongue lolled and he was only grinning and lifting a paw. "Well, all right!" I said. "Good dog!" I shook his paw and patted his head.

That was the start. After that, he'd occasionally forget and revert to his old ways but I started feeding him my leftover bits of hamburger and French fries. And I think it was the French fries that finally did the trick. That dog flat loved potatoes. So we became pals. But when I eventually unchained him to set him free, it was a sad moment. I'll have to tell about that.

But later.

First, I had a regular ongoing battle with Myrtle over the clothesline. Or that was the surface subject. She wouldn't win. Or in the end if you could say she really did win, it was a Pyrrhic finish. Like Tacitus described an ancient Roman battle, she created a desert and called it victory, only of course not in those words.

So, the clothesline and Myrtle. The first show of contention came pretty quickly but I need to put it in perspective.

We were eating. "Pass the beans, please," I was asking. The bowl was on the other side of the table in front of Meenie, or in front of Eenie, Meenie, Minie, all three. They were sitting glued together and pretended not to hear me. They kept stuffing their mouths. The beans in the big speckled bowl were set about a hand beyond my reach. To get it myself I'd have to raise from my seat and stretch my arm across the table, but this was supposed to be a Sunday family dinner, our first, and I wanted to show I had table manners. Why, I don't know. It was a complete waste of higher standards.

I spoke again, louder. "Beans, please." Myrtle nudged Meenie with her fork. Meenie wiped her mouth with the back of her hand. "Whut?" Myrtle told her prissily, "Now, honey, be nice and pass the beans to your new big brother." New big brother! Meenie hung her mouth open full of chewed food. "Huh?"

Mouse was on my left picking beans from his spoon to drop on the floor. Billy on my right was hunched over his place with his forearm laid out around his plate as if having to guard it. Charlie at the end of the table was mute and barely a presence, he was so hard to notice, but I can still see him very clearly mincing at his food, and in my mind I can see through him, on through his body and vague bones to the buckled wallpaper at his back, and beyond the wall, beyond the house itself in the flat nowhere, I see the shimmering image of the day he retired from the post office and dropped dead of a heart attack. That would be in another twenty years and I wouldn't hear of his death until later. I would be in Dallas at the time. I'd think, well, he's gone and I never really knew him. Who was he? Given another life, we might've shaken hands and parted friends. But another life is never given.

"Beans!" I said, Jesus! Meenie finally moved to pass the bowl, greedily ladling herself another gloppy spoonful before pushing it on. But she only pushed the bowl a little so I still had to raise to reach it. So much for table etiquette. I'd asked politely and been slighted, okay, I would never ask for anything in that house again. I pulled the bowl to my plate. I'd already had one helping but I wanted seconds, the way I usually did. Or, normally, when I was hungry, I'd have three or four helpings. And I was nearly always hungry. I was still growing, and going to school, working, playing football, I needed fuel to burn to keep up my energy. I spooned down and scooped. My spoon came up empty. I tilted the bowl and looked in. The beans were gone. Only a brown scum remained at the bottom where the spoon had scraped furrows in a land of drought. It was like some kind of geography for starvation. A fly buzzed the bowl. I pushed from the table and went to the stove. A big smoked-up pot sat on the front burner but it was empty, too. Its crusty insides would take hard scrubbing with wirewool to get clean. I stared down at the pot. No more beans. No more food. I stood.

This was supposed to be a Sunday family dinner. That should have meant a big table of food with more than enough to eat. But we'd had only beans and mashed potatoes and hardly a taste of that, one small helping each. Well, the calendar kids had stuffed their mouths with more. Meenie had swiped the last spoonful before letting the bowl come to me. Besides, if this was Sunday dinner, where was the dessert, the pie, the ice cream? There wasn't any. Oh, sure, you could pour syrup on a slice of bread but you don't call that dessert. When I was little, I remembered, Sunday dinners had been special. Marie was still around. We'd go to Grandma's and the whole table would be loaded with heaping platters of fried chicken, biscuits and gravy, corn, okra, all kinds of good food. Grandma would make the biscuits with Gladiola flour, flattening the dough with her rolling pin. She'd let me punch up the dough. She'd batter a mess of catfish in cornmeal and fry the pieces curling and golden crisp in an iron skillet. Under the crust the fish would come out steaming and tender white. We had cracklings and potluck and redeye grease with thick slabs of ham. The kitchen was always so full of warm smells and good things cooking, my mouth still waters remembering. Then we'd sit down to eat and it was a happy time because we'd really want to eat and the pure enjoyment of everybody together smacking their lips and saying out loud how good the food sure did look and smell, Hummmmm-umm, boy, that really smells good! We'd pass the bowls and platters and fill our plates, take our first bites and grin, Boy, now that sure does taste good! We'd laugh. It was fun to eat. And you never had to ask to have anything passed to you, it was passed before you could ask, Here, you better have some more, you haven't hardly eaten a thing. I ate eight pieces of fried chicken once and could've had more. My grandma was always saying, Eat hearty now, there's plenty, you don't want to get puny. No one was puny anyway. We could have seconds for dessert, too. Big wedges of cherry pie, peach cobbler, home-made ice cream, you name it. My favorite was the plum dumpling dump dusted with powdered sugar. You never knew what was in it. And in the summertime, in the good ol' sum-mertime—watermelon! Billy and I would get to sit out in the yard with whole halves of red juicy watermelon sprinkled with salt. We'd have seed-spitting contests and I'd win every time. Billy was older, he'd let me win. We'd wash our sticky faces and hands in the bucket of water drawn from the cistern.

I think we were happy. Food was love. Then Marie was gone. I was five. I was told years later she'd felt trapped. "Suffocated" was the word. In Dalton, in that dead-end place, she'd gone loony or had some kind of hysteria. She liked the fast life, they said, or who knows, she liked men in uniform. The war had come along and soldiers looked so clean-cut in their polished khakis, she decided to follow one off to war one day and never came back. It was goodbye Dalton, goodbye kids, she was off to live her life and do exciting things. She was twenty-three and still a kid herself, just another country girl with the hots to trot. I imagine it now. I see her getting stuck in some truckstop in Oklahoma. She's hired to wait tables and lives in a trailer in back. She shacks up with the frycook and pretends to have fun.

Then she catches a ride with an eighteen-wheeler passing through and goes on down the road. But not far. She's stopped next in Missouri. Then Kansas. And back again in Oklahoma. This is her territory and she makes a circle not really going anywhere. Pretty soon it's not very exciting, it's not much of a life, but it's too late to turn back. She's getting married and divorced and living with different men. Some of them treat her rough. She gets slapped around and beaten. It's not a good life, it's a mean and stupid life, and I think, christ, my own mother. But why do men treat her that way? Why does she take it? Because she's defiant, she won't back down, and she's asking for it. She has contempt for men and needs them at the same time. Her problem is she's messed up. The world doesn't fit her longings and she never learns. It's the long path to self-destruction.

I missed her. Like the time on the square in front of the movie. I was six. I saw a woman with a pretty print dress blowing against her legs and I ran after her and grabbed her skirt, Mom! I was so damned happy. The woman looked down and patted my head. Oh, poor baby, she said, did you lose your mother? I think I was really lost then. Where was my mother? Where did she go? I wanted her to come back. I can still catch the loneliness. But I finally wanted her to come back so bad, I got mad and quit wanting anything about her at all. So when I was eight, I remember the time, I buried her. It was the middle of the night and I was lying awake. The ceremony was ordinary, a plain casket, no flowers, no sad mourners at the grave. I stood straight. I didn't pray. I simply said goodbye and lowered the box to the bottom of my heart. Out of sight, out of mind. I thought. Of course, I saw Marie from time to time after that. As I said, she would appear occasionally with little presents and pretend everything was fine. I spent some days with her in different summers, but otherwise she was gone from my life.

Except sometimes I wondered if she ever looked back. Did she remember those Sunday dinners where we all sat down smacking our lips and it was really fun to eat, the catfish in the skillet, the fluffy Gladiola biscuits, the cobblers, the day I ate eight whole pieces of fried chicken?

Those were happy memories and that's what I was remembering looking down at the empty pot with the crusty bottom and no beans. This was supposed to be a Sunday dinner, too, but it had been only a few miserable beans and potatoes. I looked back at the table surrounded by the new stepfamily lumped in their places. We'd eaten in silence and without the least enjoyment. We'd gulped down fodder like animals, and for what? Because we were supposed to be a *family* and this is what families do, they hunch around a table and grab at tasteless food there's not enough of? And this is what I'm supposed to be stuck with in the same house in the same scroungy life?

I started out the door. "Oh, Bobby Jack—" Myrtle's lilting call. I stopped. "About that clothesline," she said. I told her I was late for work, I had to go. "Well, it's Sunday," she said, "I guess you can go." As if giving me permission! I let the screen door slam behind me. The damn clothesline. I was walking hard. She was going to keep after it, she wasn't going to let it go.

That was a day. I was walking the dirt road back to work. The sand was blowing. Only this time it was more like a real sandstorm, and the bad thing was, you couldn't escape it, the damn sand was always blowing. Why couldn't there be one calm day, just one, for chrissake, where you could walk in simple peace without having a damn forty-mile-an-hour damn wind blast your face off? Why couldn't you comb your hair without having greasy damn mud clog up your comb? Why didn't they make anything except Fitch's cheap damn hair oil? Or why anything? I was mad. It had been the whole aggravating show, the stingy *family* dinner, the ugly stepmother, her whiny brood of gargoyle brats, her dumb clothesline, her pet monster, Sybil. What kind of name was that? And it was the sand in my face, in my eyes and ears and teeth, every day the damn blowing sand and I couldn't get away from it. I started fighting it, swinging my fists at the whorling grit. It was me against the great face-less mass, the forces of nature, and I couldn't win, I knew I couldn't, but I had to fight.

So I did. I flailed the wind all around until I had fallen down in the middle of the road like some hopeless retard. Someone might have seen. I'd gone apeshit with my first solid nervous breakdown, and there I was. Now what? I might've wanted to give up and lay out in the road forever. A part of me did. Then another part of me rallied and I got up and went on. I could put that momentary craziness behind me. After all, you're human, you're allowed a little leeway. You break down, you pull yourself together and keep going. That's how you build charac-ter.

Anyway, I'd fought the wind and cleared the air, I felt better. I'd fallen apart and bounced back, I walked on whistling. Yin and yang, the only way, especially when you're young and stu-pid, you feel immortal. You're traveling the road of youth, you're riding a blind horse. But I also had hopes and dreams. Darlene was in my future. She didn't know it. Who could've known? Still, it had to be. Even today, I write her name, my heart jerks. And because of her I was going to make my first major investment in good ol' American ingenuity. I was going to buy my first car, my first piece of really cheap junky machin-ery, and I was going to change the course of my whole crummy juvenile existence. All I needed was a little luck.

Now I say luck, which everyone needs at least once in their life, like being in the right place at the right time. For example, Isaac Newton sat under a tree, an apple supposedly fell on his beanie, and whataya know, the Law of Gravity. But it was luckily a particular kind of tree he sat under and a specific time of the year. In the winter it wouldn't have happened. Apples don't fall in winter. Or if the tree had been a sycamore. Apples don't grow on sycamores. The same with Einstein. Suppose he'd been born in Lower Sloblovia. Forget Relativity. In Lower Sloblovia they scarcely have arithmetic. Or the really bad timing, the Donner party trapped in the snow in the Sierras. Who survived? The lucky ones had someone to eat. Or say you're born white in the twentieth century, that's a leg up, but suppose you're born again a missionary and sent to the jungles of the Amazon to convert the Zingu. You make it to the headwaters full of zeal, you're rapt with the spirit of God's love, but a minute later a big green boa constrictor drops from a tree and squeezes the living pee out of you. You see what I mean.

The point is, a person needs luck in this world and that's what I had with Darlene. Though not quite yet. My time with Darlene is coming and I'll get to that. Right now I'm still dealing with Myrtle.

Incidentally, I'm a little surprised by the way I'm describing the Dalton step-setup. I seem to be writing it around the edges as a kind of burlesque and I wonder why. It may be I'm trying for a bit of levity. But even at the time I'm not sure I felt the situation was very heavy. Oh, I had my fits, I didn't like Myrtle, she didn't like me, and I didn't like living in the same house with a bunch of strangers, but maybe in my mind it was just some sort of unpleasantness, the daily confrontations a kind of game. I didn't know it was going to affect the rest of my life. If I'd known the words to use then, I would've said, look, this is ridiculous. Still, it was war, metaphorically speaking. Myrtle was never going to surrender. Neither was I. My personal hubris was at stake. With her it was probably her secret Gestapo training. She was determined to have the say-so, that I should obey her. I was temperamentally unfit to obey anyone. That was the standoff and it might have lasted forever. Every week or so, when I could make her turn blue in the face, it was actually kinda fun. Then I found out one day she was more determined than I knew. She announced what I call her nutrition attrition strategy. It was more plainly her outright decision to starve me to my knees. She probably thought she could.

But it didn't just happen. A series of small tactics led up to the final skirmish.

The first I remember was the door rule. I'd skipped study hall at school and gone home in the middle of the afternoon, something I'd never done before, but for some reason I was going to work early that day and needed to change into my work clothes. So I naturally trotted up to the house and on in the front door. Myrtle was on the couch. I hadn't known. She was laid back snoozing with one leg hanging, an arm crossed over her eyes. But I'd bounded in. She was startled upright with her hands out in fright, *Eeeeek!* I was stopped in my tracks. Then she saw it was only me and collapsed back. "Lord, you gave me a scare." She was patting her chest to breathe again. Her bad conscience, I thought. "I was resting," she said. But in the middle of the afternoon? In the daytime people were supposed to be working. "I'm supposed to take my rest every day," she said. But from doing what? The breakfast dishes in the kitchen were still piled in the sink. The floor was unswept, the corners of the room thick with dust curls. I could see through their open bedroom door the unmade bed. If she'd done anything to rest from, it didn't show. A black banana peel lay like a dead tarantula on the end table.

"It's my heart," she said.

"An attack?" I might've hoped.

"If I don't rest." She affected a long-suffering face. "I have a weak heart. I don't let on, but I'm not supposed to lift anything heavy and I have to watch getting tired. The doctor said if I do too much, it might be dangerous."

Oh, sure, I thought. But a person with a heart condition, I'd never run into that before. She might've had a bad ticker.

"I didn't mean to scare you," I said.

"Well, you didn't know. I don't talk about it. It's just something I have to live with."

"Yeah, well—" I was trying to walk on by.

"But next time—" She let it hang and gave me a look. Then she smiled demurely. "I mean, next time, if you don't mind, you can start using the back door. Opening the front door lets in the draft so."

From then on, past Sybil snapping and leaping at me before we became friends, I would slide along the back wall into the house. It would take me longer but I would never use the front door again. I thought about it—sneaking up, then wildly jumping in like a mad fiend to damn sure give her ol' heart a real jolt—but I never did.

Another thing was the iron. Every place I lived, I always ironed my own clothes because I was particular about my Levi's. I liked them creased just right, which in those days was a mark of being neatly dressed. So one day I set up the ironing board in the kitchen, piled on my wad of Levi's, and reached in the cabinet for the iron. It wasn't there. Neither was it under the sink with the pots and pans or anywhere else. Myrtle was on the couch again but finally pretended to notice me rummaging. The iron? Well, if I wanted to iron, she said, I could use the handle-iron propped against the door. The handle-iron was the kind of thing they used back in the Stone Age, a flat-bottomed lump of solid metal you had to heat on the stove and lift with a detachable wooden handle. It weighed about ten pounds. Okay. But what happened to the regular electric iron? Oh, that, Myrtle said, she'd put that away. The brads on my Levi's were ruining her good electric iron, scratching the bottom. She patted her chest, her heart condition, and continued with her daily snooze on the couch.

I heated the handle-iron on the stove and pressed my Levi's, not as good as with the electric iron, it was slow going, but I worked with it. Except the more I ironed with the lumpy block of heavy metal, the hotter I got around the ears. What the hell did scratches matter? They were ruining her good iron, Myrtle said. You probably couldn't even see the damn scratches. She just wanted to lord it over me. I could hear her snoring.

I took a peek. She had one arm crossed over her eyes, the other hanging. Her fat legs were spread slovenly. The banana peel still looked like a dead thing crouched on the table. An omen, I thought. The house could fall down around her and she'd never know. Or the house could burn down around her. It could be an accident.

Maybe I thought that. I left the iron on the stove and turned the burner on high. In another ten minutes I pictured the iron glowing red-hot. It might even melt a little and weld itself to the burner. Who knew what else the melting would do? I threw the wooden handle to Sybil in the backyard and watched him crunch the thing to splinters, the last detachable wooden iron handle on earth. The kitchen was already heating up. I took another peek at Myrtle still sleeping and secretly tiptoed away.

At the Sinclair that afternoon, Puddles wandered up. "Hey, Bobby Jack, whatcha doin'?" I was fixing a flat and he could plainly see what I was doing, it was broad daylight, but he had to ask. I told him, "What's it look like, I'm fixing a flat." He appeared satisfied. He'd only wanted to know. But he was like that, always asking the obvious. I'd be walking into the movie and he'd be leaning against the box office, hanging out, he'd say, "Hey, Bobby Jack, where ya goin'?" I'd answer, "Whataya think, I'm going to the movie." He'd appear informed. But it would get to you after a while. A dumb question now and then, okay, but every time, you knew it was coming. I'd try to anticipate him. I'd be in Wimpy's, say, chomping down on a hamburger, he'd come lumbering in, I wouldn't wait. "Don't ask," I'd say, "I'm eating a damn hamburger." He'd appear culinarily educated.

So Puddles watched while I worked on the flat tire. My best friend in Dalton. And I should say, my sidekick, since he was always tagging along wherever and I accepted that. Don Quixote had his Sancho, I had my Puddles. Except Puddles was six-four and weighed about three hundred pounds. He looked like a natural potential earth mover and might've been if he'd ever gotten mad. But you could never get Puddles mad at anything and he was completely harmless. He was the tackle on our football team, he was the whole front line almost, but he would never tackle anybody. He'd just sorta stand there. If a ball carrier happened to go blind and run into him, Puddles would lift the guy off the ground, the guy would be kicking and thrashing to get loose, Puddles would maybe give him a little squeeze, then lay him down nice and easy on a soft spot of grass. Coach would be going crazy on the sidelines, screaming, "THROW him DOWN, Puddles! God-amighty, boy, THROW him DOWN and FALL on him!!" Before each game, Coach would pull Puddles aside and tell him, "Now, Puddles, this time I want you to go out there and get MEAN, understand? I want you to make up your mind right now to go out there and HURT someone. Do it for your mother, you can make your mother proud of you, Puddles, just go out there and get MAD and HIT someone HARD, okay? Promise me." And each time Puddles would promise, but the meanness just wasn't in him. You could look up at the stands during a game and see people rolling their eyes, Puddles on cleats was such a goofball Goliath.

Our school colors were puce and purple, and I still have nightmares playing football covered with puce. The colors of our main rival, the Wylie Wildcats, were blue and silver. They looked good. Their mascot was a cute little alleycat. But we were the Dalton Dustdevils. Our mascot was a bucket of sand.

Anyway, my focus at this point is Puddles and I mention him purposely to remember my first exposure to the hidden nature in a lot of people, myself included.

Now, right off, when you looked around Dalton, it was like stealing had never been invented. You wanted spending money, you had to work for it, so every kid in town had a job. Unless your family was rich like Randy Caudell's, then you got an allowance, but you wouldn't admit that in public. Red Stulislavsky, our All-State halfback, worked at Moore Hardware. My brother worked at the feed mill. My job was at the Sinclair, of course, and Puddle's was with his daddy's salvage yard at their house. He worked with his daddy scavenging the good parts still left in the old wrecks laying around, but it was mostly Puddles performing the labor. His daddy was usually drunk. That's the background.

Puddles and I would talk. I had no doubt he admired me. For instance, I'd been sent to the principal's office one day for being a disruptive annoyance in Miss Dowd's English class. It happened a lot. I told Puddles afterward, "The thing is, you stand in front of the principal, you gotta know how to act. He said it was my last chance but I think I can work him a couple more times."

"Boy, I wish I could." Puddles gave one of his three-hundred-pound helpless looks.

"Just act stupid," I said.

"I do, but I can't never get away with nothing."

"You gotta learn to think on your feet."

"I get too nervous."

"Yeah? Well, you probably do."

"I wish I could be like you."

"Nah, c'mon."

"You know what you're doing, you know how to act."

"But you don't want to be like me."

"Yeh, I do, too."

"You're like me, Puddles, you'd have to fight all the time and you don't like to fight."

"If I was like you, though, maybe I would."

"C'mon, Puddles, you'd have to hit someone."

"Well—" He ducked his head. "Maybe I wouldn't then."

That's the way we talked. He had a bruise on the side of his face and I poked it. "What's that?"

"Whut?" He put his hand to his bruise.

"It looks like you've been in a fight already."

"I fell down."

"That's what you always say."

"Then I must've bumped something. I forget."

Puddles nearly always had a bruise on his face or arms, or somewhere on his body. He'd come to school with bumps on his head. As big as he was, you could believe things got in his way, although I never saw him exactly blundering around. In fact, for his size, Puddles was fairly light on his feet. I saw him dance once and he was really pretty graceful with that surpris-

ing buoyancy many big people have. But the bumps and bruises would come and go.

Big ol' dumb Puddles, I thought. Then I found out. We were
at the Sinclair and just sorta loafing. It was probably a Sunday
morning, a slow time. Puddles sat on an oil case in the grease
stall and crushed it. I said something like, "Dammit, Puddles,
watch where the hell you sit, jesus! You don't know your own
weight, you don't know the godawful effect you have on things."

He hung his head. I'd hurt his feelings and I immediately felt
bad because Puddles was really the best person I knew. He'd
give you the shirt off his back. He'd do anything you asked him
to and never expect a thing in return. So I shouldn't have
jumped on him. At the same time, I didn't try to smooth it. We
sat. Finally Puddles shook his head.

"No, I know. I know how I do," he said.

His voice sounded different, his words definitely articulated.
It was a weird moment. He was hanging his head, a big oafish
shape in the dim grease stall, my ol' giant sidekick I'd always
known, and from out of this an intelligent brain had spoken?

"You do?" I said.

"Yeah, I know how I act." He was rubbing his knees and I
could tell it was going to get serious. Or worse, it was going to
be some kind of truth and I didn't know if I wanted to hear.

"I act dumb," he said, his expression completely calm. "And
I don't fit. Look——" He was a squeezed-up blob bigger than his
place. "I don't even fit sitting down."

"Maybe not on an oil case."

"Everybody gets a regular desk at school, they have to get me
a table."

"But being big, you're lucky, too. Guys see you coming, they
don't mess with you."

"I don't like to fight, though."

"Which makes you lucky, you don't wanna fight, you're big enough, you don't have to."

He sat rubbing his knees.

"You see my point," I said.

He looked at me hard and fixed me with his eyes. "But that's not the point."

I had to turn my head. "No, I know it's not," I said.

The point was—and it was suddenly crystal clear even if we couldn't say it—he was someone stuck in the wrong body and that body made him look like someone he had to imitate because that's what people saw. It was that simple. And for me, a surprising revelation. A human fact had been in plain sight all along but overlooked. I'd never seen the real Puddles before, I probably didn't now, but I could see the big overgrown blimp beside me wasn't him. Someone else was peeping out of those sad eyes. Some other body's lost soul was trapped inside that great lump of misplaced flesh.

He told me about his grades, that he made C's and D's to pass, but until the sixth grade he'd made A's, straight A's. I could see Puddles back in grade school, a big oversized baby-faced kid just wanting to be liked but he was so big he had to be careful not to hurt anyone. None of the other kids would scuffle with him, he was so much bigger, and if he showed he was smarter, they really wouldn't like him because being both big and smart was being too different and pretty soon too different was too lonely. You had to come down a level to get along. I thought that was what he was saying. It was also more.

"And my dad," he said, "I don't think he likes me, y'know? I used to bring in my report card with all A's, he'd say, 'Boy, you think you're a real smartass, don'tcha?' He'd get on a tear and whup me for being a smartass."

"For making straight A's?"

"Well, he'd hit the bottle. I kept growing and got big. I think he's ashamed of me being such a big lummox. I couldn't be his, he says. But I know it's the whiskey and him just being smaller. He hates that so he's gotta show he can still whup me."

I could see his bantam-size daddy in his baggy overalls and skullcap raging over his worthless life salvaging wrecks, a drunken little red-eyed maniac. I imagined him staggering around hitting at his giant son and that's why Puddles had all those bumps and bruises always. It was so damned sad. But it was his daddy, his personal family matter, and no one else's business.

I remember we sat quietly awhile. Whoever he was, or I was, and whatever our lives, we were only there and nowhere else. If Puddles had revealed a secret self, I didn't know that it mattered. Others would still see him the same and it would be hard for me not to. He was still going to reflect what other people saw. And he was going to end up with a horrible fate in another year but we couldn't know that then.

Puddles nudged me. "Anyway, I still wish I could be like you."

"Now, c'mon, Puddles, don't start that again."

"Well, I do, you're on top of everything."

"Get off it, I'm not on top of anything."

"At least you're happy."

"Happy?"

"You are, aren'tcha?"

"Compared to what?"

He couldn't say and we both simply sat in the bleak grease stall and silently stared out at the whole bleak world as far as we could see. Happy? That's what you wanted, but where? Here and there, a few moments maybe, but never always. And why not? You bring up happy, it's not a subject to explore. You want it simple, it's a can of worms.

As usual I worked until ten that evening and left when Max arrived to take over the night shift. Which was like taking over a graveyard, because after midnight the town was embalmed and there were never any cars pulling in. Max would curl up behind the counter and sleep. I'd accuse him of having a cushy job and he'd admit it. He'd say, Yeah, I'm just here loping my lizard. Or he'd say he was pulling his pickle. You got the idea he was whacking his weenie to a frazzle every night. But Max was also the only guy I ever knew who could pee over a telephone wire. He'd bet you a dollar he could. After a while you knew better but you'd pay a dollar just to see. He'd take his dong out, which was no big deal. It was completely ordinary-looking. In fact, it might have been a little undersized. It was kinda stubby. He'd pinch it off, hold it a second and aim, then without the least expression of effort, let go. A yellowish stream would go up, and it would keep going up and up. At the right moment, Max would give his dick a little flick and the stream at its height would dip and loop on up over the telephone wire. It was an amazing sight.

But I digress. Time to return to the iron on the stove.

THE HOUSE WAS USUALLY PITCH-DARK when I got home but this time the lights were on and everyone was waiting in the kitchen. I felt surprised, I'd forgotten about the iron.

Myrtle was standing hands on hips waiting to confront me. Her four kids were ganged behind her. Billy was sitting at the table. Charlie was more or less out of the way in a corner. I didn't have to count to see I was being outnumbered.

Then Myrtle couldn't wait. "So! You have the nerve to come back!"

"Why?" I was open-faced, innocent. Charlie avoided my eye.

Billy shook his head morosely like he knew I was always causing trouble. He'd had to save me from myself too many times.
The calendar kids merely appeared anxious to see blood. They
hated me.

"Why?!" Myrtle pointed. "Look at that!"

I looked. The stove top had exploded and the handle iron
was on the floor where it had burned into the linoleum which
had evidently flamed a little and caught the edge of the cabinet.
A rivulet of fire and tar smoke had climbed the cabinet to the
ceiling, then crossed the wall with a few licks to the window
and caught the kitchen curtain. The linoleum had turned into
a patch of mushy black tar around the iron. The paint on the
cabinet had curled. The curtain was a feathery scrim of ashes
still dropping an occasional flake. I didn't think it looked too
bad.

"Now what've you got to say?" Myrtle was red in the face.

I shrugged. "I dunno, looks like we had a little fire."

"A little fire!" She was purple now. It was kinda funny.
"Look at that cabinet! The house nearly burned down, I
could've been burned alive!"

The four snivelings repeated in unison behind her, "Yeah,
burned alive, Mama coulda been burned alive!"

"And it's your fault!" Myrtle screeched. "You did it!"

"Yeah, your fault, your fault!" The chorus again.

"You did it on purpose!"

"On purpose, on purpose!"

The kids were jumping up and down idiotically, Myrtle was
apoplectic, and I was just standing.

Myrtle was ranting, "Just look! My whole kitchen!
Everything burned! My pretty curtains! And you did it!"

Her brats repeated after her, "Yeah, everything burned and
you did it!"

Billy was shaking his head like, Yeah, you're the problem all right. Charlie was patting the air trying not to see or hear anything.

"You were trying to burn the house down," Myrtle said. "It's lucky I smelled smoke, I could've been burned alive."

I pictured her roasted body in the smoldering ruins, a lot of bubbly fat. Not an appalling picture. I'd thought to melt the iron and have a little fun, was that all? You're a teenager, you can see about three minutes into the future. With long-range imagination, you might see four. But maybe I really had wanted to burn the house down. Who knows what goes on in the void of a minimum-wage mind? If you read Freud gullibly, a secret wish is possible. I was at least guilty of causing an accident. Maybe I could admit that much.

"Okay," I said, "if I did something wrong, I'm sorry."

"Oh, so you're soorrry." Myrtle chewed the word. "Did you hear that, Charlie? He says he's sorry."

Charlie shuffled. "Well, he might be."

She turned on him. "What!? He says he's sorry and you believe him!?" I thought she was going to hit him.

Charlie ducked. "Well, no, I dunno."

Billy spoke up. "He's not sorry, look at him."

I stared at him, my own brother. We'd grown up in the same ignorance together and shared the same fate. Now he'd turned on me.

Myrtle egged him on. "See there, you're his brother, you know what he's like, don't you?"

"Yeh, I know all right," Billy said it dully. "And every day it's always something. He can't let a day go by without stirring up trouble. I tried to teach him but he wouldn't never listen. Since the day he was born, he was probably just born to cause trouble."

The kids harmonized, "See! Trouble, Mama, always stirring up trouble! Born that way!" Mouse was running in place, yelping the loudest.

I felt suddenly lonely. Where was the understanding and warmth of humanity? We were like animals. Or more, like different species of animals, not exactly dissimilar in origin but separate in the limbs of evolution. We might graze the same savannah and lift our noses to sniff the air but we were essentially different, gnu, hyena, wildebeest. We had no way of talking with any sort of understanding.

And in the future, I would remember—for the next forty years in every dead-end spot, when there was no communication, when I wanted to speak my mind and couldn't—I would remember that moment.

To hell with it, I thought. I turned to leave.

Myrtle moved to block me. "Now just where do you think you're going? I'm not finished with you yet." She grabbed my sleeve.

Now, in those days, someone grabbing me needed to be smiling first, she wasn't, so my instant reaction was to jerk my arm away pretty roughly. I might've even looked a little mean. Myrtle fell back against the wall as if struck and appeared to freeze. Her eyes got big and she clutched her chest. "My heart, my heart," she gasped, and started sliding sideways along the wall. We could only watch. She was staggering and catching herself. I thought she was acting. And not too badly. She was cleverly imitating someone with bugged eyes struggling to breathe and I believe I almost admired her performance. I had a natural appreciation for good acting. She was sputtering and reaching out with her hands to climb the air.

Meanwhile the calendar kids were yowling, "Mama's heart! Her heart condition!" A strangling Myrtle was staggering to the corner and back again making croaking sounds. She stumbled against the kitchen table and crashed two chairs.

"Look! Mama's dying! Mama's dying!"

Charlie was patting the air. Billy was shaking his head. Myrtle careened along the cabinet and rebounded from the sink. She was clutching her chest desperately and rolling her eyes, her face beet-red, her mouth wide open. She reeled across the room and hit the door, where she abruptly stopped in mid-reel, stiffened, and collapsed to the floor.

Nothing moved. Myrtle lay stone still, facedown. There was a moment of silence, of deathly realization. A weight in the room descended. Everyone was staring down at the body.

Then they were turning their heads and glaring at me, Charlie and Billy, too, their eyes accusing: *See what you done?*

I gave up. "All right, all right!" I blurted. "I'll put up the damn clothesline!"

Now hold.

Why in the world did I say that? My mind must've freaked. It was a flaw in my character, a compromising weakness in my soul. I'd spoken without thinking and God knows I didn't mean it. Me? Don't kid yourself, I wasn't about to put up that clothesline, not then, not in a million years, and I knew it. But I'd spoken, my words had sounded loud and clear, and everyone heard. So I was caught. When you say you're going to do something, no two ways about it, you have to go ahead and do it. That's the law.

And a big problem, the law of ignominious personal honor. But my mind was already clicking in opposite directions. Maybe I could figure a way out. I'd have to give it some careful devious thought.

At the same time, not surprisingly, Myrtle experienced a miraculous resurrection. It took her about another minute to get to her feet with her kids helping her. She would pretend to convalesce a few days and survive overall with no ill effects except she'd been dead, she claimed, and had risen from the dead. She'd done it before, too, she said. She'd had lots of strokes. But it was chancy and when a stroke struck she never knew if it would be her last. That's why, she said, she was dedicated to savoring to the last dregs every precious moment she lived. Being dead now and then also reaffirmed her belief that she was surely put on this great earth for something. What exactly, she never said, only that the all-seeing hand of Jehovah worked in mysterious ways.

I went to the back porch and laid on my cot in the dark. Billy came in and laid on his and for a while we were quiet except I could hear him breathing. He was twenty months older and from the time we were little, being the big brother, he'd always wanted to watch over me and look out for me. I wouldn't let him because I considered it bossing, even at four years old, it was an uninvited restraint against my headlong leaps into unbridled freedom and mindless anarchy. Once I jumped in a creek over my head and he pulled me out. He said I was drowning, he'd saved me. He didn't know, the third time under I might've learned to swim. And he was always telling me what I "better" do. Like, you better do this and you better not do that. He had the "better" theorems down pat. His patience, though, had evidently worn thin. He'd turned on me and spoken against me in the kitchen. My own brother. I could've slugged him. But I'd tried lots of times to get him to fight me, he wouldn't, he'd never hit back. So we were only lying in the dark, breathing, two bodies with similar genes but with two different minds in separate worlds.

He spoke. "Lemme tell you something, you better start straightening up." I told him I was straightened enough. He said, "You better start learning how to get along with people, too." I told him I knew how to get along with people, they didn't know how to get along with me. He accused me of thinking I was better than everyone. I told him maybe not everyone. His response was a long tired-out sigh. He said, "Look, you're doing good in school, you got a good job making good money—what do you want?" I said I didn't know. "That's what I thought," he said. "You better start straightening up." He went to sleep.

I lay awake and tried to figure it. Our grandparents had both died the year before. Since then Billy and I had lived with Charlie in the revamped garage. It was called a small rental. Charlie was closed-off, Billy was very nearly the same, and we'd lived like strangers, but I hadn't been bothered. I'd gone my own way as I pleased. The town, well, the town was limited, you had to admit. You could look at pictures of other places and compare. You're a kid, though, you're stuck where you live. The world is not made for kids. Then you start growing and things change. You're experiencing feelings you can't express. Your feelings become restless and clamor to get out. But where? You look around, people are living the same general lives, mouthing the same general words, they're going nowhere. They're settled down, they say. You see in their eyes they never tried, they never questioned. Or they did and gave up. Then it's routine. And this, you think, is *it?* Your soul wells up, No! I want to live, really live! Your soul starts gnashing its teeth. Meanwhile in real life you don't know what's wrong and there's no one to ask. No one can possibly have the same feelings you do. So you're in a fix. You're alone.

Still, why fight it, why not just go along with the program? And why all the crazy pent-up feelings in the first place? What made me want or even think there ought to be more? I had no idea. Maybe I was born that way.

Ah, the thought: born that way. I was my mother's son and Marie was born the same. She had crazy impossible longings, too, and finally had to get away. That's why she took off, she couldn't help it. Except she should have taken me with her. Why did she have to go off and leave *me*?

Well, I can think, why didn't Marie take me with her? Meaning, of course, why didn't my mom love me? But that's inventing a way of looking back and not the Dalton time I'm talking about. I can even say aloud, "Oh, why didn't my mom keep me, poor me," and make it sound pretty traumatic. I'm good at that. And I might go on about distrusting women. You'd expect that. Actually, some women you really can't trust. But that goes for some men, too, and I don't want to get into a lot of dumb psychology. The truth is, lying on my cot that night, I can't remember having the least grasp of anything I now pretend. If I felt life was unfair, I was also optimistic. But I knew so little. I'd read nothing, the funnies on Sunday, the sports section maybe. There was never a book in any house I lived in, or what might be called a good magazine. People I knew didn't read. In fact I was twenty before I read my first book, and only then because of Grady, an unlikely friend. He went on to become an author and college professor, which most authors today seem to have to be to survive. But that's another story.

Anyhow, I said no books. I have to admit I did read some poems, and for the simple reason we were forced to in Miss Dowd's English class. She'd have her students stand and read a poem in front of the room. She made me stand and read "Trees" once, by Joyce Kilmer, a man, she said, but his first name was Joyce. I offered the comment, in that case the poem was probably a fairy tale. I couldn't help it. Miss Dowd still sent me to the principal's office. Another time she made me read "How

Do I Love Thee?" Imagine, in front of the whole eleventh-grade class, a dumb losing-team linebacker reciting, ". . . to the depth and breadth and height My soul can reach, when feeling out of sight For the ends of Being and ideal Grace." It nearly killed me. I also had to read "The Highwayman." But I liked that one. It had a real feel to it. "And the highwayman came riding— Riding—The highwayman came riding . . ." Like Errol Flynn. The highwayman rode to see his girlfriend to let her know he had a robbery to attend to but he'd be back, she could count on it. He raised upright in his stirrups and promised, "Then look for me by moonlight, watch for me by moonlight, I'll come to thee by moonlight, though hell should bar the way!" He tugged at his reins in the moonlight and rode away to the west. Now that's something you can see. Moreover, he got away with repeating moonlight three times and I've never forgotten those lines. But then I always remember the moonlight with Darlene, maybe that's why.

Footnote: Predictably, on the road back, in keeping with his promise to return as he was bound to do, the highwayman was shot down like a dog by the authorities. Tim, the ostler, with his eyes hollows of madness, had secretly ratted on him.

So, a few poems, nothing more. My storage of knowledge was mainly the sameness I saw from day to day. Which meant I was lying on my cot that night in a solid state of ignorance trying to figure my situation. I couldn't. Except I knew I was caught. I'd announced I would put up the clothesline. Everyone heard. So I had to, only I wasn't going to. A dilemma. How to do what I said and at the same time not do it?

Then I did something bad. It was probably midnight and I was half asleep when I heard a sneaky sound under my cot. I reached down and grabbed a handful of messy hair. It was Mouse trying to steal my shoes again. I yanked him up. "You make a sound," I said, "I'll bust your face." I held him out at arm's length. The little creep. He was wriggling to squeal and I squeezed his neck. He sputtered to a gulp. "I'm going to have to teach you a lesson," I said. He started to whine. I gave him a rap on the topknot and he stopped. "And I know what, too," I said. Maybe it was the way I said it. His eyes widened. He was about to scream. I clamped his mouth and grabbed him up. He was thrashing to squirm free but I had him locked. I carried him to the back door and opened it. At that, his scrawny body stiffened like a plank. Sybil was already lunging. I held the Mouse by the nape of the neck and the seat of his pants and swung him out and back . . . one . . . two . . . Sybil's face was contorted with anticipation. His jaws were slathering and snapping. On three, I heaved.

Now, during the past years, I've reflected on that moment a few times. Of course I didn't really throw the Mouse to the dog. I only pretended I was going to, but I wonder if my doing that didn't contribute to the boy's future mental outlook. It may have.

When I put him back on his cot that night, he was stiff and traumatized. His face was frozen with fear. But I can still see his little beady eyes in the dark like fiery dots burning with hate.

Anyway, after that, I slept like a log the rest of the night and woke with a plan. My mind was clear and I knew exactly what I would do with the clothesline. I said I was going to put it up, okay, I would. I'd prove I was as good as my word. But that didn't mean my work had to be the same. I was a novice clothesline builder and inexperienced beginners make mistakes. If a product happens to turn out faulty, well, it happens. The thing can be manufactured with built-in obsolescence, call it the American way. Think of appliances, new cars. Nothing is warranted beyond mechanical puberty. Think of ordinary products with shelf life. You stick a live item on a store shelf one day, in no time it's history and discounted as dog food. The same might be expected for the average backyard clothesline. It could have instant unendurance built in. It could have rickets and suddenly expire from a deficiency of outdoor vitamins nobody could prove. Yes. I decided my problem could be finessed.

Now I use that word, I wouldn't have known it at the time. But I'm thinking finesse. You practice at it, you can easily acquire the habit. Before you know it, you're doing the old softshoe and a regular song-and-dance for every occasion. It can get to be your daily MO. The only thing, when you're finessing, you can't worry about not having a conscience.

Which bothered me with Tracy years later. Same as with the clothesline, I was trying to finesse the situation and still be as good as my word. But with a clear conscience, too. If you could call what I had a conscience.

Or what am I saying? Obviously I'm trying to make a connection between my Dalton days and my later problems in Dallas. In that case, we need to skip back to the final mess with Tracy in 1970, the Chinese year of the rat. Hold the clothesline.

I T WAS LATE MORNING WHEN I WOKE. Tracy was still sleeping and I was badly hungover but clear enough to remember the pistol. I sneaked it from under the bed and hid it in the garage behind a box. Back in the bedroom, as always, even on low wattage, I was momentarily stopped and transfixed by Tracy's perfect profile on the pillow. A flawless face softly asleep. Beneath the covers, the curves of a luscious lubricious body. Lust at rest. And this was a new day. I almost weakened. How could I not be truly in love with that? She was so beautiful, and a good person, too. Despite her murderous impulse to kill me, she was really a warm and loving woman. I was unworthy. I wondered what she might be dreaming at that moment. If I could see, surely her mind would be filled with dewdrops and rainbows. Mine was stuck with nits and cockleburs. She was right, something was wrong with me.

I left her asleep and dressed as usual without giving much thought to sartorial fashion. What was good enough that morning was probably the sport coat with the crimson lining. I liked that one. The coat left unbuttoned. Regular shirt. No tie. Don't put me in a tie. When I thought I needed one for a meeting, I'd knot a scarf around my neck, let it hang. You're a commercial TV/film producer, it's okay to be a little offbeat. Clients expect that in showbiz people. They see you flouting corporate convention with a bit of flair, they trust you're a harmless authentic type, a personality. Otherwise you'd be like them. Which is not to say business people should be stereotyped as dull. Some are deceptively interesting. Top execs especially can often come across as pretty natural. You're convinced they must know something or they wouldn't be top execs. What they know of course is how to act like they're on top. That's their secret. It sounds duplicitous, but playing a role is the way of life. It only depends on the particular culture you're in. Take the farm culture. Invariably farmers act like farmers. In street culture, sociopaths act like sociopaths. Only perverts act normal. That's how you can tell they're perverts. In business, the lesser execs on the totem pole speak their lines of jargon and crank out departmental reports. The secret of the top execs is nowhere in their job description. Yet the ones in these lower ranks are probably the better actors. They confirm expectations.

That may have been my half-baked attitude in those days and it might still be but from a different angle. Obviously I didn't see myself in tune with "business." Or with anything.

No doubt I made my way along the fringes of the business world in spite of myself, and being in the so-called creative category, I was perhaps given some slack. I had only a partial idea of what I was doing except it seemed a way to be halfway independent. But to stay that way, I had to succeed, meaning I had to make money, the key word in civil society. Let's face it, in business you need that ol' cash flow, so I had to learn to price my product at about triple my costs and promote the fiction that the best costs more. Occasionally a client would plead low-budget poverty and want a cost-plus deal. Fine with me. My costs would simply automatically triple. But I was only a small turn in the screw. Other producers I knew were making really outlandish profits. Dallas after all was a town with plenty of loot to spread around. It was also a nonunion town for filming and less expensive than the West Coast. National advertisers were beginning to discover they could save a bundle doing their commercials in Dallas. So the way I made my living wasn't all that rapacious. I'm only a little ashamed. But I don't know why I'm explaining. The subject doesn't interest me. I guess I'm trying to say I was lucky to be in on the ground floor of a growing industry at the right time and to make money, although money wasn't something I especially cared about. My brain, I know now, was never a money brain.

Anyway, I didn't like my life at the time and I didn't like myself living a life I didn't like. Even the good life. But what to do? More precisely, what did I *want* to do?

I was dressed and out of the house driving blearily to my office. I called it my national headquarters for MorningStar Productions, a name I invented on the spur of the moment when I signed the lease. I should've given the name more thought. My lease occupied an older building on McKinney Avenue and included a small sound stage, recording room, editing room, and two offices. Not exactly a Byzantine labyrinth. The offices were painted burnt orange. The sound stage was limited to simple sets for talking heads. The recording booth was closet-size, technically two-track and barely adequate for voice-overs. The editing room contained a movieola. A purposely lean operation. For most productions I hired freelance crews and rented equipment as needed.

Irving and Vicky were my two full-time people. I didn't call them employees. They were cohorts who wore different hats. Irving was an optional cameraman, sound man, film editor, and all-round gopher. Vicky was my gal Friday coordinator and organizer for everything, my official assistant. So the two together were my multi-threat workforce but also friendlies. Vicky especially was an intimate. I had sex with her in my office maybe a week after hiring her. The only time. I'd been drinking, she'd been smoking a little pot, then it just seemed to happen on the floor. A sporting event. After that, she would tell me about her men. Like she was always falling in love with a new one nearly every week. They'd leave her heartbroken and she never understood why men couldn't stick around. She loved men, why couldn't they stay in love with her? And why couldn't we do it again? She was in love with me, too, she said. But it wouldn't be a good idea, I said, the old line about mixing business with pleasure. She said it was healthy, though, and more so mixed with business because a little pleasure, a little quicky now and then, toned the skin. She told me anytime, just say the word, I could have her body. It became a daily joke between us but I don't think ever exactly a jest with her. She was twenty-five and I was amazed, even in blithering turmoil with her sex life, she still managed the niggling details of every production with unnerving competence. She was invaluable and I've thought often since that she was really a loyalist at heart and would've been a faithful woman for the right man.

Irving, on the other hand, was a skinny guy with thick glasses and scraggly hair who kept his personal life to himself. I don't think he had a personal life, but at MorningStar he did everything I couldn't and probably felt secretly superior that he knew more about cameras and editing than I did. And more about lighting and sound and all the rest. That's why he was needed. He might've been his own producer but without the initiative he was content in his place being an underling. He told me once he'd been born a serf. I didn't argue with his self-perception and in an odd way I sorta admired him, he was so quietly dependable and versatile. It's too bad that thousands of Irvings pass in the street every day and no one ever sees them.

On both sides of my building the street was lined with antique shops, pricey little boutiques, and a couple of jazzy bars, the "in" places for airline attendants in the days when airline attendants were still stewardesses and always young and pretty. The Chateau Club was one block over. I pulled into my parking space at the rear of my building. They'd promised to pave back there, they hadn't. I didn't care. A hair of the dog, I thought. But the bottle under my seat was empty. Never mind, I had a couple more stashed in my desk. Vicky would bring me coffee, I'd pour in a quick nip to pick me up, then another to carry me to lunch, and so on through the afternoon. The nip was both an anticipation and a gloomy prospect. I would keep my interior weatherized enough to survive most daylight encounters and people wouldn't know, or if they suspected, they could believe I was also a cheerful soul. But my day was ahead, the desk and phone, the calls to make, the calls coming in, the day-long series of incidentals, the whole eventually a setpiece of trivialities. Nothing of significance would occur. The world wouldn't change. Within a few boundaries the work would live a life of its own. I'd get through the hours and a calendar of days would be one day less.

Now I write that from the present distance and make it sound dismal. I exaggerate. Because I remember I had fun, too. A lot of people I dealt with were surprising characters and variously engaging personalities. What was bad for me was the glamored mindlessness of filming and TV and that day after day what I did was of no real importance. Also I'd come to that work not by choice especially but through a process of elimination. I'd drifted from place to place. After a lot of different jobs I'd learned the kinds of things I knew I never wanted to do again. Like selling. I wasn't a salesman. I did carpentry work. At one point I was working for a construction outfit that happened to have a contract to build a set for a movie filming on location. During that job I switched to working as a grip on the movie crew. I got to know a few film people and became a prop man, then a production assistant. I wasn't technically inclined, but within a year I was hired to produce a simple training film on my own. I was surprised at the amount of money I made and how really easy it was to do. I called on ad agencies and promoted myself as a training film producer. Being glib helped. Then one job led to another and pretty soon I was doing simple TV commercials. No capital investment required. I was a name on an office door and without quite planning it, I became a production resource for advertising, for dissembling meaning.

Finally, however, I was seeing the manipulation involved. And that was *me?* Early on I'd dreamed, I'd imagined myself special. Most children do, then they grow up and take their place in the food chain. Accepting that place is known as being mature. Maybe I wasn't. Maybe my feelings were still infantile.

"So go," a voice whispered in my ear. "Just walk out and close the door and don't look back."

I say whispered. It was more like repeated. The thought was always in the back of my mind. I could go. I'd done that plenty of times. Leaving Dalton, I'd damn sure closed that door behind me. And all the places after that, I'd leave the scene and never look back. What for? I had no place called home or personal attachments that I felt belonged ultimately anywhere. With the exception of Jimmy, but before and after, my sense of the world was that each person in it was solitary and alone. Certainly that's what I saw in myself, an essential aloneness, maybe loneliness, too. I wrote later in my third novel that loneliness was something we all lived with, that it was as old as creation, maybe even a condition of creation itself, but it had its uses, you didn't have to let it make you feel sorry.

With that kind of outlook I didn't think of being attached. I thought instead of being free, whatever that meant, but FREE in big letters somehow to be as I imagined myself. Which was, well, I imagined myself probably as the lone rider on the hill. At that level, I was a man to be reckoned with. Again, whatever that meant. I was a man of some sort of purpose. Naturally the image was blurry and my future figure was more like a blur on the hill, a blur to be reckoned with. The need however was basic, to take the lump and reshape it, the lump that was me. People say, hey, just be yourself. That's the problem.

"So go." The voice in my ear. A powerful impulse. The question was where, and not a definite place on the map, but where in the dark. As if it mattered. I needed to do something, I should just go. What was so complicated, anyway? I was a man of action. You're unhappy, oh, too bad, feel sorry for yourself. Or, look, it's easy, this or that, flip a coin and get on with it. And don't look back. Now that's what you do, okay?

Okay. I was confident.

Which reminds me, you're confident, you can fake it, but you either are or you aren't. That's known. The thing is, while some people are afraid to take a chance, others are natural-born gamblers and for them it's not the risk especially but the game itself. Easy come, easy go, what the hell, shoot the works. That's their attitude. They're gambling fools.

Of course it helps if you have nothing to lose to begin with. And I believe that's how I felt when I left Dalton and took off for California. I might have considered the odds but it wasn't even a bet. Besides, I'd grown up winning fistfights and a few school things, I was cocky. The payoff of the great unknown was before me, I could afford to lose the penny ante of the past, what the hell. So I headed west to the world of genuine honest-to-god nymphomania and imported palms and immediately landed in jail. After that I was nearly murdered one night, a couple of bullets in the stomach, I might've become deceased, but then I was lucky and did all right if you don't count my last few turns in jail. It's not fun being locked up in Juarez, not to mention Pensacola. The Little Rock slammer is not exactly four-star accommodations either. Although you can learn some diverting manual skills behind bars. A spacey Navajo cellmate in Albuquerque once taught me how to roll my own with one hand, a neat trick I can still perform. You pull out your Bull Durham in most places and roll a nice tight little smoke with four fingers of one palm, all eyes are riveted. You twist off the end and light up, preferably with a kitchen match, you can squint your eyes and pretend you're pondering important issues.

Anyway, Vicky brought me coffee and I poured in my morning nip. The first sip made me sort of shudder, then I felt better. My opinion of my desk became kinder, more benevolent. I could see living at peace with my desk and forgiving all the papers on it. Go and sin no more, I would say. And with the grace of another nip or two I might even begin to live in communion with my telephone and all the faceless voices flowering through it.

It suddenly seemed an epiphany, communion, grace, the spirituality of things. Nothing existed without spirituality, and I should have known but the connection had escaped me. What's more, the whole spiritual world was totally impersonal and common to every earthly form. So you didn't have to take it personally. In fact you couldn't, it was just *there* like the air you breathed. You only had to breathe more of it. And not think.

"You know what?" I told Vicky. "I need to be more spiritual."

"Is that right?" Raised eyebrow.

"It just came to me."

"Last week you said realistic."

"Last week I was uninformed."

"And next week?"

"I won't be here. I'll be in Canada."

End of confession, which was about as far as I ever went with inner revelations. But Canada was a fact. I'd scheduled a shoot in an underground coal mine north of Montreal where Dresser Industries had a giant earth tunneling machine they wanted filmed. Or, actually, immortalized. I would ride an elevator four thousand feet down a mine shaft, light the space, and film the monster machine drilling eight-foot diameters through solid rock. Boring stuff and dirty work. I'd have to wear a safety helmet. Maybe I'd work it to just send Irving and a crew alone. It would take them a couple of days and they could overspend their per diems.

"But what am I doing?" I said.

Vicky answered with a laundry list of projects, impending or not. For one, the AT&T spot with Bob Newhart was postponed. Newhart had agreed to do a version of his phone comedy routine but a prior engagement was interfering. Okay, that could wait. I liked Newhart. He was an easy guy in person who made you think he was also a good listener. But the Power and Light company wanted some changes in their new spot. Reddy Kilowatt was a little too cute, they said. The word had come down the chain of command from Top Management to the ad director to the ad agency and then to me. This was routine. Reddy was an endangered species the power company was paranoid in protecting. The little cartoon character was supposed to inspire confidence in today's future and tomorrow's revoltage. Whatever. At least the First National Bank was on track with their personalized customer service. That is, their tellers would not know a customer personally but have to smile at them anyway. Also, Butch was coming in later instead of earlier for her voice-recording session. The beautiful kids we'd used in a milk commercial had enunciated their words too distinctly and maturely, they were intellectually advanced, so, to make them sound more endearingly childlike, Butch would dub the kids' voices with her professional babyish patois, a common tactic in the trade. In fact half the kids' voices in most local commercials were Butch's. The public didn't know. You wanted a lovable child's voice, Butch was the best in the business and in real life a crew-cut rough-as-a-cob forty-year-old woman. She sported a swastika tattoo on her right biceps and Vicky had to be careful to not get stuck with her in a corner.

"But what am I *really* doing?" I said.

"You're sitting."

"I'm dying."

"B.J.—" Vicky wagged her head.

She claimed she never knew when to take me seriously. And usually I never wanted her to take me seriously. That might mean I was declaring some feelings. I might reveal a lost soul and she would feel touched and want to cuddle me in her arms to make it all better. That would turn me into a hurt creature someone needed to care for. Then I wouldn't like them.

But this time I wanted to talk. If I could pretend I was also still in control. I wouldn't have to make anything sound too serious. Flaubert had it right when he said that of the most passionate things, we should speak dispassionately. Which sounds better in French but that's the idea. The same with the most confused things, we should speak of them unconfusedly. In that case, the approach needs to be oblique. That's why we engage reality with metaphor. In other words, you have a confusion, you don't want to scare it off and make it worse, you need to sneak up on it.

So I tried sneaking and backtracked, "Or not dying, maybe I'm just getting old." I wanted Vicky to draw me out.

She joked instead, "I could make you feel younger."

I followed along, "You just want to use me."

"Tell you what, guess the number I'm thinking between one and ten, I'll give you a free blow job."

"Six."

"Unzip."

"I misspoke, I meant to say three."

"Same thing, you win every time."

"You're toying with me."

"Door open or closed, your choice."

"What if I can't decide?"

"Time's up. Now here's the deal, you stand, I drop to my knees. Rules say you can look down and watch if you want, or close your eyes and smile. Your job is easy, I handle the hard part."

"Sounds like dirty work."

"It's a career, keeps me off the street."

I remember that particular conversation gratuitously, but also because it was typical. If anything was about to get heavy, Vicky would lighten the air with cold-blooded sex talk. She liked to pose as the model modern nasty woman and I never pretended to see she wasn't. So we had a sort of amateur vaudeville act going that kept the more serious stuff offstage. But I enjoyed our bantering. Vicky had a way of making even low wit sound very nearly threatening.

In any case, I wasn't going to resolve a life crisis being a straight man for Vicky. Or with Irving, who worked fastidiously with small things but held his mind in reserve. Neither saw me, I don't think, as a person in trouble. We were doing business, we were on top of things, right? Actually, they wouldn't see me in trouble if they needed to feel they had an untroubled place to be at MorningStar. A crew doesn't want to know their ship is sinking if they only see it's springing leaks.

The day proceeded. An appointment. Figuring a bid. The usual details of "getting it done." At one point my accountant called. A cash matter, not exactly a problem. I could pay the interest on a loan or roll the loan. I said roll the loan. The accountant sighed. I never learned, he said.

Then it happened Jack Rowe came in later that day. Remember, I mentioned earlier that he just wanted to be a great artist but found he had to make a living instead. In my mind, my standby artist. That is, I didn't have Jack on retainer but I advanced him a little money now and then and he was always available when I needed artwork rush-rush. So he came in with a storyboard. The project, I can't recall, maybe a Celanese spot. But Jack also had in hand one of his own paintings. He held the canvas to the light. Proudly. What did I think? It was a painting of a woman sitting on the ground next to a weeping willow. She was leaning back and looking up. Amazingly, it seemed every leaf in the tree was focused separately. The woman's face was pensive but clearly serene. It was a beautiful painting. But what I really remember was Jack's face. He was happy. It took me a couple of months, he said. Like it was something to shrug. He might better have said, look, that's two months of me, the real me, and that's who I am. Otherwise he was existing offhand in disguise and the real Jack was not being lived except in snatches. Like Puddles, I thought, trapped in the wrong body. Someone else's lost soul was peeping out of those eyes. I felt sad for Jack but at least he knew in his heart he was an artist, though that had to be a hard fact, too. The same as not for kids, the world is not made for artists either. It's made for specialists. Or more, the world is really made for professional specialists. Like in the law profession, we're lucky to have a legal specialist for each contingency where everything is somebody's fault. You walk out of your house in the morning, no telling the liability lying in wait, you need a legal eagle at your side. Your cup of coffee at the corner cafe turns up lukewarm, it's okay, your lawyer can grab the evidence and sue for thermal failure. The waitress doesn't smile, that's good, you can nail her for customer neglect. And in bed at night, it's generally a smart move to have your family attorney waiting in the wings. With proper legal exposure, sneaky perpetrations that happen under the cover of dark can be nipped in the bud.

Anyway, Jack showed his painting and went his way and I was left curiously affected. His painting of the weeping willow. Normally you look at a tree and see leaves pretty much altogether, not separately. The wholeness of the tree is what registers. Yet Jack had looked at a tree and seen each individual leaf distinctly. Then he'd reproduced his view in meticulous detail.

Forget whether a tree can actually be seen that way. Jack had expressed an individual point of view and in that way it seemed to me he had come to grips with himself as an artist. I had a new feeling that Jack knew who he was, that he had an identity, and when he was doing his art, he was doing himself. Even if he could only manage that in snatches, in those times he must have felt a purpose I had never known, and I was envious.

Now this is all hindsight trying to come up with reasons for my big decision later. It may be that Jack had no influence at all on my deciding anything. We say we make decisions. Well, maybe, if it's quantitative, we can decide a certain nut fits a certain bolt, that's mechanical. On the other hand, in personal matters, it might be more truthful to concede we're simply compelled this way or that by the ghosts of lingering influences, the urge of atoms. That's life. Meanwhile the latest fad is to confess, "Well, yes, at that point in time I see now I made a wrong decision." The clinical authority of that term, "wrong decision," is reassuring. It sounds finally clear-headed. But I wonder. In our own emotionally screwy personal lives, the fact is we hardly ever just sit down and coolly make a decision, right or wrong. When it's personal, we're disturbed, muddled. Feelings swarm. We can't think. So in the end we probably simply act or react in a way that turns out okay or it doesn't. If how we act is dumb, we can say we should've known better, but don't call it a "wrong decision." We should know what arrogance first coined those two words.

But what to do? The great cosmos all around is so infinite and we're so tiny in it all, it's truly mind-boggling. Yet this is where we find ourselves. Plot the coordinates, we're here. Then, too, we find we only live once in this particular place and for such a short time, we imagine there must be a larger scheme involved, or a larger will. Call it Yahweh, Zeus. Put a name to it, we think it exists. But within this larger will, we also imagine a smaller will is allowed each of us to use as best we can, and that the way we each use this will makes the difference between order and chaos, hope and despair, and that difference matters. Like in control, certainty, and if not in purpose, at least direction, otherwise we're exposed willy-nilly to the whims of the larger nightmare and anything might happen.

So decide, I thought, take control, do something. I needed to. I couldn't. I was sitting in my office in my small place in Dallas, a tiny tic on the globe, not even a speck in the cosmos, my smaller will in traction, the larger scheme entirely beyond me—and there I was. By any long-term reckoning, perhaps not even there. That's how I felt.

It sounds trite and the amount of self-pity involved is hard to recall but I believe that kind of self-telescoping was always my perspective. The universe was overwhelming and I was too small in it all. I pretended it was a philosophical view. It was a wrong measurement of worth. You feel small, join the club, you're already in the parade. The thing is, size is not the point. Time is. And especially the time known as *now*, the present moment, which is neither exactly present nor a moment. As soon as we say *now*, it's gone. Say it twice, you learn. The word can never be nailed to the spot. Except we live in the here and now, we think. The past is past, the future is yet to come, yet the here and now is also elsewhere. Still, it's something, we butt our heads against it every day. Maybe it's a point of departure.

To repeat, there I was sitting in my office. In simple appearance I may have looked all right. Some appearances count but I was thirty-five with half my life gone and the next half unimaginable. Or worse, predictable. I could see continuing in the filming game meaninglessly and slowly disappearing. I didn't want to do that. I needed to know myself even if the examined life is worth nothing. At the same time I'd just seen Jack who somehow knew who he was, with his art, his talent, he could ID himself as an artist. Why couldn't I? Not as an artist, of course. I was a realist. And an artist was the ineffectual sort. In polite society, an aesthete, the nice word for dainty. In Dalton, you never saw an artist. Not out in the open. A few old ladies did watercolors but they were members of the Garden Club and needed something to pass the time. The land was desert, gardens didn't grow. At any rate, being an artist in Dalton was not an option. It wasn't even a thought. The ideal was a good wage earner. You got credit for being a steady worker. Besides, in my mind art was only painting, maybe a piece of sculpture. I felt lucky I couldn't draw. Music, dance, those things were entertainments. Even after I started reading books, it didn't occur to me a book might be a work of art and the writer an artist. Which is probably how I came to writing. I didn't know it was cultural or that in writing I might be an artie. I couldn't have faced that.

I was still at my desk. I had seen Jack's weeping willow. Irving was off recording Butch in the sound booth and Vicky was somewhere. I had some moments to myself.

In that space, as he sometimes did, Jimmy came into the room with me. Like always, he was so full of energy, he was fun. My son. A regular little towheaded boy. Given half a chance I could see he would find his own way and become his own man someday. And I was proud, he was a good kid. But he was still just a kid and loved to play. So we did. We played monsters and gladiators. We tussled and roughhoused childishly. His first pure innocence had been an astonishing thing to hold in my arms. Now he could ride his bike. Then he had to go. My allotment of time was over. I thought of it that way. I pulled into the drive, he jumped from the car, Okay, Dad, see ya! A bright shining light running off. He never said goodbye and neither did I.

So, a space. It happens.

Then Marvin arrived with his copy for a MorningStar brochure. Marvin was a freelance copywriter. The brochure was Vicky's idea for a handout. We'd never had one, we'd never needed one, but Vicky, being the whiz-kid type, decided it was time we had something more than an ordinary business card to leave with potential clients. Something we might mail as well to a select number of big spenders. We were a going concern with a first-class story to tell, we needed a four-color brochure. Four-color was first-class. The copy filling it would need to be first-class, too, to explain the company's capabilities and higher purpose. Our operation would have a solid business philosophy and proven method of operation. It would have a definite character and unique personality distinct from the usual run-of-the-mill producers. The copy itself would need to be informative but memorable, straightforward yet scintillating. Above all, it should be sparkling copy to show MorningStar as an exciting thriving company busily employing skilled professionals and top-notch experts. In short, the brochure would be a marketing tool. I like that word. At Harvard Business School a flat piece of paper is a marketing tool. You're talking on the phone, you're utilizing a maximizing communication tool.

That's the world I was in. Now it was going to be focused in my own company brochure, and I felt suddenly cautious. I was living a lie but it was about to be known, it was going to be put into words. My future bugaboo. Words were going to explain MorningStar. But MorningStar was also me. I would be exposed.

At the same time, it wasn't that clear in my head. I only casually questioned Vicky. So, you think we need one, I said, a brochure like that? Yes, she was sure, and to grow as every decent business should, we needed not only a brochure but we should start a regular media campaign, put up a few billboards along the expressway, hire a sales rep or two and get with it. I could see a conglomerate looming and suggested maybe we didn't need to grow. Vicky said it was inevitable but, okay, we didn't have to do it overnight, we could expand incrementally. I like that word, too. In marketing talk, you don't sell products, you sell items in incremental units. Bags of potato chips get sold, in the Frito-Lay boardroom they're mapping out marketing strategy with each snack bag a unit of incremental value. The original Herman Lay may have believed he was selling incidentals. His consumers now are demographically targeted digits munching incrementals. I won't mention displays, packaging, promotions. Ol' Herman night turn over in his grave.

But now Marvin was waiting, the best freelance copywriter around. It was an open secret he could type a hundred words a minute and write as fast as he typed. He didn't want anyone to know he was that fast, of course. He charged by the hour. He said the brochure copy had taken him a week, that he'd really had to work on it. I figured he'd written the whole thing in a few minutes. It didn't matter, he presented the copy and Vicky and I gave it a look-see. As we did, Marvin waited to one side with pen in hand ready to take notes and make changes. It was his copy, you'd think he'd have some conviction about it, but he was a professional, he'd agree to your worst suggestions and cheerfully revise everything to taste. If you needed a senior citizen's point of view, he'd rewrite his grandmother. I don't mean to sound unkind. Marvin was a good guy personally. But he was also a creature of the underworld of syntax. He lived his life in the promised hope of a commuted sentence. In another two years, he would move his wordsmithing to Hollywood and do very well rehashing movie scripts.

His copy for the brochure had all the right words in it, particularly a lot of dedicateds and committeds. He emphasized quality and exacting standards, creativity and expertise, dependability and efficiency. He said MorningStar had a policy of working closely with each client, that we paid strict attention to the smallest details and accomplished desired results beyond expectations. And so on. The slogan was a Marvin inspiration: "We know how to do it better." We were the best in the business. References on request. A list of award-winning commercials attached.

Vicky loved the copy, especially the slogan. She thought it was great, really great. She was a modern American. Marvin was flattered. Even a professional writer likes praise. I said I thought the copy was just fine, too. Marvin hastened to say he'd be happy to go over it again and give it a final polish, y'know, to make it perfect. I pictured Oscar Wilde polishing one of his poems, deleting a comma in the morning, then in the evening replacing it. So I told Marvin, no, no, it was the end of the day, I'd take the copy home and maybe tinker with it myself. I had a bad habit of revising copy that wasn't mine anyway.

So that was one day. And that was how I happened to take the brochure home with me that evening, a thoughtless act that was both a good and bad idea. Who could've known the change it would cause? And the hurt. In attempting to rewrite the portrait of MorningStar in the brochure, I would erase my own and jump-start the final craziness with Tracy.

I WENT HOME, it could have gone peacefully that evening. As sometimes happened, my nipping was still floating me and not yet depressing. Life was airy and I felt lightly full of good-will in general. Tracy was also in one of her best moods.

I walked in, all was forgiven: Hi, darlin'. Hi, honey. A famil-iar domestic scene, the husband home from work, a friendly kiss and hug. Tracy still believed the Six Flags spot was in the offing and she'd had her daily workout and massage at The Spa, finishing with their special arctic shower so her body felt nice and taut. See, feel. I did. A firm and plush female thigh, the grabber for every red-blooded man ever born. I might have reached for more, a year earlier we would have used each other right there in the hallway, but Tracy wasn't exactly offering. A caterer was going to deliver a platter of snacks any minute. I'd forgotten, we were having a couple over for poolside drinks, and as always Tracy was looking forward to a fun time.

The couple, Tracy's best friend, Sara, and her latest sugar daddy, Spencer. Sara was a sometime model, one of those slender classic beauties with high cheekbones, and I kinda liked her. She was poised and exotic. But I liked her better in a crowd. When we'd been occasionally stuck together alone, we'd had nothing between us but her poise and my forbearance. Her newest, Spencer, I had yet to meet but I imagined he would doubtless be into "investments" and otherwise married. All of Sara's men were. I imagined he would also be a pleasantly mannered fiftyish sort solicitous of a woman's every comfort. Sara's keepers conformed to that type and she seemed satisfied to accept what each offered without conniving to get more. For the most part then she was not a greedy soul but a sensual one who genuinely appreciated the finer parts of each of her men in turn. And I suppose each of her men also appreciated her finer parts. Or we can state that as a given. You're into investments, it's your deal to leverage.

For the pool, we'd wear swimsuits. Tracy would start out in a Samoan lava-lava with a string bikini beneath. As the evening progressed and a good time was being had by all, we'd probably end up en masse in the pool naked. Tracy and Sara would for sure. Spencer might not, I hadn't met him yet. He might be shy of going public with his middle-age sag. In that case, I'd be a pal and stay partners with him at the poolside to play ogling audience for the girls. Which is what they wanted anyway. And naturally so, I think. You're a woman proud of your body, you probably should want to show it off. You're a man attached to a woman with a good-looking body, the dance of the seven veils is a perk you can expect.

So the evening was coming up. Another get-together to be with friends. The only friends in this case however being Sara and Tracy. Spencer and I didn't know each other and probably never would. Meeting for the first time as upscale experienced men, we'd keep the chit-chat on the surface the way you're supposed to. If voiced in small talk at all, you learn, slight differences of opinion become slight detours to agreement. You can write the script ahead of time. Spencer was going to be a man of means at some undefined level living an unexposed presence out of an undisclosed past. At least to me he would be. And as a married man with Sara on the side, he'd play his cards close to his chest. If he had a joker in the hole, he'd keep it covered. I wouldn't get to know him in passing and I probably wouldn't like him. I was going to be bored.

That's what I figured. Well, maybe I could stay only half snockered but bleary enough to get through it. I know now when you're doing something absorbing with your life, that keeps you concentrated and occupied, a break is welcome, even if it's a nothing poolside thing, even the banal is enjoyable. But if your life is empty, you believe everything else is, too. You anticipate boredom, you get what you anticipate.

Anyway, Sara and Spencer would arrive in another hour. I changed into my matching swim trunks and shirt to appear at least visually coordinated if not mentally. Tracy was taking time as usual getting dressed, thirty minutes for the bikini, thirty minutes for the lava-lava. You'd think a couple of minutes but she always did a lot of emery work on her perfect nails. At least it wasn't the two hours to dress to go out. But I was waiting, cooling my heels. I was always waiting, no wonder I drank.

Right, no wonder, I think, place the blame. But I was by

myself, so I mixed another drink, a half glass of Old Charter with a jigger of water to mask the obvious straight liquor.

I sat on the couch. Earlier I had pitched the brochure copy on the coffee table. I picked it up. The words . . . committed, dedicated, professional, quality, results . . . I mouthed the words and they were all distasteful sounds. But they were the expected words to use and placed in the proper order designed to make sense, to persuade and convince. Look, this is the essence of MorningStar. No, this is the *thrust* of MorningStar, the portrait of high performance and dynamic action. Expect magic. But don't worry, we're also grounded in sound fundamental business practices. And this is me, committed, dedicated . . .

Okay, it was going to take some changing. It was artificial. I'd need to make it believable. And lie. Because a good lie is always believable. And the best way to lie, the old tried-and-true way, you've got a story to tell, put a face to it, make it human. Like Billy the Kid, the myth from my past. He'd hidden in one of the salt flats around Dalton. But with small hands, small as a girl's, which is how he slipped a pair of handcuffs once and got away. The sheriff had taken those handcuffs for granted, they were such familiar tools of the trade. But at MorningStar we don't do that, we don't take the tools of the trade for granted. You've got a Billy the Kid product on the loose, we can turn it into a legend in its own time . . .

Or that was stretching it. I'd have to think about it.

Sara and Spencer arrived, and sure enough, Spencer was fiftyish, well-mannered, and decent. Sara was exotic and this time, to fit the occasion, a little Hawaiian-looking. Tracy came down the stairs in her lava-lava slit up one thigh and we all said pleasant things to each other in the living room. I played convivial bartender and mixed the drinks. Spencer was a Cutty Sark and soda man. Sara took her wineglass from me cozily in both hands and lingered against my arm, the only woman Tracy never minded being flirty with me, which was only for show. When we were alone, as I said, Sara and I had little but blank space between us, especially between our minds. I asked her once if any man could warm her without money. She said, "Let me put it this way: no." But if they had money, well, how to say it, she was "transformed." So, she felt the chemistry? She shook her head. "No, the alchemy." Not a bad answer.

We strolled out to the pool, where Sara and Spencer changed clothes in the cabana. Sara emerged in a sarong—last week's tablecloth, she said—and Spencer, the same as me, came out in matching shirt and swim trunks. We didn't have to comment on our apparel. We were men. I couldn't help noticing, though, that Spencer's legs were a couple of pretty pitiful things to have to show. He'd never been an athlete on skinny white stems like those, you could tell, certainly never a linebacker. You're half-crouched behind the line, eagle-eyed, ready to stop the run, you need a little muscle above the knees to throw your weight in there and plug the hole. It takes some heft from the ol' thighs to really launch yourself into the breach like you mean it and sacrifice your body. That's how you play linebacker, you break a few bones, get a little bloody, whack a tooth out, you can feel good about doing your job. But I could see Spencer had never known that kind of world and I felt a passing flicker of contempt for his legs. As a kid, he would've been the teacher's pet. Miss Dowd would've had him up front reciting Robert Browning.

You see how my past keeps informing me. Meanwhile, we were playing compatible as if members in good standing from the same club. The evening was pleasant. The light at the bottom of the pool was luminously glimmering. It was like a moon under the water. Looking up, the starry sky was forever and the

night air was warm and balmy. And not sandy, I thought, not full of daily blowing grit. I always made that comparison and checked myself. I should just accept it. Yes. The air was clean, the grass was green, and this was living, I was fortunate.

At the pool then—I can remember generally but not in detail. I know I didn't ask Spencer about his business and he didn't inquire into mine. I think it was just accepted between us that we were solid in whatever. We were naturally men who knew how things worked. We could afford to be private. And obviously we had discriminating tastes in women. So we were a lot alike. No need to mention it. Spencer made references to golfing a couple of times. I'd never golfed but I pretended to be interested. He told about a funny incident at the Petroleum Club, a waiter spilling something. I'd never been in the Petroleum Club and the incident wasn't funny but I chuckled and shook my head anyway. It went on in that vein. When I try, I've been told I'm an easy person to be with, and since I was still feeling good, I was trying. It wasn't that hard. Sara and Tracy spoke now and then but stayed mostly only beautifully native in lava-lava and sarong. Tableclothes designed by Blass. A topic with them once was a favorite comedy show on TV. It might've been Carol Burnett. One show had been particularly hilarious and a lot of laughing went on remembering the jokes. I joined in the glee without a clue. Then we jumped in the pool and splashed around—not skinny-dipping yet—and got out. A refresher. Spencer was right there with towels for the girls. He helped them with their chairs. A gentleman. I was attending to the drinks, pouring myself straight tumblers. Tracy as usual was barely sipping one. Spencer was being moderate. He would. Sara also. They were social drinkers. But for that reason, you could reason, why drink at all? You live in this world, you drink to get out of it, to escape, the same as in every family of man since the beginning of time. You drink to dream. And for no reason, why care? Get happy. It's all the same in the end so live it up while you can. A voice in my head was beginning to talk.

You get the picture. The get-together was pleasant enough overall but pretty dull, too. I was beginning to feel restless. Sara and Tracy talked about the newest styles at Neiman-Marcus and it occurred to me that might be the one idiotic thing we all had in common, we were Neiman-Marcus patrons. We had the store credit card. Tracy would soon use her card to fill a vault with furs. But that was later. The caterer had come and gone and trays of snacks were laid out on the poolside table, a multitude of tidbits displayed in decorative shapes and colors. Exactly what you expect from a caterer, aesthetic appeal. If it's only gobs of food it's not supposed to be appetizing. With the decorative stuff, though, you can't eat it regularly, you have to take your time, which for me in years past had been a learning experience. For instance, a little tire patch of a sandwich is less than bite-size but you're supposed to encroach on it in nibbles to get it down, and that's not natural. Normally you raise food in front of your mouth, your mouth sees whether it'll fit or not. If it does, your brain doesn't say, now wait a minute, just a taste. If the lunk of food looks like it fits, zoomph, in it goes. Your jaws chew automatically. You're a human, not a rabbit. Picture masticating with four-sided mandibles, that's how you eat. But you can't do that with gourmet delights.

Spencer was offering the trays to the ladies, tiny sausages, anchovies, shrimp, smoked oyster, cheeses—wait. Back up.

Smoked oyster. A ping in my heart. An old memory. My first smoked oyster had been with Darlene in the sand hills. The thing had been stuck with a toothpick and tasted exactly like a moth but I said I liked it. That time had also been my first encounter with pâté and true love. No other word for it. Darlene had prepared the picnic herself and we were alone. She told me I was wonderful. You are, she said, believe it. And I wanted to. *Wonderful.* Lord, how that word lifted me. Then she leaned against me and we watched the moon rising but I couldn't tell her my feelings. It seemed enough just to be with her and for that moment all in the world I would ever want. I still remember.

A tray with crushed ice and shrimp. I picked out a shrimp. The ice should've melted but caterers have their ways, the tray was probably insulated. The shrimp was fresh and plump. And since this kind of eating was a learned experience and not natural, I never failed to plan—let's see, one shrimp, little booger's about two inches long, size of small pinky, should take four bites, tail excluded, no rush, chew politely. And look pleasant. Eating with friends is supposed to be enjoyable. With friends. I looked: Sara and Spencer, faces. Tracy, a body. The three were opaque and I was invisible.

Or maybe that's too existential but when you're lost, it's like being an exile in a foreign land. The inhabitants can be friendly but you're still the outsider. You can learn the language and adapt the mannerisms but a certain strangeness will always remain. If the populace eats with chopsticks, you can learn to eat the same and acquire the manual dexterity, but thirty years later the skill will still never feel completely natural. Deep down in your heart, your fingers will continue to believe they were born for the spoon and fork.

By the way, speaking of eating, I think of Erasmus of Rotterdam who helped set the standards for polite dining back in the sixteenth century. For example, it's interesting, he ruled when more than one person gnawed on the same bone, it was impolite to place the slobbered-over thing back on the platter.

The last person at the bone should toss it over their shoulder to let the dogs finish it off. Another thing, he said you should never blow your nose or wipe your greasy hands on the tablecloth. Grease could better be absorbed from the hands by pressing a chunk of bread. For the nose, he advised using your sleeve. Also, when sharing the same drinking mug, you should avoid swirling the contents. Swirling, he said, tended to stir up the less hefty dregs from the bottom. Remember, too, he said, never stick your hands straight into the food the minute you sit down. Let others take that chance first, you never know where food has been.

Anyway, I was sitting at the pool with three faces around me. I knew their names, Tracy, Sara, Spencer. I smiled and nodded at the small talk. You wouldn't know I wasn't participating. I nibbled my shrimp. Thank you, Mr. Erasmus. Inside my head, the same old feeling of being detached. It was my house, my legal terrain, but I wasn't exactly there. I didn't belong just as it seemed I'd never particularly belonged anywhere. But so what, I'd never especially cared either. Except what did I want?

I think of my father, Charlie.

Charlie's place in the post office was always behind the General Delivery window with its little brass bars in front of his face, and that's still my picture of him, a small man with big ears sitting in a cage looking out. In a way he's a metaphor like that. But there's a vagueness about him, too, and he's not at all substantial. He's thin and airy and in my mind nearly a transparency. I can see through him to the mailbags in the aisle behind, and on through to the rear doors and loading dock, to the vacant track and beyond to the beginning of the desert, and just there, in the air itself, the absolute predictability of every day Charlie ever lived. Which is sad to say, no life should be predictable, but that's what I'm seeing. Also the line of telephone poles sticking up and traveling out of sight with their long droopy wires in between like ragged strings in places, they're so worn you can hear them singing. Little birds light on the worn spots to fry their feet and fall to the ground with exploded feathers.

At the same time Charlie sits at his General Delivery place and waits on people calling for their mail. He knows them and they know him and since he's already sorted the mail into the pigeonholes to his right, he knows without looking if a person has a letter. When they don't, he tells them without looking, Nope, nothing today. You could take his word for it. But no one liked him doing that, it was like not caring and dismissing them. They wanted him to check to make sure. Mail was something to look forward to, a letter from some relative or married daughter, even if it was never anything new and only about the weather and who died, it was still a human contact. These people had their lives blowing away, with only a desert all around and nothing to break the wind—with the sand blasting their faces, with their kids' scalps scarred from ringworm, their teeth stained from alkaline water—a letter was something to count on.

Starting in the morning. The mail was always put up by nine when the post office opened its windows. A few minutes before, the line for General Delivery would've formed, and year after year, it was the same line of people almost, waiting, shuffling forward. A scraggly row of baggy overalls and squinty eyes is imprinted in my brain. Charlie would sit behind his window and pass a few words with each person as they came up. How ya doin' this mornin'? Oh, awright, I reckon, how 'bout yourself? Words like that. But he would wait for the question, I get any mail today? If there happened to be some, he'd say, Yeh, believe ya did. He'd pick a batch of letters from a pigeonhole and flip through them, tossing out the ones meant for that person. They'd watch him thumbing the batch to be sure he didn't miss their name. If there was no letter to begin with, Charlie wouldn't look. He'd say, Nope, nothing. The person before him would get a different look in his eye, of hurt or irritation. You're sure now? I was kinda expecting something. Charlie's mouth would tighten, then he'd pretend to look, but not really. He'd sorted the mail, he knew without looking, so he'd only slap his hand at an empty slot for show and shake his head.

These small confrontations went on five and a half days a week his whole post office life and it might have been a joke but Charlie was serious. He was saying, Look, trust me, I know my job. He wanted people to believe him about their mail and give him credit, a little respect maybe, but no one ever did. In his own way, then, every day Charlie sat with his big ears behind his little window and kept on. I feel pained for him. Of all the great obsessions in this world, of all the really consuming drives and passions a man might have, Charlie's fix was this tedious preoccupation with the smallest sort of recognition. He never spoke of it. He never said three words to me about anything. He was so mute and closed, we never talked. But looking back, I can still see him feeling insulted, slapping his hand at the empty slot, and the way he'd say, Nope, nothing, I can still hear him. The tiny trust he wanted was so incidental.

All the while, General Delivery was perhaps the only place he felt any real confidence. But to what end? It's almost an embarrassment. He never had friends. He didn't hunt or fish. He'd read the local paper about eight pages long, that was it. The post office finally had a bowling team but he wasn't on it. So what did he do? He didn't drink. He didn't go to church. He'd spend his vacation in the fall picking beans. I played football on Friday nights but he never came to watch. He was in the army three years, he might've been sent overseas and stuck in a war, he could've seen something, but he was stationed at Fort Hood out of the way and never left the States. I imagine him in his uniform looking the same as a million other soldiers in polished khakis but while most of them are out on weekend passes getting drunk and having fun, Charlie sits on his bunk in his barracks and shines his shoes. He wore a size 7-AAA, his feet were so narrow, and he had such a scrawny frame, he never weighed over 130 pounds. At fourteen I was bigger than he was and in every way it seemed we were simply completely different. I wanted to do exciting things, I had dreams and hopes, but what was he, sitting behind those little bars at his window looking out, what did he see? Growing up, he'd never had a girlfriend. He was shining shoes at the local barbershop when he married Marie. Or she married him. Neither had any choice. He was twenty and working for dimes. Then he'd somehow married again eleven years after Marie left him, he found Myrtle, or she found him and took over, but in all his life in that one little Dalton spot, in the long empty nights before he retired and suddenly dropped dead, what did he ever truly want?

I was sitting by the pool. I became aware of the two naked bodies in the water. Tracy and Sara had slipped in without a sound and their bare limbs were glimmering in the illumination from beneath them. Naked, but I'd been seeing their thighs and most of their breasts anyway. It seemed the only difference now was the actual nipples and the small pubic patches that had not been shaved to fit a bikini. The bodies were both luxuriously undulating and performing. The usual show. Then—no matter how many times you see it, it's always interesting—they dove and two round bottoms briefly mooned the surface of the pool. Spencer nudged me and grinned. He was sitting beside me and since he had not stripped to join the nymphs, I hadn't either.

He may have had his own personal sense of propriety, he may have been naturally inhibited in public, or maybe he just couldn't let go and have fun. That was probably it, he lived in Highland Park, I figured he was a piker. But I was playing congenial host, I didn't want him to have to feel silly sitting alone. Besides, he was the only other man around and buddies stick together.

Actually, I was feeling resentful. I didn't want to sit with Spencer. I liked skinny-dipping, swimming naked with naked women's bodies. Your balls are free in the water and there's a larger freedom in floating weightlessly. You're suspended in watery space with the touch of slippery skin like quicksilver. The buoyancy of the reach between a woman's legs in the depths is almost mystical. Especially if you don't know the woman.

So there I was keeping Spencer company but two nude women were gliding the pool. I should drop my trunks and jump in with them. And for a moment I thought I was going to do just that. Then I remembered it was Tracy and Sara. I'd been naked in the pool with them before. They liked to pretend it was all very natural and nothing sexual. Their bodies were purely innocent. Or I never knew what they thought. Sara was a closed shop. And Tracy and I were married. It wouldn't be intriguing and I'd end up going along with the play-acting just to be nice.

I try to figure it now. Obviously I was plopped down in the middle of the basic American Dream including the fantasy of beautiful women openly displaying their wares. I'd been the poor high school dropout who'd come from nowhere and obtained to some degree the prescribed ingredients of that dream, house, cars, clothes, furniture, those things. Of course some bad things had happened along the way, no one gets off scot-free, but it was a good life now. Look, gorgeous wife, my own business, enough money, gourmet treats laid out for the picking. The drinks were embalming, the pool was glimmering, and the night was calm. A small breeze now and then was nice and pleasant. Call it easy living. All the parts were there.

Or not all, exactly. I'd hidden the pistol in the garage, so that part was missing. And substance as well, where was that? The word popped into my head and I suddenly focused on the little decorative snacks. I saw they were almost ephemeral and I was nibbling style not substance. And I should have known, that's why I was always hungry. I was starving for those Sunday dinners at Grandma's where we all sat down and smacked our mouths at how good the food sure did taste and you didn't have to ask to have anything passed because it was passed to you before you could ask and it was fun to eat. Food was love. You could have double helpings and all you wanted. You could eat hearty and have eight whole pieces of fried chicken at one setting and never get puny.

Those were the days. But that was past and the past was gone. Now the food was for looks. And the living, too. The style was surface. The living itself had no meat on its bones and beyond the bones, no heart and soul.

I'm sure I had that thought. As I said, I was sitting with Spencer. Which could've been the title of a sad poem, "Sitting with Spencer." With any real lead in his pencil, he would have piled in with the naked women in the pool, what the hell, but he was being properly middle-aged and self-contained. That's how you learn to act when you grow up, and I was stuck with him. Actually I was sticking myself but I was blaming him. Still I played the congenial host and offered a couple of times,

Would you care for another drink? Each time he declined. Anyone else, I'd say they passed but with him I have to say declined. He said he was already feeling a little tipsy and gave a look like, wow, he'd come close. Tipsy was his traffic signal programmed to stop him on red. The yellow light blinked, he was automatically braking. So he controlled his drinking, the worst kind of person to be around, he'd probably never been completely blotto once in his life. What kind of man was that? You'd think he'd need to blow it occasionally just to clear his head.

Anyhow, Spencer was keeping Sara. To his way of thinking maybe that was more interesting than really boozing. I couldn't imagine the two of them doing anything very inventive. Sara was the picture of vacuous poise in any position. Spencer was the portrait of the nonversatile. My point is, Spencer had Sara as his playpretty to show he was a man who could get a beautiful younger woman. That it was his money that lured the woman and not his personal self didn't need distinguishing. Mammon/self in the better circles is one specie. Or that's my old resentments talking.

Spencer and Sara. Their relationship was their business but it occurred to me Tracy and I were perhaps similar. I'd gotten Tracy. In our case, we'd married, even if I hadn't planned it, I'd married her because I said I would. Or because she said I said I would and I said I was a man of my word. It was stupid. The fact remains, I had gotten her, a beautiful woman who could pick and choose but with a yen for display. Tracy had believed I could afford her and do things for her. I produced TV stuff. So with me, she could become displayed. It happened she was also a terrific fuck, a definite plus at first, but with fucking all the time and little else in between, well, to gloss it again, I'd burned out. I don't need to review it. Sex is half in the mind but not exactly the best reason for thinking. The question was, if I hadn't been able to afford the display, could I have gotten her? Meaning more than once. Suppose I was still working at the Sinclair and she pulled in for gas. Would she have given me a second look?

Darlene would drive her daddy's big Lincoln Continental into the Sinclair every Saturday and fill up with ethyl, the highest octane, the finest premium. It was the only car in town that didn't use regular. Her daddy owned the Dalton State Bank and she'd say, "Just put that on my daddy's account, wouldja?" The way she smiled saying that word, wouldja, it sounded innocent, but the look in her eyes had all the meaning in the world behind it: *wouldja be my man, wouldja let me kiss you, wouldja, huh?* The words of a song. You'd stand there feeling like mush.

Without a doubt, Darlene was the most beautiful, sexiest girl in Dalton. Her body was perfect. Her hair was jet-black sin. Her lips were like rose petals. Which sounds pretty corny, rose-petal lips, but pick a rose and take a petal in your hand to see up close. It's so light and delicate, so soft and downy, it feels almost tender. It's so full somehow, it's plush. You want to put it in your mouth and taste it. Squeesh it in your fingers, a sweet juice comes out. It's luscious. That's why I still think roses and Darlene remains my perfect fantasy, and back in those days, not only mine but every other local yokel's, too.

With three of us working the Sinclair on Saturday, the big day, Darlene would drive in and it was like we'd all been just waiting. Well, we had been just waiting. What else was there in Dalton? She'd come gliding up to the gas pump in that long sleek Continental without a sound, it had to be like driving a couch, and everything would stop. I'd be fixing a flat, I'd drop it. Alvin would rush from the wash stall in his rubber boots and apron. Denzel would be charging a battery, he'd leave it dead. We'd be onto that big Lincoln like a pack of swarming rats, under the hood and all around, checking the oil and water, tires, fan belts, spark plugs, you name it, we checked it. Of course the oil was never low but whoever got to check that got to show the dipstick to Darlene and tell her, "Looks like your oil's all right, Darlene, right on full." You'd say it gently and show her the dip-stick at an angle, holding the drippy end on a rag. She'd say, "Oh, good, thank you." But in that special sexy way she had. It made you weak in the knees. The best though was cleaning her windshield, especially on a hot day when she was wearing little huggyass shorts and maybe only a halter. You could look down over the wipers and see the Exotic East, across the plain of the dash and the moon of the steering wheel, suddenly rising into view, the pagodas of Bangkok, the road to Mandalay. It was hard to take your eyes away. I used to pray Darlene's windshield would come in every day completely bug-splattered. But better, even better, was when you vacuumed her floorboard. You'd have your head down where she was lifting her feet to give you room and her warm brown thighs would sort of ease up off the seat—it was wonderful. You'd want to keep going forever with that vacuum and suction everything.

I'd think so near yet so far away. By sheer accident my timing into this world had been off and I'd been born too late. Darlene was a year older and a grade ahead. She was a senior, which put her on a different planet almost, so how could she even think to notice me? Besides, she was rich. She lived in a beautiful house with a big lawn and flowers and a circular drive all around. It was the only lawn in town with underground sprinklers. She drove that big Lincoln that only used ethyl, and lemme tell you, the way she dressed was really inspiring. She came to school one day in a see-through blouse and for the whole day nearly we had a breakdown in education. Guys were walking into walls and falling down stairs. It was the event of the year.

Then I saw Darlene one night on the way to a De Molay dance at the country club. It took money to be in the country club and to join the De Molays, so those two things were out for me, but that night I saw her driving by with Randy Caudell in his new two-door Ford Deluxe and I still remember. She had on a strapless blue formal and he was wearing a white dinner jacket with a black bow tie. I was working the late shift at the Sinclair, I happened to look up, and there they were gliding by. Darlene was laughing and Randy was smirking. He was conceited. His daddy owned the peanut mill. Or I shouldn't say anything against him. He was all right. In recent years a lot of people have seen him on TV giving advice on mutual funds. But that night he was with Darlene and I'll never forget, they both looked so comfortable and careless, it was like they were happy maybe. And they had time, my sudden thought as they drove by, that they had all the easy time in the world to simply go somewhere and dance and have fun and not think a thing about it. They had time and never the least worry about what anything would cost, and I wondered what that must feel like, to never look at a price tag, to never see the cost of something, to just get what you wanted, new Levi's and big juicy steaks, and say, "Hey, let's go to the movie," and never think a bit whether you could or couldn't because *of course* you could, and you never had to work and save up and feel sorry for yourself because the money was always there like air. And every day, every time you breathed, the money was always simply there.

I wondered what that would be like. Would it feel peaceful? I figured it must. But then what would you have to think about if it wasn't the hand-to-mouth ways you had to scrimp to scrape by? I couldn't imagine.

In my mind then Darlene was so far above me I didn't stand a chance. I was just another ogling face in the crowd, another dumb kid full of wild hopes and nowhere to go and that was all. Except for one thing. And the thing was, I didn't care if I didn't have a chance. Or it was more like who cared, who really gave a damn? And the answer to that was easy. Nobody. Which comes from living where nothing has a chance to begin with and you're supposed to know your place and accept that, where if you feel and think and want more, forget it, you're lucky to cope. So quit wanting things you can't have, be happy with what you've got. That was the message.

But I couldn't accept that. Like at the time my social life was pretty much only a few school things now and then and Fayette under the bleachers. Or Fayette in the back of her father's furniture store on the square. Fayette had a key. We'd sneak in at night to be on a mattress for a change. I don't remember if they were Serta Sleepers in those days but they were all new with the latest in modern back support, firm or soft, we had our choice. A new mattress got a little spotty, we'd flip it over.

Now this wasn't exactly a nightly event and Fayette had her guidelines. You had to be there. We'd be under the bleachers or on a mattress in the rear of the store, it was no problem getting that far. Fayette would practically drag me to the spot. Then we'd start kissing and she'd get hot. I'd have her dress up and be pulling her panties down, she'd push me away, "No, now I told you, we're not going to do that no more." She'd sit up with her hair messed and start straightening her clothes. I'd be rolled off in exasperation.

"You can get mad," she'd say, "I'll just go home."

"Fayette, c'mon."

"It's not my fault. You just want to get your way, that's all, you don't care about me."

"Sure I do."

"You don't. You don't even think it's wrong."

"C'mon, it's not wrong."

"Then what is it?"

"It's supposed to be exciting."

"Hah! For you maybe."

"Fayette—"

"What if something happens?"

"Nothing's going to happen."

"But what if it does? You wouldn't care."

"Fayette—"

This would go on, the same argument every time. From the beginning I figured she'd chased after me and made all the advances, bumping into me in the hallway at school, sticking little notes in my locker. I'd finally given in, I believed I was doing her a favor, but now, even after a lot of times, she'd act coy. I don't know why I bothered. She was vain, she probably thought she was cute. I thought she was skinny. So we'd argue. Then I'd pretend to give up. "Okay, you don't want to, that's it, let's go."

She'd pout, "You don't like me."

"I didn't say that."

"Then say you like me."

"Okay, I like you."

"But you don't love me."

"Fayette, c'mon—"

"Say you love me."

"All right, I love you, how's that?" Jesus.

She'd get all gooey then and put her arms around me, "Oh, you do, don't you? You love me and I love you, too, I do, I do." She'd pull me down with her and I'd almost get started. This was when her guidelines kicked in. She'd say, "Wait." She'd have to scoot her body around. I'd nearly start again, she'd say, "Just a second." She'd have to get her hair or something out of the way. She'd say, "Not yet." Then, "No, wait, lemme get straighter." Finally she'd say, "Okay, now you can." Another guy would've lost interest. I had no pride.

It's no wonder I couldn't accept my lot. There had to be something better. Then why not the ideal? Besides, I couldn't help my feelings. Even without a chance, I wanted Darlene and I was going to get her. The question was how. I could see being shot down in flames but at least I would die trying. Then I had an idea. The annual May Day Frolic was coming up at school. This would include the box lunch auction. If I worked it right, I could outbid Randy Caudell for Darlene's box lunch and she would have to be with me to share it. That was the rule, you bought a girl's box, figuratively speaking, the girl came with it. But then what could I offer? Darlene had everything. I'd need a car for sure. I didn't have one. But I'd saved. I had $200 in Postal Savings. I could draw that out and buy Skinny Bailey's '38 Ford coupe. I could push it to get it started, it would probably run. But what else? I needed to be smooth and casually confident, a man of the world. I wasn't that. Then I hit on it. In a flash of brilliance, I decided, Hey, I know, I'll just be me and act natural. It was a stroke of genius.

It was also a bad idea. For one thing, acting natural was still acting and as far as being simply me, I didn't have the foggiest blinkiest notion in the world who me was. My name was Bobby Jack, I was called that, but who in any room anywhere was really *me?*

The truth is, had I known, only *me* might've set the course for the rest of my life and I might still be today the same lowly character I was then. When I look back and see the fork in the road, the different path I might've taken, well, I don't know. At the time I may not have had a choice and perhaps what I did, I had to do. I like to say I did a lot of calculating and planning. I can recall one step leading to the next. I bought the car. I bought the aphrodisiac. Then I closed my eyes and bet my soul on a single roll of the dice. As far as I was concerned, it was all or nothing. But was that fated, or what?

When I drew my $200 from Postal Savings, it was through the Money Orders window. Charlie saw me from General Delivery, the next window over from Parcel Post. He pretended to count stamps. If I had told him I was buying a car, he would've said, "Well, I figured it was something." He wouldn't have acted interested. So we didn't speak. As I said, we hardly ever spoke anyway. I gave a nod walking out and he nodded back.

Now the $200 was all the money I'd saved from all my jobs in four years. A paper route first. I had the longest route in town, forty customers in four miles, but I liked it. I liked walking and throwing the papers without breaking stride. If I had to stop and get set, I'd take a point off. I'd walk along folding half my papers into flat disks I could sail, and the other half into wads I could chunk. I could throw floaters or speedballs and groundhoppers. If there was an obstacle in the way, that made it even better. I loved obstacles, the challenge of hitting a porch dead center in spite of the odds. Only once I threw a paper on a roof and I remember that paper stayed on that roof for nearly a year before finally moldering and blowing off. Every day I'd walk by and have to see it. My one defeat, I'd think.

My next job was at Little John's Country Fresh Grocery. Little John's had flypaper hanging in strips from the ceiling and rat traps set out along the aisles. I sacked groceries and carried the sacks to the cars, usually to somebody's old pickup parked about a mile away. It would seem that far. It would be a block or two anyway. Little John's didn't have a parking lot. And most of the time I'd find myself following along behind some crabby old granny who wouldn't tell me where she'd parked so I could hurry on and unload. They'd make you poke along behind them at a snail's pace while your arms started aching and the sacks began to split apart. You'd have to hold the eggs in from falling out. I'd say, "Ma'am, if you'd just tell me where you're parked, I can go on ahead." The crabby old granny would say, "Now you just hold your horses, young man, I'm going to show you." I'd say, "Well, I dunno, ma'am, these sacks are getting pretty heavy." Maybe I'd be carrying an armload of sacks with glass jars and bottles. I'd say, "This one's beginning to tear." She'd say, "Well, don't you worry, we're getting there." Like in time for the Rapture, I'd think. They had Eternity waiting. Meanwhile I'm playing spastic, hiking my knees, hunching my chin, hitching the sacks nine different ways to keep things from spilling out. You were a sackboy back then, you never knew, every sack could be your next exercise in instant acrobatics.

Then I worked in the fields picking beans, digging taters, windrowing peanuts. It was routine stoop labor up and down the rows. You'd be bending, picking, crunching clods all day, it wasn't thinking work. Your brain would go into a coma. Oh, you could look over and see the wetbacks on their side of the field and maybe think about them. They couldn't talk English so they were kept separated. They were lower-class. But what were you, working the same? Still, they'd come in the fall in their caravans and trailers and you'd see them over away in their own pack. They'd camp along the irrigation ditch and you'd hear them at night playing music and laughing. It was strange. They worked all day, then sat around their fires eating frijoles and chilis, jabbering, you'd think they'd just want to lay down and rest. You labor ten hours in the hot sun, you're worn out, you're tired and sore, but you'd hear them at night having a good time. They were like a foreign tribe camped with their women and kids, with their straw hats and bandannas, they were set apart and shunned, they weren't allowed in town, but they'd come in the fall for the worst kind of field labor and every evening in firelight beside some old muddy ditch, you'd hear their music. In that lonesome flat land and nowhere, in their own world, you'd hear them laughing.

So, different jobs, the last year at the Sinclair, and I'd saved $200. I could buy Skinny Bailey's '38 Ford coupe I'd been looking at. He left it parked in the alley behind his shoe repair shop. It had been hand-painted blue and from a certain slant the brush strokes showed but it came equipped with fender skirts and running boards along the sides so it wasn't all bad. Even if it took a little fixing up. The windshield on the driver's side was a busted spiderweb, the tires were bald, and it might need a battery, a new taillight, but not everything. The body wasn't completely rusted and you could give it a running push, jump in, slam it into gear, it would probably start. Then all you had to do was keep the motor running. After that, the sky was the limit, you were free, you could pick up girls and drive around drunk and hollering and litter the world with beer cans. It only took a car.

I left the post office with my savings in my pocket and walked across the square to Skinny's Shoe Repair ready to deal.

Now first off, Skinny was exactly what his name implied. He appeared to be made out of sticks. He had a long neck with a kink in it and his sleeves never reached his wrists. He had to cinch his pants double to hold them up so his belt was always too long with the end sort of hanging down limberly in front. From a distance it would look like a brown peter flopped out. Women fronting him unexpectantly would be struck dumb for a second. One old maid once supposedly fainted.

But Skinny also had a reputation for smiling due to the nature of his work. He needed to have tacks handy so he'd keep a row of tacks clamped in his mouth. This gave him the appearance of a barbed-wire grin. You could walk by his shop any day and look through his window, he'd be sitting at his last in his apron squirting tacks from his lips and going *blap!blap!*, blapping away with his tack hammer. Or the sound you'd hear was his old sewing machine stitching leather, but slowly as if barely making it, *zuk-a-zunk-ah-zunnk-ahhh-zunnnk*. Skinny though was pretty fast. He could carve a sole from a square of leather in nothing flat and with such a smoothly continuous motion it was almost mesmerizing to watch. It was the one graceful thing I saw anyone in Dalton do. He could carve a sole, slap on glue, tack and sew a shoe in ten minutes. He'd neoprened about half the footwear in town. Then it happened in another year, some joker—just kidding, he said—sneaked up behind Skinny and slapped him on the back—"Hey, Skinny!" It's still remembered. Skinny swallowed his tacks. But that was in another year.

I walked into Skinny's shop, I was a little excited but you go to buy a car, even your first, you know not to show you're interested. You pretend you're not. Which is probably a natural instinct passed down through thousands of years of bartering from the first time two cavemen sat down to trade wampum for women. They knew, you let your eyes get too wide and start drooling over the other guy's wampum, he's going to start licking his chops. He'll see he's got a live one.

So I decided to play it cagey. I ambled in and didn't say anything, just sort of stood. A few old geezers were sitting around wasting another day. They had the benches on the square and the domino parlor, but Skinny's shop was their next favorite lazy spot. They didn't appear to notice me and I pretended to only happen by with nothing better to do, the same as anyone. I had a matchstick stuck in the corner of my mouth, the idea being to let it hang and not chew on it. That way I could look nonchalant with my thumbs hooked in my belt and take in the view out the window.

Of course there was never anything to view out the window, the usual people blowing by, a few clattery cars, maybe Thumper Joe. You'd see him nearly every day shuffling along making screwy faces, his pockets stuffed with empty pop bottles. He'd pick up the bottles along the roadside and get the deposit back on them from Little John's. And people would pay him a quarter to dance his jig on the sidewalk. He'd flop his feet up and down in his sloppy oversized shoes like Thumper the rabbit and some of the men would have fun with him. They wouldn't call it taunting but they'd egg him on to keep stomping around until he was falling down, he'd be so dizzy. And they'd tease him about paying his quarter, offering it and yanking it back, making him grab and miss. They'd threaten to cut his pecker off if he didn't keep it in his pants. It was never seen that he didn't, but they'd scare him with a knife until he was rolling his eyes, whimpering and slobbering, trying to hide his privates with his hands. He was such a crazy moron, you could really have fun with him. At the same time he didn't have a family, he'd been abandoned as a child, or no one knew. He lived out of garbage cans, people gave him throwaway clothes, he was paid quarters, and somewhere along the way he'd found his place to live in a boxcar set off the tracks at the edge of town. In another ten years, Myrtle's youngest daughter, Minie, would move in with him and they would set up housekeeping together. They would lay linoleum, install a regular window, and nail orange crates to the wall for shelves. Some people said it was a shame and they felt sorry for Minie having to live with an idiot. But I'd lived with Minie and the others a few months, I felt sorry for Thumper. The freight trains passing would fill their boxcar with smoke and rattle the window, but if you put yourself in their place, you had your own home on a permanent lot rent-free, you could probably stand a little train smoke.

So I was standing looking out. Skinny was working, *blap!blap!* I was still not chewing my matchstick but letting it hang, playing it cool. I had my eyelids about half drooped like Robert Mitchum, my thumbs hooked in my belt. My weight was rested on one leg, my weight actually a vital force with lightning moves held in check. You wanna speak to me, mister, you better be smiling. I was living in my mind. Then I started listening to the old geezers grumping about the sparrows taking over the trees around the courthouse and dropping birdshit on their benches. Damn birds. The old farts were going to bring out their shotguns one of these days and blast the living daylights outta them damn birds, be good riddance, and all the damn dogs running loose, pick 'em off while they're trottin' down the road, by god, and the damn cats howling every night, draw a bead on a few of them suckers, teach 'em a lesson.

That's how they talked, spitting and dribbling tobacco juice, grousing about the same things year in, year out, and about the weather, by god, the country could sure use some rain, couldn't it? You'd think after ninety years they'd know that. The country could always use some rain, it never rained, and that's why it was desert and not about to change, so why talk about it? What good did it do? Sitting around griping about the same things every day, that's all they did, dried up and withered themselves, when had they ever done one worthwhile thing in their whole lives?

Or when had I? I was seeing myself grousing and ranting inside my skull. I'd be old someday, too, and no use to anyone either, even myself. They were my fate and I felt struck. I could see being aged and wrinkled, dribbling tobacco juice down my chin and just sitting. *Blap!blap!* The seconds of my life were being hammered flat. Time was passing with each beat, each moment. Now was the moment and with each beat of the hammer, now was gone. A million moments had come and gone without a trace and I'd let my life pass me by without really living.

Blap!blap! Gone! Gone!

I blinked. I had chewed my matchstick to a mushy pulp. I threw it down. Those old geezers could sit there and waste their lives, not me.

I turned from the window, "Hey, Skinny, you still got that ol' coupe?"

He nodded. "Yuarrh." He was saying "Yeah," speaking through his tacks. Then he said, "Wuugh?" That was "Why?"

"Oh, I was just wondering. You used to have it back out there in the alley but I don't remember seeing it a while ago."

"Nuhm, szz aarh." (No, it's there.)

"I guess I missed it. I wasn't really looking."

"Uhmm." (Uhmm.) He continued blapping at his last.

I pretended to look out the window again. So far, so good. I'd left myself open a little but I hadn't revealed anything you could prove. It was going to get exciting.

I let the suspense build, then I said, "Y'know, I was just thinking, you sure have had that ol' car a long time. How long've you had that ol' thing?"

"Uugh, uunnoo, 'maile, uh ekcon." (Oh, dunno, 'while, I reckon.)

"That ol' car must be a hundred years old."

"Utsa hurrtiaite."

I didn't quite catch that and one of the old geezers interpreted, "He said it's a '38." All the old farts were interested now and watching. It wasn't about the weather but they knew it was about something old and they could relate.

"Yeah, '38," I said. "I heard that was a bad year for cars, like they had to make everything outta scrap metal that year, tin cans and such, y'know. They had to just sorta stick the parts together any way they could." Now that was good, tin cans and such. You could see the trashy metal going into one side of a factory on conveyer belts and cheap defective automobiles rolling out the other end. You were stuck with a car like that, you'd almost have to give it away.

"Ezgh rye?"

"Skinny says, is zat right?" Old fart interpreting again.

"Well, that's what I heard," I said. "Besides, that ol' coupe's left out in the weather, the body's probably all rusted out." I shook my head.

Bobby Jack Nelson | 1 7 3

One of the old grumps thought a second, then perked up, "Rusted out? How the hell can it be rusted out, ain't no rain."

"From the air," I said.

He clamped his mouth. If air was reasonable, he was going to start hating me now and never forget.

"Anyway," I shrugged, "you could probably sell it for parts, get something out of it that way."

Skinny gave me a sidelong peek, then did a final blap with his hammer, dribbled the tacks from his mouth, and sighed. His face without tacks made him look somehow balder. "Okay," he said, "what're you after?"

"Whataya mean?" I was innocent.

"You trying to buy that ol' car?"

"Me?" The old geezers were looking at Skinny, then me, back and forth. This was drama. "Shoot," I said, "who'd want to buy an ol' rattletrap like that?"

Skinny nodded. "Okay, whataya wanna give?"

"Whataya mean, what do I wanna give?"

"You got some figure in mind, don'tcha? You been sneaking up on buying that coupe for about six months now. I seen you out there in the alley looking at it 'bout every day."

"Yeah, but just passing by. I cut through the alley to get outta the wind." That was good, too, outta the wind. That was believable.

"Well, guess I'm mistaken, then. I figured you wanted to buy it, I'd let you have it. An ol' boy's coming down from Wylie tomorra, I guess I'll let him have it."

That caught me off guard but I held tight. "Yeah, you got somebody wants it, you better let 'im have it."

"Yeah, well, I reckon I will." He went back to work.

The old geezers were disappointed. I turned back to my window and felt my presence disappear. Damn, what if he was telling the truth and there really was a guy coming down from Wylie and the guy took the car, where did that leave me? Without a car. And where would I find another one? In Dalton, they didn't have extra cars. You had a car in Dalton, you married it. Besides, the box lunch auction was coming up and I had plans for Darlene. This required a car, absolutely, and this was the deciding moment, so I had to go for it. Now or never.

I turned back to Skinny. "Y'know, this is funny." I gave it my best chuckle. "I just thought, y'know, I don't need a car, I mean, I really don't, but then I thought, well, heck, why not? You need to sell that ol' coupe, Skinny, tell you what, I'll do you a favor and take it off your hands, how's that?" I was being a friend.

Skinny shook his head.

"No, I mean it," I said. But don't beg, I thought, jesus, don't beg.

"Nah, you don't want that ol' car, you just said, you don't need it."

"But you're going to let that ol' boy from Wylie have it."

"So?"

"I can't believe you mean that. Skinny, Wylie's our *rival!*" I was striking at the age-old Dalton weak spot.

The room was suddenly perilously quiet. You could hear the blowflies hitting the windowpane like BBs. Some of them were dropping to the floor with broken necks where a black spider was waltzed over eating them still alive, crunching their skulls in his mechanical jaws and sucking them dry.

I said, "Skinny, the big game every year at Thanksgiving is with Wylie, I know what they're like, I play against them."

Skinny cleared his throat. "Well, I know it's Wylie."

"And you're just going to let somebody from Wylie come over here and take away one of our cars?"

"It ain't ours, Bobby Jack, it's mine."

"But you can do that? I mean, you can sit there and honest-ly say you can let that happen?"

"It ain't like they're taking one of our women."

"But don't you kinda hate to do it?"

"Annajean Rawlston!" One of the old geezers popped his head up like a rooster. "She run off with that ol' Wylie boy, 'member? Ain't been heard from since. When was that? Twenty, thirty years ago, I cain't recall. Seems like it was right after the war. Mighta been during the war, I'd hafta think. One of the Rawlston girls, though, name was Annajean, I 'member that. She was kinda reddish-haired, whole family was." He sat back satisfied.

I was still with Skinny. "All right, I tell you what," I said. "I'll give you a hundred and fifty dollars for that coupe, now that's it." There, it was out.

Skinny shook his head. But I wasn't going to take no. I offered him $160 and said I'd take the car as is. He didn't exact-ly answer. I didn't wait, I told him $170 and that was more than the old clunker was worth. He didn't accept. I immediately went up to $180 and said that was my last offer, take it or leave it. He left it. I said $190 and he was still only wagging his head. I pulled out my wad of bills, a hundred percent pure money, I said, and announced $200, the works, the whole bundle.

"And that's it, all I've got," I said, "my last nickel, my life's savings, and I'm not lying, that's every cent I own." I held the money out to him pitifully and felt like a dwarf. I'd envisioned myself wheeling and dealing, a regular one-man Houdini, but I'd panicked, I'd wanted that car so bad, I'd turned belly-up and ruined my own self-respect. I stood in defeat.

Skinny sighed. "You finished? If you'd give me the chance, I've been trying to tell you—look, you want that ol' coupe, you can have it. But not for two hundred, save your money. I'll sell it to you for a hundred and twenty-five. That's what I got in it and I think maybe it's worth that much—okay?"

I looked at Skinny and he looked at me. A hard moment. The old geezers were wheezing and hooting. One of them slapped his knee and poked me. "Ha! Gotcha, didn't he?" But what did he know? I'd lost my image and I knew it was going to take me a long time to get it back. An hour, maybe two.

I told Skinny, "Well, if you're sure." I counted out the $125 and sealed the deal. If there were any papers to sign, we didn't. The title was somewhere. Skinny said he'd try to find it and get it to me. But I didn't need a title. This was Dalton. We shook hands. The keys were in the car.

I walked out of Skinny's shop and immediately felt taller. I could see my future opening before me like a big boll of cotton and all I had to do was live it. Life was good. I had my first car and $75 to spare. So the first part of my plan for Darlene was in place. The second part would be the aphrodisiac. I'd have to drive to the county line to get that. No problem. I had the wheels and the means. I started humming, O-h, l-o-o-k o-u-t D-a-r-l-e-n-e, h-e-r-e I c-o-m-e.

First, though, I needed to put up the clothesline. I'd given my word I would do it, but I also had to think where. Sybil had the rear of the house guarded. Cross that off. The front was too near the road. A few steps was all the front yard was. And the west side was where the tumbleweeds stacked up. I wasn't about to get tangled in them. So that left the east side of the house, except after about six feet, the east side became a vacant lot and someone else's property. I didn't care. I pushed over the NO TRESPASSING sign and sited my spot for an end post.

The best arrangement, I'd decided, would be the house and one post. I'd simply nail the end of three lines to the wall of the house and stretch the lines to a post out in the vacant lot.

Myrtle was dying to have a damn clothesline up, fine, then that's damn sure what she'd get.

I went to the lumber yard and got a roll of nylon cord, a post, and a 2 × 4 for the crossbar. I nailed the ends of three lines to the house, fixed the crossbar to the post, then measured for distance. How far? How much clothesline? This was important. Thirty feet looked short. Okay, then how about being generous, say, fifty feet? That looked about right. I started digging. The ground was like cement but pretty soon I had a four-inch hole. Deep enough. Four inches would hold a post a little while. I set the post and attached the lines from the house.

Imagine, three long stretchy cords, the distance is fifty feet, the ground beneath is dirt. You hang a heavy wash, the clothesline sags, the wind blows. It's not something you can say was planned. The wash flops in the wind and mops the ground. Or it might not. You'd have to wait and see.

A VOICE WAS TALKING in my head. . . . Y'know, you could've gotten that car for $115 if you'd started lower, but you weren't smart, you blabbered yourself all the way up to $200. I know, I said, but it's okay, Skinny was fair. And the clothesline, the voice said. Right, the clothesline, but I don't want to think about that now. Then how about Darlene, remember? Are you kidding, in the sand, in the moonlight . . . memories forever.

I was sitting in the house in the dark. I could hear the others still out by the pool, so I guessed I'd simply left them and walked away. I had done that a lot the past year when the scene bored me. I found I liked my own company better.

Then Tracy was standing in the doorway. She had turned on the light. "—you left without saying a word, how could you?"

I raised a folder. Somehow I was holding the brochure copy.

"Have to work on this," I said.

"In the dark?"

"I'm thinking about it." And here it comes, I thought, her hurt, my blame, the same old hassle.

"You're so rude. I don't know what Spencer thinks."

"When they leave, I'll peep out and say goodbye."

"He wants you to do a promotion for United Way. He was going to ask you." Her voice was rising.

"Tracy—" It was so damned tiring.

"He's chairman of the United Way this year. The chairman! Do you know who Spencer is?!"

She was saying more and I tuned out. Who cared who Spencer was? He was an important man in town, he could throw business my way, I wasn't interested. He wanted me to do a promo spot for United Way, I didn't feel grateful. As chairman, Spencer's job was to drum up all the free help he could in the name of community spirit and civic benevolence but in my mind it would be more pointedly in his name. He'd list his chairmanship as qualification for political office someday and my promo would be a freebie, my contribution to organized charity, the operation of which is known to require most of the money for itself.

I wasn't in the best mood. I'd gotten bored, then walked away from the pool without a word and vanished inside the house. In the dark, no less. That was thoughtless, but now Tracy was chipping at me. I'd deserted our guests. She emphasized *our* guests. I said I was sorry, she didn't care, she was still chipping and I didn't want to hear it. She figured Spencer could do me a favor, big deal, he was chairman of a Big Deal, but it would be more like me doing him a favor, she didn't know. Besides, to hell with favors. If I needed a favor, I'd ask for one, but it damn sure wouldn't be from somebody like Spencer. He'd never played linebacker, his first car was probably a new two-door Ford Deluxe. Tracy thought he was worth knowing, he was keeping her best friend, Sara, in style and he could tell stories about the Petroleum Club. I'd never been in the Petroleum Club. He told stories about golfing. I'd never golfed. What's more, he'd never worked with his hands, he'd never had to sweat to make a living, so what the hell could he know?

I see my mind then as if it were only a moment ago. A switch might've clicked. It still clicks. Call it reverting to type. Earlier in the evening, I'd felt generally indifferent to Spencer, I didn't know him, but with Tracy lauding him now, I began to really not like him. He was another Randy Caudell and he probably didn't like me either, fine, he could say so, we could settle the matter right there. Spencer wanted to get smartass, I'd be happy to oblige, one pop, I'd drop him flat. He didn't know, you mess with me, you pay the price. Ask Buck Coover. Buck thought he could take me and ended up with his nose rearranged. Or Blackie Burns in his hobnail boots, he thought he was the baddest dude in Dalton. He found out. He called me out one day with a smirk on his mouth, the next day he was sipping soup through a straw. Or Buster Franklin, we were supposed to have a showdown at the graveyard one night, I was there, but Buster turned coward and chickened out. No wonder he ended up a lay preacher in the Church of the Nazarene next to the water tower. He married Fayette and they became known in the flock as Brother Buster and Sister Fayette. For a wedding present, her daddy gave them a dinette set from his store. He'd wanted to give them a mattress but the last in stock supposedly looked a little used.

Of course in those days fights were bare fists and you didn't gang up, you fought fair. If the other guy went down, you stood back and gave him room to get up. Then you won, or the other guy did, you could shake hands and be friends, no hard feelings because you'd both fought fair and that's what counted. You never thought of using a weapon.

Unless it just happened. I almost forgot.

It was one summer. Marie sent me a bus ticket to visit her in Oklahoma. I was eleven that year and the bus ride was nearly all day but I enjoyed watching the countryside roll by, the wide beautiful world I was going to see someday. Then the bus pulled into the station and Marie wasn't there to meet me. Or anyone. I stood with my suitcase, then asked the ticket agent, he asked someone else, and it didn't take long. Marie was known. Yeah, Marie, sure, works over at the diner. On the other side of town but only about four blocks to walk. I stopped in front of the place and looked in the window. Men were sitting at the counter and Marie was in a white waitress uniform behind the counter pouring coffee. I hadn't seen her in a year but she appeared the same, though also kinda like a photograph. Something was said and she laughed. Nice teeth, a pretty laugh. Her teeth were an attractive feature. She saw me looking in and rushed out to hug me. I was embarrassed with people watching and tried to stand back. I didn't like being hugged. Then she was concerned, where was Jerry? I didn't know, who was Jerry? Your new stepdaddy, she said, he was supposed to meet my bus. Well, he probably got tied up at work but somebody should've met me, she said. They didn't, I said, nobody did, and I waited. Poor baby, Marie said. She patted my head and I ducked my head away. I wasn't a dog. She'd tell me later Jerry was a paint-and-body man but his family was rich and he was about to inherit thousands of acres of prime wheatland. She made it sound good. It would turn out to be more like fifty acres with no wheat but by then Marie would be long gone and settled into becoming a recluse.

Marie paraded me in the diner and told everybody, "This is my baby." Patting my head again. Nobody could seem to believe it. I said I wasn't a baby, I was eleven years old. Men shook their heads, "Why, Marie, you're not old enough to have a son this big." Or whatever size, they acted surprised she even had a son. She laughed, she'd been a child bride, she said, *very* young. That got a laugh. Besides, she said I always lied about my age, I was really only nine. She gave me a wink. I said I didn't lie. "Well, that's all right," one man told me, "you could sure pass for older. Just be careful you don't get too big for your britches." More laughing. After that, Marie had me sit in a booth and told the cook to fix me the biggest meal in the house. When it came it was chicken-fried steak and biscuits with cream gravy and french fries and I ate everything on my plate. Then I had two pieces of cherry pie à la mode. "Look at that," someone said, "he sure does eat like a man." That's right, I said, and I wasn't nine either, I was eleven.

Marie got off work at four and we walked home. Or I should say we walked to her house, it wasn't home in my mind. I carried my suitcase. Jerry had the car, she said, but he'd be home in another hour. The car, she said, was a big blue Pontiac. Jerry had fixed it up and painted it like brand new. Maybe he would take me for a ride in it, wouldn't that be fun? I said I guessed so. A ride to the movies maybe.

Her house was on a corner lot, one of those small frame things built by the millions after the war. With a GI loan, you could get one for $99 down. I know now the new price was probably $8,000. It was the beginning of a middle class that was expected to last forever.

Marie showed me my room off the living room. The bathroom

was across the hall. I had a twin-size bed and a dresser. I emptied my suitcase in the top dresser drawer, then Marie and I sat in the living room. How was school? Okay. I'd made straight A's in arithmetic. That was good. And how was Billy? Okay. He was supposed to come with me on the bus but he hadn't wanted to and nobody could make him. Marie said she was disappointed but she understood. Billy was older and, well, she understood. She just hoped he was happy and all that. What else? She guessed I had a girlfriend. I said I didn't. But she knew, pretty soon I was going to have lots of girls chasing after me, and when I did, she hoped I would be nice. Don't do naughty things to girls, she said. Naughty was her word. I couldn't look at her. She asked if I'd ever kissed a girl. I said a couple of times. She tsk-tsked me and shamed me with her finger. I pretended I needed a drink of water and went to the kitchen. After that, I can't remember what else was said. We sat. Jerry should've been home by then but he was running late. I thumbed a *Ladies' Home Journal*. Marie changed into a housedress. Did I want to play cards? No, not especially. Then what? I didn't want to do anything. Marie said she'd have to work daytimes while I was there but I could find things to occupy me. There were kids down the block or I could go to the school where they had summer youth activities. I said I could take care of myself. It began to get dark. Jerry was still not there. He'd been repairing a gas heater in the living room and had left a crescent wrench and pliers on the floor beside it. I fooled with the heater awhile but couldn't see how to fix it. Then it was night. I went outside and looked at the stars. Maybe an hour. When Jerry still didn't show, Marie made me a sandwich and I went to bed. I'd sat on a bus all day and hardly moved but it seemed I was more tired than I'd ever been. I remember going to sleep thinking I was supposed to stay with Marie a couple of weeks, I sure hoped those kids down the block were my age and knew fun things to do.

Then I was waking. I'd been disturbed. Or it was like a nightmare. The room was pitch-dark and I couldn't see but the wall at my head was being shaken, bumped. People were yelling. Then a crash, blundering sounds came from the living room, and something like a shriek. I bolted upright.

The next I knew I was looking into the living room. Marie was on the floor and a man was sitting on top of her. He was straddling her chest, pinning her arms with his knees. His fists were raising and hitting down. I could hear his fists landing. Then he was throwing me off and I was sprawling. I'd jumped on his back but he was too big for me. The gas heater was right there with the crescent wrench. It just happened. I grabbed the wrench and hit him. His head spurted, his eyes rolled. It was like he was reaching for me and I hit him again. He toppled sideways and curled on his knees with his arms cradling his head. I could see blood in his hair. Blood was on my wrench. Marie was standing and finding her balance. Her face was a mess. The top of her dress was torn. She pulled me with her into the hall and stopped. Wait, she said. She stepped into the bathroom. I stood with my wrench. The man would be coming. If he was still alive. He'd still be mad. I heard water running in the bathroom. Hurry! I said. Marie was taking the time to wash her face, then she came out and we crowded into my room. I slammed the door behind us and leaned against it. No lock on the door.

It was still too dark to see in the room but I knew Marie had lain on the bed. I stayed against the door. The man was Jerry, blind drunk, Marie said, and when he was like that, he was mean. She didn't know how many times he'd beaten her. She'd had lots of black eyes. Sometimes she wished he'd just go on and kill her and get it over with. All she'd ever wanted was to be happy, that's all. But don't you worry, she said, it was going to be all right.

I could hear Jerry moving around in the living room. Then he was at the door shoving it but I was keeping it shut with my shoulder, my feet braced against the bed. He didn't try that hard. He rattled the doorknob and banged the panel. He was yelling slurry words. Marie yelled back and that set him off banging the door harder. He went away and I heard water splashing in the bathroom but I stayed hard against the door. He came back and slammed the door again and Marie said things I wished she wouldn't, it only made him madder. Don't, I said. It seemed to me if Marie would just keep quiet awhile, maybe he'd calm down, but it was like she didn't care, she wanted to make him madder.

Finally Jerry stumbled away and the back door slammed. A car roared off. I couldn't hear anything then. I sat on the floor with my back against the door, my legs stiffed straight out against the bed, and for the rest of the night that's the way I stayed, the wrench in my lap. Marie slept. I might've dozed. I don't think so. I was afraid Jerry would come back crazier and bust in the door or climb in the window and get me.

But the next morning, he was still gone. There were blood spots in the living room and blood smears around the bathroom sink and Marie went about getting dressed as if nothing had happened. We didn't talk. I was ashamed I'd been afraid. Marie only said once she hoped I would never start drinking. She spent some time then with pancake makeup and lipstick. Her upper lip was puffed and she had a black eye and bruises. The makeup covered her bruises but made her skin look different. She was dressed in her white waitress uniform and patted my head. When I was ready, she said, I could come by the diner for breakfast. She hid her black eye with dark glasses and walked away to work.

I didn't have to think. I didn't want breakfast. I had my

return bus ticket in my pocket. I piled my clothes from the dresser back into my suitcase and walked the alley to the bus station. It turned out a bus was leaving in the next hour. I spent the time in the rest room counting the black and white squares of tile on the floor. The bus pulled out, so nobody would see, I was scooched down in the last seat in back.

So, a wrench, that one time. I never wanted to pick up anything to hit with again and never did. At the same time, I started getting into fights. In one way you could say it came with the territory. How else could you prove your worth, that you were tough? You had to fight. Brains didn't count. With me, though, I think it was also a secret fear of not being tough enough. And prompting that probably, a fear of not being worth enough. Or that's getting psychological. I could better say I had a hole in my heart and didn't know it. So it wasn't a conscious thing. If I felt something was missing, I was still okay enough, I didn't have to worry. Now, I know, a lot of people have holes in their heart that flat ruin their lives. But I imagined I was special and I had a life to live. So what if I couldn't see the cards I'd been dealt? It was up to me to play them.

Now I was still sitting in my house thinking how I'd like for Spencer to say something wiseass so I could let loose on him. But Spencer and Sara had gone. Tracy had told them I was working against a deadline and Spencer said he understood, business came first. I believe they left around midnight.

So nothing bad happened. Then Tracy sweetly brought me a cup of coffee. I was surprised her mood had changed. She was going to bed, she said, did I need anything else? I said, no, I was staying up to finish the brochure. She kissed my cheek and apologized for being upset with me earlier. I told her it was my fault. We hugged and for once a simple good-night hug didn't turn into a clutch and the clutch into heavy breathing. It was one of those rare times when we were more naturally friends than not. A nice easy moment. And this was the warm giving person I knew Tracy could be, and perhaps would be more often if she didn't feel so constantly frustrated and unloved by me. Okay, maybe I could change and be more attentive. I could try to be more considerate.

But then I had a quick flash, a certain knowledge that her new pleasantness was also a lull, the calm before a storm. I should be prepared. As it turned out, my flash was right. The lull lasted three more days until she sneaked around my typewriter and saw what I was writing.

That night however Tracy went to bed and left me with my MorningStar copy. The word portrait of a business. But the business was also me. I sipped my coffee. The words, committed, dedicated. No. Not right. It needed to be more what I actually thought, more honest. So begin there, make it different words. I knew a lot of words.

Now I believe I've described myself as growing up pretty illiterate. True enough. I was twenty when I read my first book. Grady tossed me the book, "Here, you're dumb, Nelson, read a book." The title was *Look Homeward, Angel*. This was in Albuquerque when I had a vocabulary of maybe forty words. The biggest word I knew was mayonnaise. But if I could learn, Grady thought there was a chance I might be saved from the bliss of ignorance.

Grady Walsh. An unlikely friend. We met at a college hangout, Smokey Joe's on Central. A beer joint. I was there to pick up girls. At twenty, college girls were easy pickings. Grady was holding court with a group of undergraduates at the end of the bar. He was older. And a great talker. I'd find out later he was thirty, a veteran of the Korean War and enrolled at the university in the drama department. That's right, *drama*. I still shake my head. He also played the violin and wrote poetry. So he was definitely an artie. He should have been a sissy. But he liked to camp and fish, and what really got me, he could beat me arm wrestling. How could that be? Not that I had the strongest arm in the world but I could usually take anyone my size. Now here was this egghead who was into all the prissy stuff, drama, poetry, highbrow music, but in every other way, he was a regular guy. It was a revelation.

I started hanging around him in the bar and I think he tolerated me at first because he could see he had me confused. Then we became friends. Since he was older, you could say he took on the role of mentor and encouraged me. You've got a good brain, he told me, you oughta use it sometime. How? Hell, read, learn something. No one had ever said I even had a brain. It's still not a fact but at least Grady started me reading and over the years, off and on, I also accumulated about sixty hours of college credits. I like to tell people that's two years of college and it probably is. College however was never for me. I wasn't the scholar type and I'd been on my own enough it seemed to me college was a bloodless sort of life.

But back to *Look Homeward, Angel*. Grady tossed me the book. He said I should read. I took it as a challenge. Though not much of one, what the hell, anybody could read a book. Grady thought I couldn't probably, all right, by god, I'd read the damn book, prove him wrong.

I almost didn't. First page took me an hour. I'd read three sentences and forget the first and have to go back. I couldn't concentrate. I was reading one word at a time and guiding my eyes from word to word with my finger. What was the story about? I couldn't get into it.

Then I did. I began to see the main character, Eugene Gant, was a young guy with all kinds of feelings he couldn't express, he was a lost soul, and I suddenly thought, Hey, me, too! It was an electric moment. I had feelings trapped inside me the same clamoring to get out but there was no way. Except maybe when I got mad. Then the feelings that came out were not especially the right ones.

So I identified with Eugene Gant. His story made me think I wasn't so alone. Then, too, the book opened up a whole new world of imagination for me and it was almost like being reborn. Eventually, in my second novel, I quoted a poem from the front pages of *Look Homeward* that remains with me to this day, the first poem that really spoke to me personally and emblazoned itself in my memory:

". . . *In her dark womb we did not know our mother's face; from the prison of her flesh have we come into the unspeakable and incommunicable prison of this earth. Which of us has known his brother? Which of us has looked into his father's heart? Which of us has not remained forever prison-pent? Which of us is not forever a stranger and alone? O waste of loss, in the hot mazes, lost, among bright stars on this most weary unbright cinder, lost! Remembering speechlessly we seek the great forgotten language, the lost lane-end into heaven . . .*"

Of course all that seems a bit much to me now. I wouldn't describe this beautiful bright earth as a most weary unbright cinder. But at the time those words might have been mine if I'd been more articulate and gushy. As it was I could barely read the damn words but they went straight to my heart. A stranger and alone, that was me, and for sure I was locked into some kind of prison of my own. Even more, the language, I needed to find the great forgotten language.

After *Look Homeward*, I began reading every book I could grab. When there were words I didn't know, which was all the time, I wrote them down and looked them up. Words had surprising meanings. Pretty soon I had a vocabulary of big words I liked to use every chance I got to show how smart I was. I'd be in a bar boozing it up, yakking with some ordinary dumbnut about nothing, I'd casually let drop a good-sounding adjective like "crepuscular" or "hirsute." It's embarrassing to remember. The dumbnut would find a way to move to another stool down the bar. A couple of times I also tried to write, what, thoughts, impressions? It was too hard. I could never string together more than a few sentences. I wrote about Grady once because I admired him and wanted to describe him. I wrote, "First of all, Grady Walsh is very intelligent and knows a lot of things. He knows about life and things like that." That's as far as I got. And once in Fort Worth, feeling lonely, I wrote, "The moonlight crashes through the window and falls to pieces on the floor." I thought that was good. Then I started memorizing snatches of poetry to recite to girls. I would come out with "If I were king, ah, love, if I were king, what tributary nations would I bring to kneel beneath your sceptre and pledge allegiance to your eyes, your lips, your hair . . ." Like Ronald Colman, remember him? Imagine "ah, love, if I were king" in the backseat of some car. Girls probably thought I was being romantic. The thing was, I found I could memorize a poem and it would stick. I hadn't known my brain could retain anything for more than five minutes, but I can still recite every poem I knew in those days. Which I did with Lorne Greene one night in a bar near Paramount Studios. This is name-dropping. I walked in the bar, Lorne was sitting in a booth with a starlet. He was still wearing his *Bonanza* duds with the leather vest and the starlet was absolutely beautiful. I couldn't help noticing. I had the bartender send over a couple of drinks on me and Lorne invited me to join them. He was gracious that way, a born charmer. We hit it off. Pretty soon we were reciting poems. I'd come out with one, he'd come back with another, and we kept this up a couple of hours with both of us enjoying the sound of our own voices, except he had a wonderful voice, I didn't. He was also really terrific with Shakespeare, especially Macbeth, "Out, out, brief candle!" Dramatic as hell. It was fun. The night ended, the starlet was sitting there dead asleep.

So I knew a lot of words. And along with being glib, it was perhaps inevitable I landed in the advertising game, where it helps to be glibly wordy and not too smart. You invent a commercial, it's not like having to connect one thought logically to the next. With a little imagination, you contrive a gimmick, an attention-grabber, then mix in a few words, the fewer the better, and, presto, whataya know, a commercial. You're not digging for meaning. You can't. You're selling the sizzle. Pin it on the wall, rule one: It's the sizzle, stupid.

But what I wanted now with the brochure for MorningStar was to say something special. It was my company, my own personal involvement, I wanted it to reflect my real thinking for once. If I could figure what my real thinking might be.

I started writing on a notepad in pencil. Something like this: Okay, first, what am I doing? I'm wasting my life. No, can't say that. Stick with the business, what am I doing with MorningStar? I'm faking it. Can't say that either. Start with should, say what I *should* be doing. Which is? Well, right off, I should be living a happier life. That sounds sappy. At least I should be doing what I like. Which is? I don't know. I wish I knew. This is nuts. I'm sitting here talking to myself. I should write a book.

Just like that.

I felt surprised but as soon as it hit me, I knew that was exactly what I would do and nothing else would matter. A book. I didn't think what kind, I only imagined I would write down my thoughts and feelings, it would become a volume. I had a brain full of vague impressions, a skin plastered with dumb feelings, if I could make them into words on paper, I would *see* what they meant. Then I would understand what I meant.

I thought. It helps to start out naïve. The fact remains, in the instant, I was completely decided.

Now I wonder how I suddenly came to that point? If anyone had said a day earlier, Y'know, you really oughta be a writer, I would've said, Are you kidding, *me*? No way. So how did it happen? I think of Jack's face when he showed me his painting. He knew who he was. And I think of Grady's influence getting me to read, my late love of words, and the times a book had me nodding: Yes, I think that, too, I just couldn't say it. And the copywriters I'd been around in advertising, talking of writing seriously someday. Most never did but I heard their talk. And the age-old question deep in every soul: What are we here for, what's it all about? Maybe, finally, I simply needed to know.

Truth is, I can't explain. I think now the writing was always in me, but buried. Then it was time. I'd been muddled long enough.

I don't know that I slept that night. I felt the world had changed and I was seeing it with new eyes. I told Tracy the next morning I was going to write a book. Oh, really? Yes. I'd have to find the time, in the evenings, maybe the early mornings, whenever, but I was going to get right on it. She blinked at evenings, that was playtime. Then she was excited. In her mind a book was automatically made into a movie and in a movie she could have a role. In that way a book was still showbiz to her and she probably imagined the writing as nothing, a few days, a couple of weeks perhaps, the same as a TV commercial. A book was just another project. I may have thought the same. I believed everything in me was ready to pour out. I'd empty my brain in no time and that would be it. Then I started writing and what began as a story turned into a novel. I didn't know what I was writing. The story was an experience. The novel became a way of life.

Now this is old hat to anyone who knows but I'm going to say it anyway. When a novel takes any length of time to write, it's necessarily a continuous concentrated effort and I don't care how talented you are. You have to work at it and the writing doesn't end with the day. It stays in your mind. In a very real sense then you're living what you write. You can go to parties and carry on conversations, people assume you're present. You're not. You're still behind the scenes in your imagination. And ironically that's often when you're doing your best writing, when you're giving your fingers a rest. What's bad is when the actual scribbling is finished with a final chapter. Your world is nowhere until you can imagine another way to write it again. Or, as with most writers, the same old way again but with slightly revised characters.

In any case, the day-to-day writing life in uninteresting. Of course, in the nicer circles, nice people say, Oh, you're a writer, how exciting! They don't count. You're a writer, you sit in one spot like a potted plant for hours a day, you can't stand being interrupted and you can't talk about what you're doing. You don't know what you're doing. If you did, you'd say so in two sentences instead of going on with it for four hundred pages. Only in Hollywood can they describe a complete story in one sentence. But that's a different planet. You're a writer, your daily world is nine-tenths enclosed inside your noggin and that's not a normal way to live. It's like being a zombie, you forget to live. You go somewhere, you're not there. Bankers meet you, they don't want to know you. They're afraid you might apply for a loan and one more writer's financial statement would be too depressing.

For me, however, that night in Dallas was a turning point. I was a grown man, thirty-five years old, you'd think I should've had some clue, but without the least notion what I was about, I decided to write. Or it was decided for me. I still don't know which. In explaining, we use the word "because." Someone says, Mary was loved by all because she was good. Surely that's too simplistic. Ask a kid why, he'll say because. Ask because why, he'll say just because. Even if they can't reason it, kids somehow know the "because" is murky and not simply one thing. It is the wind that blew last year on the other side of the world. It is the infinite elaboration of that first blobby bubble in the marsh at the dawn of time. We can think a reason but most becauses are beyond our blinders to see. Still, we need to *know*. Anything can happen. So where can we find certainty? Not to worry, leaders appear to show the way. And they always appear. Look at history. Look under a rock, there's a leader ready to crawl out.

But I was decided. I told Tracy I was going to write a book. I told Vicky and Irving. And, naturally, once I said I was going to, I had to. This time however it was no problem. My mind was set and I never once thought after that night that I wouldn't write. Or that I couldn't. Or that the first book I wrote wouldn't be published. It was.

Now I think, ah, me, if I'd known then what I know now. But I didn't know. I was lucky. From over the transom and out of the gloom of the mailroom at Houghton Mifflin, I have to thank a neophyte editorial assistant named Mickey Newlove. She picked my manuscript from out of a pile and read it. She didn't know not to do that. Then she also didn't know not to pass it on up the line to a senior editor, that it's a known fact manuscripts arriving in the mail "over the transom" never get published. They never get read. The standard procedure is to let all the unsolicited stuff stack up in the mailroom. Bunches of such things come in every day. Who knows where from? Who cares? They let the packets stack up a month or so, then an intern goes in, opens a few, sticks in the standard memo rejection slips, and sends them back. That way space is cleared for more. The would-be writers don't know, poor devils, they keep sending their material in, publishers keep sending it back. But the time they take is also a kindness. A manuscript sits in the mailroom six or eight weeks, the would-be writer has to believe it's being considered and his empty mailbox only helps to keep his hopes alive.

So I was lucky to make it over the transom with my first book. It almost never happens. Of course Viking also picked *Ordinary People* from a transom heap but it was the first book Viking found in that manner in twenty-six years and so rare an event it made the cover of *Time*. Or it was made into an event in the promotion of the book. The transom angle was a way of talking about the book: Look, from out of nowhere, a star is born. Only in America. People love the sudden-discovery-and-leap-into-fame-type story. Still, the Viking transom find was true, so it does happen. But, again, almost never.

Now I'd never had an office at the house but when I came in from MorningStar that evening, the same day I'd announced my new literary intentions, I found Tracy had set up the sunroom for me with a desk and typewriter, paper and pens, dictionary, the works. She'd gone out in the morning, bought everything in one swoop, and had it delivered and in place by midafternoon. She'd even included a coffeepot. I was surprised but I have to say I was also pleased. It looked like a place to write. The windows behind the desk and to the side made the light just right and the room was off by itself. My own special place to be.

So Tracy was all for me. I could have my privacy with my writing and she'd see to it I wouldn't be bothered. Since I wanted to write, she understood, I had to do what I had to do. And it was okay, when I was writing, she'd find things on her own to keep busy. Which was a way of saying she could sacrifice for me. She usually didn't like being left to herself but she loved me, she truly did, she said, and whatever I wanted, she did, too. I felt almost guilty. I probably sensed even with her cheeriness at the moment, she was also a little desperate. She knew at a certain level I had excluded her, that she'd never been my all-in-all, and now in another way, or at the same level but more particularly, I was going to exclude her even more. Was this the goodbye?

Later, she casually mentioned, by the way, the Six Flags spot? It had slipped my mind and I had to think, oh, yeah, Six Flags, not final yet, Harry was having to get more corporate approval. Tracy's face changed. But it's okay, I said, it's in the works. It wasn't the time to spoil the moment, my pleasure with my new writing room, and her brightness at seeing my pleasure. For once she'd given me something she could see I actually liked and we made love that night in a mutually warm loving way that only became a little frenzied toward the end. But that was Tracy, as ever true to form. She couldn't help it. To say the least, I've missed a lot of that form since. Even at my age now, well, I won't say it. It's my loss.

I started writing the next morning the first thing that came to mind, about getting shot and nearly murdered. Which occurred when I was seventeen a few months after leaving Dalton. Maybe I was trying for the dramatic with my first effort but I couldn't make it more than something that just happened and not a big marker in my life at all. The next thing I wrote was about Darlene, of course. But first the shooting.

I'D HEADED WEST FROM DALTON in my little
coupe with a few clothes stuffed in a pillowcase and my last two
weeks' pay from the Sinclair wadded in my pocket. It was $80
and enough I figured to last me to California. It might last me
forever. The road ahead was forever. And I felt good. I picked
up a hitchhiker at one point, some scruffy guy without a hope
in the world, and the way you do with strangers you'll never see
again, we told each other our life stories. It took about three
minutes. He said he was going to his aunt's house, he didn't
know where else. I told him if he ever got to Dalton there was
a girl named Fayette who was hot to trot. I didn't mention her

guidelines. And I didn't mention Darlene. My feelings for Darlene were sacred and mine alone to cherish. The hitchhiker got out at the state line and I roared on into the great unknown across the flatlands of New Mexico and Arizona, the lone rider on the hill but without the hill. I was whistling and zipping along trailing a cloud of black smoke. I liked waving to people in the streets of the dinky towns I passed through. They'd wave back and you could tell by their expressions they were trying to remember if they knew me. Maybe it would dawn on them later they'd just witnessed a speeding wonder, a free spirit on the loose. Their lives were stuck in place, mine wasn't.

Then it happened my old coupe finally broke down on the outskirts of Yuma. A busted head gasket, thrown rods, probably everything. The motor started clattering and steaming and abruptly stopped. I looked at it. The thing was a leaking heap with smelly fumes rising from the carcass. Gone. No need to even pronounce the word, it had been an instant death. My first car. But it was only a car. I left it and went on. Which is what you do, you keep going. But with a sack over your shoulder? You're on the road, you gotta think image, so I stopped at an army surplus store in the middle of Yuma and bought a fifty-cent duffel bag, stuffed in my pillowcase of clothes, and started hitchhiking. But now more respectably equipped. A pillowcase is *Grapes of Wrath*. The duffel bag is professional highway luggage.

Now this was still the '50s when rides were easy to hitch. A few hours, I was dropped off at the seaside in San Diego. The ocean. What an amazing sight. I'd never even seen a lake before. It seems now I just stood and stared at the ocean a long time. Then I found a deserted spot, stripped to my underwear, and dived in, the sea itself a huge ponderous weight deep down but at the surface, magically light. The taste, hey, it was salty! It was supposed to be, it really was. I lapped it up.

Anyway, that's how I made it to California after leaving Dalton but I'm trying to get to the part about being shot so I'm going to skip the scroungy stuff the next few months, like sleeping in parked cars and bus stations, being picked up for vagrancy, making it to Los Angeles, washing dishes, stacking boxes in warehouses, selling blood, getting caught shoplifting, a couple of fights, those things.

The shooting part comes after Los Angeles. I was hitching to Bakersfield, a fairly new Mercury stopped, I piled in the back seat with my duffel bag. In front, two guys in their early twenties maybe, I didn't get their names. One had acne, the other had buckteeth. Both were badass talkers like, what the fuck, they didn't give a shit for anything. Living was a ratfuck. The last town was a goatfuck. Just driving along was a pissfuck. They looked to me, ain't that fucking right? I said I was just trying to get to Bakersfield. Yeah, well, that place was a pile of cowfuck, too. And would you fucking look at that, the dumb fuckbutt in the car ahead was going too slow. Acne pulled up to the car's rear bumper and started pushing it faster. The guy in the car began frantically waving his arms to stop. He couldn't stop. Acne was stomping the gas and whooping it up. Man, was this fucking living, or what! Toothy was laughing his ass off. This went on, the speed up to 70/75, it was wild. The car ahead finally careened from the road and skidded onto the shoulder in a whorl of dust. But it didn't fucking roll, it came to a stop fucking upright. Well, fuck. Acne and Toothy were looking back, throwing the finger. What a pigfuck.

Beneath my feet on the back floorboard, five or six car license plates from different states. Why? Acne and Toothy were passing a bottle back and forth. They passed it to me, here, have a fucking swig. I'd only tasted wine before and that had been with Darlene. I tilted the bottle and took a sip, the sip nearly gagged me, my eyes watered. It was like fiery perfume. I know now it was probably gin. Toothy was laughing, pointing his finger in my face. His slobbery overbite was like a moron laughing. I slapped his finger away. He turned back in his seat. Then he got on his knees on the seat and started pissing out the window, though not very well. The wind blew most of the piss back in the car and I had to duck behind my duffel bag. A minute later Acne tried the same trick while Toothy held the wheel with the car still going. But Acne couldn't quite reach his window. His knee stance was too short and he ended up mostly only pissing on the door inside. After that, Toothy came up with a pistol. Hey, look what I fucking found! And fucking right there under the fucking seat, man. I could tell the gun was a genuine surprise, a first-time discovery, and I think that's when my small-town brain finally began to put two and two together. The license plates were stolen. So the car was stolen to be fixed with different plates. I was riding in the backseat of a hot car with the two guys in front nothing but bad news. What if the cops stopped us? "But, officer, I was only along for the ride." "Yeah, like Santa's little helper, right? Up against the wall." You're ranked with the company you're caught with.

Toothy was pointing the pistol straight in his own face to see in the cylinder if it had any bullets. Guess what, fucking loaded, man. He aimed at Acne's head and cocked the hammer, *klic-klac,* the sound I would remember later with Tracy. Acne knocked the gun away and the thing went off. A loud explosion inside the car. A sudden hole appeared in the dash. Hey, man, you're killing the fucking car. That was funny, killing the fucking car. They were both laughing. Toothy cocked the hammer again and fired out the window at the wide-open country. Then he jerked around and shot at a passing car, but too late, the car had already whizzed past. Shit, fucking missed. He pointed the gun back at me and cocked the hammer, Say your fucking prayers, mister. That was funny, too, fucking prayers. He fired out the window again at nothing. Gotcha, he said. About that time Acne decided he wanted the gun, Gimme that. Toothy wouldn't give it up so Acne grabbed for it and in the next second they were pushing and shoving. The car was swerving all over the place. Acne finally slammed the brakes and pulled to a stop. Now gimme that fucking gun, he said. Toothy handed it over. Acne was the leader. Now you fucking drive, Acne said. They both got out of the car to change places, I jumped out with my duffel bag. Toothy turned, Where the fuck you going? I'm going to walk, I said. Acne squinted his eyes, What's the matter, you don't like fucking riding with us? He said a few more words, I didn't argue. I said I wanted to walk to stretch my legs. They got in the car and drove on, I was glad to be rid of them.

Then it was crazy. The car had driven away but it was no longer moving out of sight. It was returning, backing up full-speed. Oh, shit, I thought. The car screeched to a stop in the road directly across from me. Acne leaned out the window, Hey, you don't like fucking riding with us? He leveled the pistol straight at me, cocked the hammer, and fired. And immediately fired again, bam! bam!, that quick. A stone is thrown hard down into water, if you're underwater you can see, the stone zips in, then loses its force and lazily floats on down. That's the way the two bullets felt going into my stomach. They didn't hurt but I could feel them zip into me, then slowly float the rest of the way. Acne kept pulling the trigger but the pistol was only clicking. No more bullets. The car roared away and I fell down. I'd been left murdered on the roadside in the middle of nowhere. Then I was lying there, I didn't know why. It was probably like when you're a kid, you're playing being shot, you think you're supposed to fall down, but I wasn't in pain, I didn't feel hurt, so I sat up and looked down at my stomach. A couple of red spots on my shirt at midlevel. No real bleeding. Maybe inside. I touched the spot with my finger and tasted. Blood all right but still no pain. I stood and felt only sort of numbed. If I started walking, though, I was going to start hurting. I didn't want that so I sat down on my duffel bag and stuck out my thumb. I was going to need a ride. Maybe to a hospital. I folded my arms across my stomach to hold in the numbness. No cars in sight. The world was empty. Pretty soon I began to feel a little funny. A tingling sensation was beginning off in the distance somewhere, in my toes. Somebody better give me a ride, I thought.

It wasn't long, a car slowed and stopped about a hundred yards down the road. A green Chevrolet. In my mind, the finest car I'd ever seen. I got to my feet, I had to stay bent over. I was hurting now. Also my duffel bag was suddenly too heavy but I could still drag it. I may have stumbled. I couldn't walk right. The guy in the car probably thought I was drunk and decided to drive on without me. He spun away in a spray of gravel while I was hobbling toward him.

The moment remains vivid and I still feel sorry for myself. I watched the green Chevrolet disappear, then sat down again and held my stomach. By the time the next car stopped, I had keeled over. Which may be the best way to catch a ride, just keel over on the roadside and look dead. Anyhow, I knew a car had stopped and a man was bending over. My eyes were open. He touched at me. I said, Hi. He jerked back. It was okay, I told him, I was shot. I might've said twice. He helped me up but then I couldn't lift my foot to get in the car. He pushed and managed to load me in anyway. My duffel bag, I said. He tossed it in the car somewhere and started driving. He told me to hold on, he was driving as fast as he could, he was going to get me to a hospital. I guessed in Bakersfield. Which was good, I thought, I probably needed to see a doctor pretty quick. I could feel blood sloshing around my ribs and more pain. After that, I don't know, I think I rode doubled over until I passed out.

Since it's boring to hear people gleefully tell about their latest surgery, I won't describe mine. Besides, I don't remember it. I woke up in a white bed with tubes streaming from me in three directions. Maybe I had a vague memory of bright lights when I was first rolled into the hospital from the car. They stretched me out on the gurney, I definitely remember that instant like my stomach was being ripped apart. Then nothing. When I could think, I was embarrassed they had me dressed in something like a gown that only opened in back. The nurses would roll me onto my side to see my naked butt where I couldn't and stick me with a needle. Four days of that, I walked out of the hospital with a line of stitches up my belly and one bullet still lodged in a back rib. For no reason the bullets had missed my vital organs and only pierced a few loops of intestine. Someone else might've had their kidneys riddled.

A day or so later I was sitting in Lilly's Room & Board in west Bakersfield, the rate three dollars a day. I was sitting in the bath with my swollen stomach stretching my stitches, so I used a razor blade to cut the stitches one by one. I jerked them out with my fingers and laid them on the side of the tub like a little railroad track, fifty-seven in all. My stomach began to feel relieved right away and I went on and healed just fine. The scar down my middle however is wider and uglier than it should've been but I hear that's what happens when you take your stitches out too soon. You should consult your doctor first. If you can afford a doctor.

A question: I was shot, did I think I was going to die? I don't believe the thought ever entered my head. Maybe that's why when I first tried to write about the event eighteen years later in Dallas, I thought I could make it dramatic, my god, I faced Death! But I could remember it only as something that just happened, no big deal. I couldn't imagine Death and still can't. I don't think most people can. Oh, okay, the possibility maybe, but the possibility is not the real thing. We can stand on the edge of a cliff and look down, it's scary, we can see falling, so we step back. That's the dumb survival instinct, but we can't actually see Death itself. We're influenced by myths. Or I'm confused. Jimmy is gone and shouldn't be. He's still with me and yet he's not. I use the word gone.

But I don't want to get into that. I've tried, I can't. All I'm saying is this: I know the physical embodies spirit, whatever that is. Call it soul, that's fine. And there may very well be another way of being beyond this world, something's in the air, we can feel it, but at the final exit from this world, I don't think there's a gatekeeper we can see. We'd like to. We represent him as a skull in a hood, as a wispy ghost of sorts, but he's really not there to open the gate. A vision of Death surely has to be illusional or delusional. We see people who've been killed and bodies slaughtered, so we say we've seen death, but it's perhaps more the shock of the aftermath, not Death itself. Even at the last moment, I don't believe Marie imagined Death per se. She didn't say she did, so she probably only imagined sleeping. She was so damned tired of living, she just wanted to go to sleep, that's all she could think.

End of subject. A morbid subject anyway.

Now I need to acknowledge this. The man who drove me to the hospital that night returned the next day to see how I was doing but I was still goofy. If he said his name, I couldn't remember, and he never came back, so I don't know who he was. Except, whoever, he was a damn good man who came from nowhere and took the time to help someone in trouble. If he's reading this now and needs a friend, I'd like him to know I'm here. I owe him.

Which reminds me, I also continue to owe the hospital, I don't know how much. Though maybe I shouldn't concede that in public. Even if it's been forty years, their bill collectors may still be out looking for me, and those people are relentless. They have no pity and never sleep. Believe me. You say, hey, c'mon, bill collectors have to make a living, too. But stop and think, what kind of person is it who can wake up in the morning smiling and look forward to a wonderful day of busily hounding poor debtors to the grave? And with zeal and glinty eyes? Your cousin maybe, but you never hear anyone admit some of their best friends are bill collectors. It would be too demoralizing.

Three days, then, I wrote in my own special place in the sunroom. First, a couple of pages about being shot. I couldn't make it interesting, I didn't care, I was writing. I called Vicky at the office and told her I was staying home, she and Irving would have to do without me unless it was important. She called a couple of times to ask whatever it was and I told her, Vicky, you do it, just take care of it, all right? She was worried I'd flipped out, it wasn't like me to pass on details. I told her I was fine. Actually, I was happy. I wasn't drinking, I didn't think of drinking. I was into writing about Darlene and that first turning point in my life when I left Dalton.

The only interruption came after three days when Tracy learned through a friend there was no Six Flags spot in the works and hadn't been. Six Flags already had its commercials for the season. So I had lied. Tracy confronted me. You bastard, she said. She was hurt and mad at the same time. I tried to soothe her, "Now, sweetheart—" "Don't sweetheart me, you sonofabitch, you lied to me, you don't love me—" And so on.

I knew her tantrums, they went on for hours, and I usually faced them but this time I walked out. She wouldn't be any calmer when I came back. In fact, she'd read what I had written about Darlene and really go crazy. I'll get to that.

Right now I need to get back to Darlene, the clothesline and Myrtle, and the end of my beginning.

THE BIG DAY, the annual school May Day Frolic. It was supposed to be that time of the year when the earth sheds its mantle of winter white and turns green and blooming again. In Dalton it looked the same. The desert was year-round.

The May Day idea of course comes from the old pagan rites of spring, the celebrating of fertility, the sacrificing of virgins, a lot of dancing and drunken revelry. But we had the Baptists and were expected to hold it down, no drinking, no dancing, forget the virgins. Which meant we were left with the cakewalk, the Maypole, and the box lunch auction. This last, my aim.

It took place in the gym. I was sitting in the bleachers with

Puddles and the rest of the student body. Why it was called student body, no one knew. Most of the students' bodies were slouchy barnyard types, scrawny or fat, misshaped, but slouchy nonetheless without a whit of grace or poise. Only Darlene was the exception. Her body was every inch perfection, curved, smooth, taut. The others, well, Dalilah Lou wasn't bad. She had a terrific rear end. Wanda Sue had great knockers. She was so short, though, she was nearly all knockers. And it was said Fayette was pretty cute. I thought she was too skinny.

Anyway, collectively the student body, and on this occasion that meant everyone from the squirmy first-graders on up to the twenty-two-year-olds in their sixteenth season of occupying free desk space. You could look out around the gym and count three hundred head of illiterate, me included. The younger kids performed their usual Maypole wind missing the over-and-under with the ribbons until one kid got wrapped to the pole like a blister. The junior highers had their cakewalk. A girl winning would squeal and jump up and down. A boy would act puffed. The cake was Betty Crocker.

I watched from the bleachers and bided my time waiting for the box lunch auction. Darlene was sitting in sinful beauty across the gym near the stage. Randy Caudell had planted himself beside her. He was wearing loafers with tassels and gray gabardine slacks, a real clotheshorse. In fact he was the only guy in Dalton who wore slacks to school pressed and creased. He'd sit down, he'd pull his pants up at the knees with his two pinkies sticking out so his creases wouldn't bag. He'd show off his argyle socks. He was also the only guy on our football team who never got his uniform dirty. The rest of us would come out of a game looking shredded, like we'd been attacked by Tasmanian devils. But Randy was our quarterback, he didn't have to get messy. He'd come out of a game with his numbers spotless and his hair still neatly combed. The way it was, his daddy owned the peanut mill and headed the Booster Club so Randy was automatically quarterback. He was also Most Handsome and Most Popular and Homecoming King and Class President. And guess what, right, Mr. Most Likely to Succeed. How could he help it? He had a new car and a white dinner jacket. He had Darlene and together they were considered the Perfect Couple. I'd hear that, I'd want to chew glass. I pictured him going to bed with her in his argyle socks. He'd hang his pants up first to keep the creases straight. Then he'd do everything by the book, Mr. Sex Manual. The little creepy spidery touches first. He'd start at her elbow with minnowy kisses and go up to her shoulder. He'd stop there with his eyes open and look deeply into hers perhaps an inch away, he'd be seeing about six eyes. Then he'd nibble her ear and whisper, Oh, ma chérie, ma petite chouchoute, in French no less, and he'd breathe on her neck, his body held slightly distant, none of that crude body stuff yet, and slowly, very slowly, he'd trail his finger down her neck to her perfect right breast, circle her nipple, then slither his finger on down to her navel, circle that, then digit down to her curly patch, give that another circle, and in a line he'd go down her thigh to her calf to her toes, the whole trip with just the wormy tip of his finger, right out of the manual, and this goes on until he groans and moans, Oh, darling, dearest, what do you want, tell me what you want. He's asking her but what the hell does he think she wants? She's been lying there bored out of her gourd, she's probably asleep by now, and any man with an ounce of common brains would know that's *not* how you do it. You gotta act like a man. A woman wants to be treated like a woman. So what you do is, you walk up, you don't talk, but you let her know you know what you're after, and you don't just walk up either. You move in with this heavy sort of animal magnetism and right up close you stand there exuding this power over her so she sees what you've got boiling in your veins is honest-to-god real lust and while your eyes are stripping her naked, she'll feel her legs turning to jelly. The next instant her last resistance melts and she surrenders helplessly with her whole limp body gasping, *Take me! Take me!* So you do.

Now that's the way it should be and every red-blooded man in this world knows that. So why isn't it? What happened to just doing it? You're born five thousand years too late, you have to research what you're supposed to do. You get a sex manual and study it to death, then you get with what you're after, you have to talk it to death, it's so damned programmed it's finally not worth having the urge in the first place.

Or I say that. I don't mean it. Truth is, anything is worth it and especially when you're sixteen, let's face it, you're a guy that age, you're a walking hard-on.

But Randy and Darlene. Actually I didn't know what they did when they were alone. He might've been the honorable type and all they had was some dull platonic relationship. I could see them parking but what else I couldn't imagine. I didn't want to imagine it. I only knew Randy was the honcho I had to shoot out of the saddle and I was afraid I couldn't. He was handsome, rich, Mr. Everything. How could I hope to compete?

Well, there might be a chance with the advantage of surprise. He didn't know I was waiting at the pass and laying for him, and if he'd never lost, maybe he wouldn't know he could. I was telling myself, What the hell, easy come, easy go, shoot the works. I was a gambling fool, the only way to be. Besides, I'd already been to the county line and picked up the aphrodisiac, which I'd hidden in a sack in my car. It was a half gallon of wine transferred to a big Welch's Grape Juice bottle so no one would know. Then, too, I had my $75 snug in my pocket so I was really only sitting, waiting to spring my trap. When the auction began, that was when. The horse would come out of the pass empty-saddled. Ol' Randy Caudell wouldn't know what hit him.

It seemed forever but finally the cakewalk ended, the Maypole was cleared away and it was time for the box lunch auction.

Since bidding was involved and couples paired off, this was for high schoolers only. The younger kids were herded out and Mr. Ferris moved onto the stage with a pile of box lunches on a janitor's rollaway. Mr. Francis Ferris, the history teacher. His name gives him away. He had capped teeth and square horn-rimmed glasses and was always putting his hands on guys in the hallway between classes. He liked to squeeze biceps and rub shoulders so we tabbed him Ferris the Fruit. He gave a speech in the auditorium once about hobbies, how everybody should have one instead of being idle, the idle mind being the devil's workshop. He said we could have hobbies like collecting stamps or building model airplanes, making it sound like we could really be bored. Then as a personal example, he said his own favorite hobby was needlepoint. It was one of those moments. Did he really say needlepoint? No one moved. He went on to show a sample of his handiwork by holding up a burlap-looking thing with a big flower in the middle. There was dead silence. Then it hit. The auditorium erupted. Guys were hooting and rolling in the aisle with tears in their eyes. I can't tell you how bad it was. It took an hour to calm the place back to normal and all the while Mr. Ferris had to stand there looking foolish. I felt kinda sorry for him. A rumor started next day that he was going to get fired because queer teachers turned their students into queers, too. That was a known fact. But apparently nobody could be found to replace him. It was also known that teachers went crazy in places like Dalton.

Anyway, Mr. Ferris was allowed to stay, and since he doubled as director of school plays, naturally, he was also the designated MC for most school events, including the annual box lunch auction.

Now it was supposed to be a secret whose box you bid on, but then you'd have to sit with that girl, and since no guy wanted to chance getting stuck with the worst girls, and the girls felt the same about the guys—even Lumplumps Laurie didn't want to have to eat with ol' Scabs Toohey—the girls told so everybody knew in advance whose box was which. Then nobody really competed and it wasn't much of an auction. Blackie Burns would get Melba Glee's box. Billy Bob Hilman would take Eula Mae's. They'd go through the motions of bidding fifty cents, maybe a dollar, no one else would bid, and that would be it. Randy Caudell would bid the most, like two dollars, for Darlene's box, which was always the picnic hamper. I was expected to bid for Fayette's inevitable mustard-and-baloney. I'd bid a quarter and Fayette would get mad because it showed everybody, she said, how much I thought she was worth. She had a point. But she'd get mad when I put the correct name to things, too. I'd call a tit a titty and Fayette would accuse me of talking nasty. Now I'm not going to put up with that nasty talk, she'd say. I'd tell her she didn't have to.

Sitting beside me, Puddles asked for about the fifth time who he was going to bid on. I told him to be patient, when the time came I'd let him know. He found it hard to wait and like a three-hundred-pound kid all excited, started bouncing on his seat, rocking the bleachers. I had to make him stop.

Mr. Ferris was blowing on the stage microphone, *wuust, wuu-uussstt!* He was tapping it, *Buufp-Buuft!* "Testing, one, two, three, testing." *SquEEeek-SQUaaawk!* This went on. He finally held up a sack lunch and crooned into the mike, "All righty, it's that time again, boys and girls, is everybody ready?" The usual groan rose from the bleacher. "You big spenders, now, get out your money." Somebody let out a loud kissy smacking sound and titters went up. Mrs. Bledsoe turned in her first-row seat and glared and the titters stopped in midair. Mrs. Bledsoe could glare a gorilla to its knees. She took Raymond Zahn out of class for discipline one time and Raymond was never the same again. He'd been headed for prison, people thought. He'd stop cars on the road for no reason and bust out their headlights with a bicycle chain. But when Mrs. Bledsoe brought him back to class that day after discipline, he was changed and sat like a mouse with the blood drained from his face. The word got around that Mrs. Bledsoe had taken Raymond out in the hall, looked him in the eye with a smile, then reached down and crushed both his balls with one hand. It might've happened.

As the auction began, the usual bids were made. Mr. Ferris would hold up a box or sack, somebody would hold up a hand and bid fifty cents, and Mr. Ferris would try to keep it going. "Fifty cents, do I hear more? Fifty cents is the bid, do I hear fifty-five? I have fifty, fifty, fifty, going once, going twice—" No one else was about to raise the price but every time Mr. Ferris had to act like it was exciting and go through his song and dance. A guy would bid, he'd have to sit through all the blathering, then he'd have to walk up to the stage in full view to claim his sack or box with god knows what in it, the girl would walk up at the same time to get claimed herself, then both would have to walk off together in full view to eat at the end of the gym or out behind in the parking lot. That was the routine and you knew what was bound to happen but Mr. Ferris would have to monotonously string it out.

Blackie got Melba Glee's box. Billy Bob got Eula Mae's. Nobody knew but Melba Glee was already pregnant. She and

Blackie would have to get married in another month and drop out of school. Lumplump's box was almost passed over but Scabs Toohey finally raised his hand and got it for a dime. There were a few more bargains, then Mr. Ferris held up Fayette's box wrapped like a Christmas present with a bow on top. It was as if Fayette considered herself a present. Mr. Ferris patted his belly. "Ho, ho, ho, it's jolly Saint Nick!" Nobody laughed. Only Fayette appeared vainly pleased. "Now what'm I bid, do I hear—" I didn't raise my hand and since it was known I was supposed to, no one else raised his hand either. Mr. Ferris kept trying to get a bid and Fayette started looking at me with a terrible smile and I could feel her thinking, Okay, you're teasing now, you sonofabitch, but you better not go too far or I'll never let you do anything nasty to my wonderful body again.

I nudged Puddles to bid. He was confused, Fayette was my girl, but I told him not anymore, I was giving her to him. He didn't understand, he'd never had a girlfriend.

"She's hot," I told him. "She'll let you play bunny in her little briar patch."

"You said it wasn't worth it."

"I lied."

"You said it was boring."

Mr. Ferris was auctioneering. Fayette was looking at me with real daggers now. Time was running out. "Dammit, Puddles, she's a girl and you're a guy, okay? A girl and a guy, Puddles, think about it." He thought about it and raised his hand. Fayette could see what was coming and clutched her throat. Then Puddles lowered his hand. He was afraid she'd be mad. I told him he could handle it. He said he didn't know how much to bid. I told him it didn't matter, anything. He fished in his pocket and all he had was a nickel. So bid the damn nickel, jesus! He raised his hand again but this time with a new thrust of confidence. He'd seen in his mind the dark goal where the sun never shines and he'd come up with the means to get there. "I got 'er! I got 'er!" he yelled. "I bid a nickel!"

Fayette screamed.

What happened next is a little vague. There was general havoc, but not exactly. You have to imagine, here was this giant sex-starved sixteen-year-old bounding down the bleachers with his nickel held out. Faces were upturned. There was a moment of stricken disbelief, then a kind of simple panic swept the faces of the more innocent girls and you could see that look in their eyes, the ancient fear women have held in their breasts since time immemorial, of the plundering horde, the barbarian at the gate, the rape of the Sabine women. Girls huddled. Fayette fainted.

It was a critical moment. You could sense mass hysteria building. The crowd could turn into a mob. A riot might break out. Then what really happened was almost as dreaded. Mrs. Bledsoe stood and let loose with her glare. She went from left to right, and like a wave along the bleachers, from left to right whole rows withered. Fear was replaced with abject submission. Puddles reached the stage with his nickel and Mr. Ferris handed him Fayette's box. At the same time a couple of girls were trying to revive Fayette, fanning her face. She finally came around fluttering her lashes and saw Puddles waiting and immediately swooned again. She had to be carried to the girls' room and the last I saw, Puddles was standing at the door knocking but Fayette wouldn't come out.

The auction continued. A few more boxes were routine. Finally Mr. Ferris held up Darlene's unmistakable picnic hamper. "Ah ha!" he said. "I guess we know whose this is, don't we?" He leered at Darlene. "And I guess we know who's going to bid for this, too, don't we?" He leered at Randy, and right on cue,

Randy flashed his brilliant Most Handsome smile and bid two dollars. Mr. Ferris chanted, "Two dollars, I have two dollars, do I hear more? I have two, do I hear two-fifty? Now I have two—" He continued. I waited. He started winding down, Going once, going twice—

I raised a finger. "Five dollars."

Mr. Ferris was stopped with his mouth open. The gym was suddenly silent, eyes were turning, but I sat normally as if nothing had happened. Mr. Ferris blinked. "Did I hear five?"

"Right, five dollars," I said.

Murmuring rippled the bleachers. Darlene gave me a quick glance but without expression. Randy fixed me with his pupils as if sizing a gnat. Then a small corner of his mouth curled and he appeared to write me off. Mr. Ferris collected his wits and announced brightly, "Well, all right! I have a bid, I have five dollars, five, do I hear six?"

"Six." Randy spoke strongly.

Mr. Ferris turned to me. "Six, I have six, do I hear seven? The bid is six, what about seven—" He went on. I pretended to be finished and you could feel the letdown in the gym. I'd only bid to be obnoxious, to make Randy have to pay more, right? It would be talked about for the clownish act it was worth and forgotten. That's probably what everyone was thinking. Mr. Ferris was still chanting, "Six, do I hear seven—" I stayed deadpan. Mr. Ferris looked disappointed. "Then that's it, six is the bid, six it is, going once, going twice—"

"Ten," I said.

Mr. Ferris choked. The gym buzzed. Randy lowered his sights to give me a newer harder appraisal. Darlene's eyes caught mine, and the way they did, I knew she was with me. She was smiling and I felt her smile fill my heart. The instant rush, who would've known, she was with *me!*

Mr. Ferris was still stopped. "Ten?"

"Yes sir, ten."

"All right, ten—"

Randy didn't wait. "Fifteen!" He sat back with his arms folded, daring me.

I shrugged. "Twenty-five."

Mr. Ferris was out of it, looking at Randy, then me, back and forth. Randy was trying to appear unperturbed but I could see he was beginning to be concerned. His jaw was more set. I'd jumped the bid $10 to an incredible $25, an unheard-of figure. No one had ever bid over two, and only Randy had done that. He was probably thinking, when was I ever known to have money? I was poor. I wasn't even in the De Molays. So I had to be bluffing, trying to pull a fast one. I was jacking up the bid to make him have to pay more so I could laugh about it. Or he could quit bidding and I would be stuck, wouldn't I? I'd have to admit I didn't have the $25 and look like a fool. He'd have the laugh then, and the whole school, too. But—and this was a big but—what if I *did* have the money and he stopped bidding— I'd walk off with Darlene? It was going through his mind. Did he have the nerve to call my bluff and chance losing Darlene? That was the question. He was looking at me steadily. Then he cracked, his nerve failed. "I bid twenty-seven," he said.

I smiled. Mr. Ferris was still flustered but picked up the count. "Twenty-seven, I have twenty-seven, do I hear—" I let him chant. I was looking straight at Darlene and she was looking straight back at me and smiling. It was like a thousand movies. It was wonderful. My brother, Billy, clambered up behind me and started spewing in my ear, "What're you, crazy? You better get aholt of your senses, now I'm telling you, do you know who you're bidding against? You better straighten up and start acting like you know the meaning of money." He scooted away. I wasn't bothered. Mr. Ferris was still chanting. When he got to the going once, going twice part, I figured the suspense was about right.

I flipped my hand. "Fifty."

A mind-boggled babble rose all around—Fifty! Did you hear that! He said fifty! Did he say fifty!? Gawd! It was music to my ears, the wonderment and bafflement of the crowd. Darlene's eyes were looking into mine and saying, This is real, isn't it? And my eyes were saying back, Yes, I promise you, this is real. Then hers were saying, And this is fun, too, isn't it? Mine were answering, Oh, you betcha, fun, too. Like every living day should be, fun and real, and real and fun, the only way.

Mr. Ferris was dumbfounded. "Did you say *fifty?*"

"Yes sir."

"Now you know we're talking dollars."

"Yes sir, dollars."

"Well, just so it's clearly understood, you're saying you're going to bid fifty dollars, is that right?"

"No sir."

"Oh, so now you're not going to bid fifty dollars?"

"No sir, I meant I'm not going to, I already did."

He regarded me balefully. "Are you sure you know what you're doing?"

I took a moment, and not because I wasn't sure. I wanted to sound the right note for history, one giant leap for man, one small step for mankind, that sort of thing. I needed to be equal to the moment but also properly modest. I looked at Mr. Ferris sincerely and spoke. "You ask if I'm sure—" I let it float and I can still feel the portent in the air, Nathan Hale, Patrick Henry. I finished, "Mr. Ferris—it's only money."

He looked at me like I was an idiot, as if he couldn't believe what he was hearing. I'd taken a stand for a larger reality but he was still stuck in the teacher's world of borderline thinking. Did he hear, *only* money? Good lord, $50 was a year's supply of needlepoint, a vacation for two to Carlsbad Caverns.

I sneaked a peek at Randy to see him defeated. He'd be sitting there shell-shocked and bewildered. Or that's what I thought I'd see. But he was totally calm with only a sardonic smile tracing his lips. He was calmly smoothing his creases.

For the first time I felt a twinge of doubt. I'd upped the bid from $6 to $10, from $15 to $25, then all the way up to $50 without blinking an eye. I'd given it my best it's-only-money shot. What did I have to do?

Then I knew. I'd said it was only money, but Randy's daddy owned the peanut mill and the only richer person around was Darlene's daddy, who owned the State Bank. To Randy, then, money was like water and he was a fish swimming in it. He lived it and breathed it. He didn't even know it was water. Which meant money wasn't *only* with him, it was nothing. It was simply there and always there.

I felt myself sinking. Whatever possessed me to think I could win? And with so little? Darlene was looking at me the same but she didn't know. In another bid or two I'd come to the end of my paltry $75, my last cent, and Mr. Everything plopped beside her would bring out his bottomless moneybags and blow me away. I'd be left sitting with a blasted face and no hope, a born loser. I should've known my place.

Mr. Ferris was prattling on, "—I have fifty, now fifty, do I hear—" Randy raised his hand. "Fifty-two." I felt weaker. "I guess I'll make it fifty-five," I said. Mr. Ferris picked up the count but I couldn't listen. The end was coming and I just wanted it over and done with. Then Randy said fifty-seven. Another cheensy two-dollar raise to draw it out. He wanted to nickel-and-dime me to death. Why didn't he just bid a hundred and finish me off? I said sixty. Mr. Ferris chanted. It seemed a longer interval but Randy finally raised his hand and said sixty-one. Not even two this time, but one. He was going to string it out even longer to watch me squirm. I decided to hell with it. I stood and my voice got away from me. "All right," I screeched, "seventy-five!"

There, it was done. I sat back down and looked at my feet. I couldn't look at Darlene. She was the only wonderful thing in life I'd ever really wanted but she was beyond me and I needed to accept that fact. They were right, why keep wanting something you can't have? Be satisfied with what you've got and feel lucky you're alive. Be humble. Be a Christian. Besides, I was a stupid dreamer, always dreaming of exciting things happening and they never did. And I was a whiner, too. Something didn't go right, I'd start whining about it. I called it griping, it was the same thing, and that was me, a whiny dreamer, the two worst things you can be. They'd put that on my tombstone someday: Here Lies a Whiny Dreamer.

It was my worst hour. I'd failed and I was alone. Then I heard my name. "Bobby Jack?" Mr. Ferris was peering at me curiously. "You didn't hear me?" The whole gym was waiting. "I said, going, going—" He was offering Darlene's picnic hamper. I turned slowly to see her eyes still on me and her face still smiling, only differently. She was standing as if expectantly. Randy appeared smaller, his mouth a clamped line, his expression, well, I knew. It was that old familiar strain that twists your mouth when you're trying to be a good sport. But meaning what? That I'd won? It couldn't be. Mr. Ferris was finishing, "—going three times and gone! To Bobby Jack Nelson for seventy-five dollars!" Jesus, I had won. But how? I couldn't move. Then I figured it. Randy's daddy was rich all right, but Randy himself only had an allowance, and all those small bids, he was stretching his allowance all he could, but it was like play money, not hard-earned real money, and the play stuff you can't stretch. So the outcome was inevitable. I had real money, he didn't. Which is a lesson you learn, you're in the game to play for keeps, you better have the real thing.

Mr. Ferris was holding out the hamper. "—for seventy-five dollars. And you do have the money, I hope."

"Yes sir." I was bopping down the bleachers. "Oh, yes sir, you betcha, I got the money right here!" At the same time Darlene was walking to the stage from her side of the gym. It was a great moment. We were both in full view. We'd meet on the stage, I'd carry her hamper, and we'd walk off together with every mouth in the place hanging open and every lonely envious guy in the world eating his heart out. But I'd done it, I'd won Darlene.

I T WAS THE MEETING OF TWO OPPOSITES, beauty and the peasant. The whole gym was goggle-eyed but I believe I can honestly say I behaved with my usual aplomb. Which is the key in a moment of glory, you play it cool. It's 10 on the Richter scale with buildings toppling, people running amuck, what the heck, finish your breakfast.

Darlene and I arrived at stage center at the same moment and acknowledged each other with a socially acceptable nod. We were dignified. The ceremony was simple. Mr. Ferris took my money and handed me the picnic hamper. If it was heavy, I didn't notice. Then Darlene and I walked from the stage like two ordinary people except I was polite, I graciously allowed her down the steps first. Four perfect steps. Every eye watched in awe. The air was filled with stunned silence.

Now, as I said, the routine was to sit on the end bleachers or you could go out in the parking lot. I had a third alternative. At the end bleachers, I said, Tell you what, how 'bout the parking lot? Darlene said that was fine with her. We went out the rear exit to the space in back and, whataya know, my little blue coupe just happened to be parked right there. I pretended a brainstorm. Hey, I got an idea, I said, how 'bout the State Park? I acted excited. Darlene laughed and flashed me a really neat look with a daring twinkle in her eye. It was against the rules to leave school, but that was the point. We made a dash for the car. I threw the hamper in the trunk and hurried to open her door. She was right with me. And let me tell you, that moment remains, the way she touched my arm just barely and brushed against me sliding in, the careless, yet utterly graceful way she swung her legs in without bothering to hold her skirt. She was so beautiful, and up close, the closest I'd been, she was even more beautiful than I knew. Her skin had such smoothness, her face such perfection, I stood transfixed and filled with love. Aching pure love. I was unworthy. But proud, too. God, I was proud. Darlene was in *my* car. And after all these years, I still remember. I can still smell the fresh scent of her skin and my arm still prickles where she touched brushing past me. It was a hot day with not a breath of air anywhere but the picture I see is always cool and balmy. The glimpse of her golden thigh as she swung her legs is imprinted in my brain like the sliver of a moon. Only now I don't see the auction as a stunt. I imagine I stole her and carried her off. I imagine, too, my old coupe was not a car but a blue stallion and somehow that's the reality. The highwayman would've ridden a blue stallion.

I closed Darlene's door and hurried around to my side. The car wouldn't start. Well, I didn't expect it to. That car could sit parked ten minutes, the juice in the battery would drain completely dry. I think it was a short somewhere. Whatever, the thing wouldn't start, I gave it a push on my side with the door open until I was nearly running, jumped in, stuck it in gear, we were off in a splatter of gravel and billowing smoke.

I took the first corner on two wheels and glanced at Darlene. She was smiling. My kind of gal. I took the next corner the same and the car survived. Yahoo! And hot damn, I thought, what a car. I'd made a good investment. I turned onto the highway, the State Park was five miles ahead.

The pliers? Darlene asked. Right there, I flipped open the glove compartment to show her the pliers. And the wood's in the trunk, I said. The State Park was barren landscape the same as the rest of the country. The only difference, it had an entrance with a wrought-iron sign overhead: STATE P RK. Inside, a few sand dunes but no grass or trees. And no wood. So you needed to bring your own wood if you wanted a campfire. Also the park had water but it was a hydrant with the handle missing, a stem with no knob, and that's why you needed pliers to turn on the water. And you had to think pliers especially because nobody else was going to loan you theirs. Which was understandable. With the law of the desert, whoever had water had survival. You'd see whole families in the park backed in a circle guarding their pliers with their lives.

Or not that bad. I'm joking. But fortunately the State Park was a place nobody wanted to go, so most of the time you had the run of the area to yourself. And naturally that's why I picked the spot to bring Darlene. With no one else likely to show, and particularly on a weekday, I figured we'd have privacy. Just the two of us, a boy and a girl, but all alone.

Meanwhile I was driving and feeling good. The way we talked as I recall was like this:

I said, "I hope you don't mind I kinda aced out ol' Randy."

"Oh, no," she said. "But guess what I thought, I mean, what I really thought."

I couldn't guess.

"I thought, finally, it's about time!"

"Hey, that's just what I was going to guess."

"No one ever tries to get me."

"Well, guys look at you, they see a wallflower."

"But that's only my exterior. I'm really—" She was lowering her eyes, pausing for effect. "—well, I guess you know, I'm really a nymphomaniac."

Now that was good, nymphomaniac. I came back without missing a beat, "I didn't know that, but you know what, I was kinda hoping you would be."

"You know what that means."

"I'll look it up in the dictionary."

"It's under the N's."

"I'll have to remember that. I'm reading the dictionary this week but I'm only up to the F's."

"That's where it starts getting interesting."

"I hope so. The A's were pretty boring."

"Wait'll you get to the P's, the suspense builds."

"Don't tell me the ending."

"The Z's."

"You told me, now I'm not going to be surprised."

"The plot's always the same."

"Yeah, but I like to figure it out for myself."

I couldn't believe it. We were on the same wavelength, we had the same funny brain. Yet how could we? She was royalty, the upper class. I had no class. She moved close and hugged my arm. Her breasts pressed my arm. "I like you," she said. "You're dangerous."

Dangerous, I thought. Then I couldn't think. Her breasts against me zapped my mind and for about a second I experienced near insanity. She had my arm snugged between her breasts and I could feel their soft rounded mounds. I could feel their softness protruding, they were so infinitely deep and soft. And I say soft. I want to be clear. They were not mushy. No, definitely not that. They were soft and firm. Or firmly soft. It was hard to tell. They were such tender perishable morsels, you'd need to caress them gently with care. At the same time they were so firmly uplifting and inspiring, they were everlasting. They could be used and reused for months and years and still be good. I felt pain and misery and paralysis. It was the happiest moment of my life.

I pretended I was still sane. "Well, I kinda like you, too," I said. "But I'm a real rotten guy, y'know, I dump girls all the time, I might break your heart."

"Oh, wouldja? I want you to." She nuzzled my shoulder, then pulled back to fix me with sloe melting eyes—*wouldja let me kiss ya, wouldja be my man, wouldja, huh?*

It made me weak. And I saw at once exactly how it would be. I would be a fool for her and love her wildly. I already did. But I wasn't going to break her heart, she was going to break mine. Then I'd wander the country and spend the next half of my life in dumb honkytonk joints listening to ignorant songs about lost love and cheating women. I'd compare every woman and every drunken one-night stand with Darlene and not a one would halfway come close, even the ones I might've loved, because I'd feel I'd had the best, the sexiest, smartest, most beautiful girl in the world and that girl would stay in my dreams forever. That's how it would be. You love without thinking, without reservation, it's true love and never leaves you. And especially true love, you can't forget, you don't want to forget.

So, all right, we were driving along. I saw how it was going to be but I was young and stupid, I didn't care. How could I? I'd just gotten with her, we hadn't done anything yet.

I concentrated on the road and for a while we were quiet. It felt natural and pleasant. Darlene had moved away to sit with her back to the door, her beautiful knees curled on the seat between us. She was watching me. Appraising me?

"I can hear you thinking," I said.

"I'm reading your mind."

I hope you can, I thought. Then I felt caught. What if she could? I had things in my mind no one knew, that I'd purposely hidden. Families had skeletons in their closets, I had weirdos locked away in a back room. You could come to the front door, maybe you wouldn't see, but going around back, and in the dark, you'd see a secret door and if you passed close, you'd hear sounds like people inside scratching to get out, and they would be, they didn't like it crammed in there together. In fact I had some real kooks in that room I was scared to let out. The kleptomaniac. The future alcoholic. I had a potential suicide chained to the wall and a couple of plain imbeciles. I suspected one was a real sex fiend. If I let those guys loose, no telling what would happen. And if Darlene *could* read my mind, what if she saw behind that door? I passed it off. "I'll bet," I said.

She didn't reply and only sat with the hint of a smile on her lips. It seemed a long time. Then she said quietly, "Don't be afraid."

It was like a punch in the kidneys. I laughed. "Who, me?"

"I'll make a bargain with you." She put her hand on my knee. "If you won't be afraid of me, I won't be afraid of you."

It was an uppercut right in the gut, my legs were gone, but I needed to hang on, if I could spar for time and use the ropes— she leaned across and kissed me on the cheek.

"That did it," I said.

"What?"

"That. You just turned the prince into a frog."

"Oh, so now you're gonna croak." She goosed me.

"Well, how'm I supposed to act? You changed the game right in the middle of the damn rules."

"You don't want to be honest?"

"I don't know how."

"Oh, c'mon."

"I'm too young to be honest. My whole life is ahead. You start being honest, you get hooked, you gotta lie to save yourself. I've seen guys hooked on that honest stuff, they get thrown in jail for being honest."

She patted my knee. "There, there, it's all right, it's going to be fun."

I turned into the entrance of the State Park, a space in a wire fence, and it was only a trail heading into more desert but in my mind it seemed a choice, either the gateway to heaven or the rutted road to hell. It was one of those roads you travel without knowing where it'll end and you can't predict. I only knew my soul was at stake. A healthier-minded kid might've become warped. But Darlene was right, it was going to be fun, too.

Picture rippling waves of burning sand, not a cloud in the sky, a white-hot sun beating down, that's the park. Or the sand is not that burning. Dig down a couple inches it'll be kinda cool. But the air in the distance is filled with shimmering lines of heat so this is Sahara land, lonely nomad and camel country, only without the nomad and without the camel. For one thing, your normal camel wouldn't live here. There's nothing to do.

You want to cruise the strip at night, it's to the top of the next dune and back. You want entertainment, you're left to your own devices. Or make that singular and around Dalton the main device is the opposed thumb.

In every direction then, acres and acres of drifting sand. But for about the second time in the year, no wind, the air was pleasantly still. My plan was to get Darlene drunk. Which was old-fashioned even then but I was in love. You're in love, you're into trailer-park mentality. I had my wine in the Welch's Grape Juice bottle so Darlene wouldn't know. And I wouldn't tell her. I'd just say, Here, have a taste. If she wanted to pass on it, I'd say, Aw, c'mon, try it, you'll like it. I'd get her to take a sip, a few more sips, then sit back and wait for her eyes to turn glassy. The procedure is called getting-a-girl-snockered-and-taking-advantage. Fathers of teenage daughters hate this procedure. The next day girls claim they can't remember what happened. But next day also they suddenly want to go steady and start following you around with moony eyes. You have to tell 'em, Look, you gotta understand, I need to find myself, I can't get tied down. They don't understand but they keep hoping, they're so miserable. Finally they start going out with someone else to make you jealous, which is like employing grade-school tactics, it's so obvious. Except it usually works, then it's your turn to start following them around. It becomes a test of character.

I stopped at the hydrant, a two-foot pipe sticking up out of the ground, and turned off my motor. The engine on its own rocked and sputtered until it coughed and died. An autopsy would've revealed consumption. I glanced around. No cars. No people. The place was completely deserted, as I expected. Darlene jumped from the car, flipped off her sandals, and twirled in the sand. She spread her arms and called out, "Hello out there! Anybody home?" Not an echo came back. She ran to the first dune with her skirt flouncing, her hair flying. A child of nature, I thought, full of delight. I felt happy just watching her so exuberant. I wanted to watch forever.

Then she ruined me. She skipped back from the dune and pulled me from the car. "C'mon," she said, "let's get naked."

"Pardon me?"

"You know, clothes off, nude, bareass."

I wasn't prepared. I could feel myself shrinking. She started unbuttoning her blouse, I was staring, entranced and demented at the same time. I was being hit with reality.

"Well?" She looked at me. "You're just going to stand there, or what?"

I tried to think. "Darlene, listen, what about your mother?"

"She's not here." She loosed to top button.

"Your daddy."

"He's not here either." A second button.

"Look—it's daylight."

"So?" Another button.

"Darlene, wait, you don't know me."

A shrug. The last button.

"What if I tell?" I was helpless, I couldn't move. She stood before me with her blouse unbuttoned, but with the front only slightly parted. I saw naked skin between her breasts, no bra. Her eyes were serious and leveled straight at me. If she grabbed, I'd have to run. The firing squad was set, ready, aim—I held my breath.

Then she grinned meanly. "Gotcha, didn't I?"

I sank to my knees.

"Now admit it, you thought I was serious, didn't you?"

I had to admit it. She laughed and stepped back. "Wanna peek?" She flashed a peek, a quick flap, open and closed, but enough to see. I groaned and fell over. She stepped over me buttoning her blouse and left me sprawled in the sand. I could crawl away. Or I could lay there, the buzzards would come, it would be a relief. If I crawled away, she would follow my trail in the sand and hunt me down. She was raising the hamper and calling, "Hey, I'm hungry, let's eat."

Darlene spread the picnic blanket in the open and set it from end to end with all kinds of exotic goodies, little finger sandwiches, small round sandwiches, celery sticks spread with cheese. And more, cherry tomatoes and pickles, black olives and radishes, and different bite-size treats I'd never seen before stuck with toothpicks. Also real cloth napkins and real plates and the way each thing was set on separate dishes, it really looked nice. The pickles came sliced in long strips, the radishes were carved like little flowers. The bread on the sandwiches had the crust cut away but neatly, precisely. The celery was crisp and not a bit limber. Only the cheese on the celery appeared as if melted. I didn't know it was cream cheese. I sat cross-legged on the blanket and Darlene sat with her legs tucked to the side. The blanket was brightly colored and the food between us was a wide feast.

"So this is what we eat," I said.

"I hope you like it."

"Oh, I can eat anything, I'm not picky." I tucked my napkin into my collar. "But you didn't fix all this yourself."

"Of course I did. Here, try this." She held out a brown wrinkled thing stabbed with a toothpick.

I took it in my mouth. The taste was awful. "Now that's good," I said.

"You like it?"

"Yeah." I was trying to smile and still chew. "What is it?"

"Smoked oyster."

"Well—" It tasted like a moth. "It sure is good." It finally went down. I tried a finger sandwich next but didn't get to actually know it. It was such a tidbit, I swallowed it whole. Then I chomped down on one of the round cookie-size sandwiches and the taste surprised me. I looked inside the two dinky patches of bread. Cucumber and a little spread of butter, but an ordinary slice of cucumber, nothing more. It looked lonely. I said, "Hey, cucumber!" I tried another finger thing and it was weeds. "Watercress," Darlene said. "That's great," I said, "roughage." Another sandwich tasted sort of gummy but mixed. It was pâté, she said. "I knew it," I said, "my favorite." Some of the stuck treats on the toothpicks were like meatballs. One was pretty spicy. Then I kept eating the sandwiches. One bite was one sandwich and I finished off about twelve. At the same time Darlene had one and it took her three or four bites to get that one down. I noticed that. Also the way she had spread her napkin on her knees, not like me. I made a mental note, next time, napkin on knee.

I picked a flowery radish to crunch and grinned at Darlene crunchingly. "I like to eat," I said.

She smiled back and our eyes met.

It was a romantic moment. There we were on a beautiful blanket with a beautiful picnic between us in the midst of nothing but beautiful sand. And for once the sand really was beautiful. I'd never seen it that way before, or a day like it. Not a speck of wind anywhere. The sand lay perfectly still in dune after dune of calm waves. The sun was hot but with the air baked dry, it was the kind of heat you could stand and never sweat. It was the kind of sun that showed the sky almost white. A long V of cranes flew slowly overhead and disappeared and for a while the world appeared empty and without a sound. We were sitting on the blanket like two souls on a raft becalmed in a sea of sand and it was like we were drifting aimlessly, carried by a deep current we couldn't see.

"This is peaceful," I said. Darlene nodded and it seemed a soft agreement as if something magical had settled between us. As if there, in the air between us, we had melded into one. I felt caught in a spell. And this is love, I thought, the spell of love. We were two souls in one, two minds and hearts in one. What she felt, I would feel. When she breathed, I would breathe.

"I like it here," she said.

In my mind, *I love you, Darlene, I love you.* I didn't want the spell to end.

"But a tree," she said. "If I had to say, I think the place could stand a tree."

But we're alone and I love you, Darlene, forget the damn tree, I love you!

"I'm thirsty," she said. She was unscrewing the thermos and I felt cheated. The spell was broken. But thermos, something to drink. I snapped back to my senses.

"Hey, you're thirsty!" I said it too quickly but I don't think she noticed.

"We have lemonade." She was setting two glasses to pour.

"Wait!" I jumped up. "I've got something better." I ran to the car and came back with my bottle of Welch's Grape Juice. "Here, let's have this." I showed a happy face.

She looked at the bottle. "Grape juice?"

"It's good, try it."

"I don't think I want grape juice."

"Taste it, you'll like it."

"It'll make my teeth purple."

"Not this, it's new and improved, full of vitamins. C'mon, just a sip." I poured her glass.

She took a swallow and I waited. Did she know?

It was a dumb question. Of course she knew. She looked at me gravely. "Thunderbird?"

"Mogen David."

"A good vintage. What year?"

"I got it Thursday."

"Thursday was a good year for Mogen David." She finished her glass and licked her lips. "You know something, I may have underestimated you." She held out her glass for more. "Let's get drunk."

"Hey, that's just what I was going to say!" And boy, oh, boy, I thought, here we go. I poured her glass again and one for me and raised a toast, "Here's looking at you, kid."

"Down the hatch."

We clinked glasses and drank. My first swallow went straight down and shot right back to my brain. "Now that's real grape juice!" I said. I downed my glass and felt my ears lift from my head. After that, I don't know. I'd never drunk wine before. Darlene had. She drank wine occasionally with dinner, she said. She used that word, "occasionally," and I pictured her sitting at a long dining table with her family. A big crystal chandelier hangs down and everything is formal. The tablecloth is pure Belgium lace and the centerpiece is a big bowl of fresh flowers. Each place has about four spoons and forks and a servant in a white jacket goes around the table with a bottle of wine filling the long-stemmed glasses. Darlene's daddy carves the roast at the head of the table and everyone sips their wine politely. Darlene's mother dabs her lips with a napkin, but nicely, delicately. They all take small bites and chew with their mouths closed. They smile and talk pleasantly about important issues of the day with Darlene's daddy leading the discussion on financial matters and the nation's trading policies. He's for higher import tariffs but everyone contributes their own view and each opinion is considered respectfully. The wine is Lafite-Rothschild '28. One bottle costs more than my whole car and they're sipping it like it's nothing. I feel awed. One sip, they've just scarfed down a new set of tires. Two sips, I could've had a motor overhaul. I kept seeing how they lived. But parts skipped and missed. Like what happened to the rest of the roast they didn't eat? Where did it go? There was enough left over to feed a Boy Scout camp but it went back to the kitchen somehow and disappeared. And who cleared the table and washed the dishes? I pressed my nose to the kitchen window and saw a cook and scullery maid kept out of sight and never allowed to appear before company. The cook had bunions and didn't want to appear. The scullery maid had smudges and it was all she could do to keep the pots and pans scrubbed. But I still couldn't see what happened to the roast. Where was it? A big juicy roast doesn't just up and disappear. Then it dawned on me, the cook and scullery maid had eaten it, that's what. They'd sat down at the kitchen table before I could get there and wolfed the platter clean. Now I didn't care. They were stuck off in the kitchen like that, overworked and underpaid, I was going to feel sorry for them, but they ate better than I did.

"You're gonna have to watch the help," I said.

"Help?"

"The cook and the pot scrubber, you didn't see 'em."

"You're drunk."

"They ate the whole roast in about a minute, and I mean the whole thing. I got there too late."

I raised my head and that's when I knew I wasn't exactly with it. My head sailed off and left my body hanging. I followed my arm to my hand about a mile away and saw the glass in my hand empty. The bottle on the blanket somewhere was also empty and I perceived with uncanny insight that the wine was gone, all gone. I'd drunk it all, or most of it, I didn't know when. Darlene had three eyes. "I'm not in," I said, "just leave the message with my secretary."

"Bobby—" She made the word sound pitiful.

"No, it's okay, I'm all right." I tried to stand but one of my legs had grown shorter and I could only mush in a circle. "My leg," I said, "I'm crippled." I fell down.

No telling how long I lay there. Darlene was pulling at me to get me up. "You need to walk." But I didn't want to get up. My head was still floating off in the atmosphere. I could look down and see a reef in the Gulf of Mexico. The reef was teeming with aquatic life. Which was brilliant, I thought. The reef's in the damn ocean, what other kind of damn life was it going to have? I could see my own brain like a reef crawling with crustaceans.

Then Darlene was covering my body with sand. I think she had me about half buried from the chest down when I realized. Oh ho, I thought, she wants to play! I pushed up and the sand fell away. Look, the mummy rises from the grave, it lives!

She ran and I caught her ankles diving. A flash of white panties and fresh thighs. We rolled and my body rolled with hers. What a luscious squirming body! But she was stronger than I knew and kicked free. She threw a handful of sand at me and I crouched. "Now you've had it," I said, "no holds barred." I threw sand back and we went into a regular free-for-all dirt brawl. It was like desert warfare, the battle for North Africa. We were slinging and kicking entire dunes at each other, fighting on all fronts. Imagine a four-handed, four-footed whirlwind dust storm. It was fun, and with sand in our hair, in our mouths and ears, we were laughing. Then she was out of breath and called a truce. I was honorable and stopped. She didn't. She immediately poured sand down my shirt and we started again. I grabbed her waist and held long enough to stuff sand in her panties. I loved doing that. She blasted me with a mouthful of sand and we played King of the Mountain, clawing and scrabbling to crawl the highest dune. I was pulling her back by the legs and wouldn't let her win until we were slipping and slogging, tugging and falling. She wouldn't give, neither would I, but finally we were too weak, too tired. We sat in the sand panting.

"You ought to see yourself," she said.

"You, too," I said. Her face was dusted completely and her hair, eyebrows, everywhere, was caked with sand. Only her eyes looked white and bright. She licked a finger and wiped a line in the sand on my cheek, and more lines on my forehead and chin. "Ha! Cochise," she said. I licked my finger and painted lines on her face, too. But I couldn't name her. Not Pocahontas. She'd become transformed. With her dusted face and sand-filled hair, and with the lines I'd made streaking her features, she'd become a primitive mask. She might have been the first goddess mask. She looked strange and wonderful and I felt mesmerized. She was the face of woman down through the ages and incredibly beautiful. Then her eyes held mine. What did she want? I was seeing an unearthly beauty beyond me. "Hey—" She was passing her hand in front of my eyes. "You there?" I came back to myself.

She shook sand from her hair and swiped at her arms. "Look at me, I'm filthy." She stood. "I'm going to wash."

"I'll get the pliers," I said.

"That's all right, I'll get 'em, you stay there." She was starting down the dune. "And don't look," she said.

I watched her going, she was so lovely—then it hit me, how slow can you get? She'd said "wash" and I'd thought nothing, face, hands. But "don't look" had meant more, like don't look at what? Could it be? We'd eaten together. We'd gotten drunk together. Or I had. We'd played footsies in the sand. Now the preliminaries were over. A vision of opportunity rose in my mind.

"Darlene, wait!" I ran after her. "Where you going?"

She stopped and I almost ran over her. "I told you, I'm going to wash."

"Right, wash, but you mean like really wash?"

"Look." She flounced sand from her skirt. "I'm covered with sand."

"Me, too. Hey, let's wash together!" I said it a little too eagerly maybe. She gave me a look. "You can wash my back and I'll wash yours," I said. "I'll wash between your toes."

"I don't think so." She pushed me off. "Now you just go back to your perch and let me wash."

I tried reasoning with her but she wouldn't change her mind so I gave in. "Okay, you wash, I'll sit and watch."

"No, you won't."

"How do you know? I might."

"Because I know. I trust you."

"What if you can't?"

"I'm putting you on your honor."

"But I'm not honorable."

"Yes, you are. Now go on." She was walking away.

I called after her, "But I'm only a man, I'm weak, I'm not responsible—Darlene?" She kept walking. "I'm not kidding," I yelled. "What if I lose control?"

She wasn't listening, only moving to her purpose, and I was left to sit on my dune. Trusting a guy, putting him on his honor, christ, the oldest trick in the book. I could look, what would it hurt? What was a girl's naked body anyway? I'd seen about four I knew personally. Fayette's being the latest. Hers wasn't worth looking at. But Darlene's—well, she'd sounded serious. What if she was? I faced away.

A moment later I heard the car door open and close. She'd gotten the pliers. I didn't hear anything next and imagined her undressing, her shirt first, no bra, then her gorgeous thighs slipping out of her white panties. I heard water splattering from the hydrant, a pipe two feet high. She'd have to bend over to wash her hair. But which way, north or south? I prayed for south. "Darlene?" No answer, only *splash-splash*, water slopping. "Darlene, I'm warning you, okay? I don't know how long I can hold out. I might have to look, okay?" *Splash-splash*. Still no answer. I imagined her golden body naked in the sun with rivulets streaming down, droplets dripping from her nipples, her sopping hair slicked back from her cheeks.

But I only sat faced away.

So why didn't I look? Maybe I thought she was really trusting me not to. But what did that matter? I'd never bothered with trust before, ask Fayette, I didn't even know the meaning of the word. I sat shaking my head. Somewhere behind me the most tantalizing female body in the world was revealed and I wasn't seeing it. Not normal, I thought. I was sifting sand with my fingers. No sir, not normal one bit.

THE SUN WENT DOWN, we built a fire and sat a long time after dark talking about life, the subject, without defining it, the way we wanted to live, the things we were going to do. At least Darlene had plans and I felt carried along. I kept saying, Yeah, me, too. I didn't have a glimmer what I wanted, only I knew I had crazy pent-up yearnings and dreams I couldn't name. But Darlene knew. She was going to Europe for the summer. She'd come back in the fall and go to college. Back east, she said. Her parents expected that, so, okay, she'd go, a year, two years, then take off on her own. That's right, just take off,

I thought. She was going to Nepal, Timbuktu, all those places, and sail the Pacific. Some guy sailing the Atlantic had been in the news. And she was going to learn French and write poetry. I couldn't see the connection, it didn't matter. She was going to float the Nile and climb the pyramids. The idea being freedom, to be free and never stuck. And I agreed. Or it would be good just to live in some green spot awhile with rivers and trees. She said she was going to have a lot of lovers, too. I didn't care to hear that, but she was so sure, so confident, I wanted to sound the same. Yeah, me, too, I said, me, too. I imagined her in different settings, riding in a rickshaw in Singapore, wearing a safari hat in Kenya. Then what? Her life was an endless dream and I finally had to ask, but how are you going to get by, how are you going to eat? She said if she had to, she could do anything a man could. I pictured her trying to fix a flat with her pretty hands greasy and calloused, she wouldn't have the muscle. But it wouldn't come to that either. With her looks, she could write her ticket anywhere in the world. She could hitchhike, the first car passing would come to a screeching halt. A guy in the same spot would be left standing.

"And what about you?" she asked. "What are you going to do?"

I didn't have a clue but I didn't hesitate. "I'm going to be a professional boxer." And in the same breath, I thought, that's it, that's what I'll be. I saw myself in the ring waiting for the bell. I had a future. "I'm a light-heavy now," I said, "but I'll probably end up heavyweight, I'm still growing."

She was surprised. "I didn't know you boxed."

"Well, I don't really box. I just have fights."

"You have a scar." She traced the scar in my left eyebrow with her finger.

"That was a lucky punch. Usually I don't get hit that much.

I'm pretty fast. You oughta see me fight sometime." I stood to show her my moves. I let go with some fancy footwork. "See, I'm too fast, they can't find me." I shot off a few quick left-right combinations. "They're down, they don't know what hit 'em." I was bobbing and weaving, flicking lefts. Buster Franklin was a punching bag. Blackie Burns was a standing target in his hobnail boots. They were throwing the roundhouse stuff you could see coming and duck. I was moving in with straight punches from the shoulder, in and out. I had Buster down and stood over him with my arms raised. The crowd was cheering. Then I saw myself showing off and felt like an idiot. If I looked, Darlene would be rolling her eyes, is this a fool or what?

"Maybe you can't tell," I said, "the sand kinda slows me down."

"No, I can tell, you're fast."

"Well, I dunno—" I had acted like a six-year-old.

Darlene saw my feelings and patted a place beside her. "Com'ere." I sat beside her but I couldn't face her. She poked my shoulder. "Hey you—it's okay."

"I don't even know how to box."

"You could, though, you can do anything you want to."

It was a bad moment. She was only pitying me. I hung my head. Then it occurred to me, wait a minute—pity. That was good. I was getting sympathy. Maybe I could milk it. I went into a slump. "Nah, I can't do anything."

"Yes, you can."

"You don't know." I was really moping now.

"Look, I think you're wonderful—here, look at me." She pulled my arm and I allowed myself to be turned. "Now." She was seeing into my eyes with infinite tenderness. "You're special. You are. You can do anything you want to."

"I wish I could."

"Believe it. How do you think you got this far?"

I looked around at the empty sand leveling off and going nowhere. "I must've gotten lost," I said.

She laughed and pushed me playfully. "You're a nut." Then she pointed. "Oh, look."

The moon was coming up. She leaned her shoulder against mine and for a long time, with not a sound around, we watched the moon rising. We were only sitting, and the feeling of simply doing that and nothing more seemed enough. Especially with someone I loved. It seemed all I'd ever want.

I drove Darlene home and stopped in her circular drive. She smiled. "I had a wonderful time, I really did." No girl had ever told me that. She put her hand on my chest, her face close to mine. I felt my heart banging against her hand. She murmured, "And I think you're wonderful, too." She kissed me on the lips but with her hand still rested on my chest. A guard. Or not a guard. We barely touched and I started floating. She pulled back and I felt left in midair. It had been the lightest, sweetest kind of kiss, unimaginably delicate and feathery.

I watched her go in the house. She turned at the door to smile good night and slipped inside. I let the car roll down the drive and into the street before pushing, it made such a loud roar starting. Then I was driving in a cloud. I should've told her my feelings, now it was too late. Did she mean it saying I was special? You're wonderful, she said. How that word lifted me! But she could say terrific words like that because I didn't matter. Besides, a wonderful person would've taken wonderful in stride. But me, I'd made a stupid fool of myself getting drunk and boxing thin air. I'd acted like a moron.

I drove around the empty town and finally went home. As usual I flattened my body against the house to slide the wall to the back door. But it was out of habit. I'd forgotten Sybil wasn't making his regular raving leaps at me anymore. We'd become friends. So I gave him a pat on the head, good dog. Poor guy, always chained, one-eyed, slobbering, wagging his stubby tail, I scratched his leathery ol' hide and went on in the house.

I might've had some premonition. Except for Billy not being there, I don't know where he was, the scene was the same as the time I'd left the iron on the stove and burned the curtains. Myrtle was waiting in the kitchen, hands on hips. Her four squirrely kids were ganged behind her. Charlie was vaguely off to the side. I walked in, again Myrtle couldn't wait. "So! You finally decided to face up!" I blinked. Face up to what? My mind was still in the sand. Myrtle waved a flashlight. "Don't give me that innocent look, you know what you did and I'm going to show you. Now you just come with me." She stomped out the kitchen door with her progeny flapping behind. The world's future, I thought. Charlie reluctantly followed. Well, okay, it was outside, it was going to be the clothesline, right? Might as well take a look. I wanted to see anyway.

Myrtle was shining the flashlight from the house to the vacant lot, sweeping the beam back and forth. "Look at that! See? See that?" She shined the light in my eye and I couldn't see. Then I could. And it was a real mess. It was like the tornado ruins of some used laundry store. The clothesline was down, all three lines, and a long path of wet tangled things lay strewn on the ground, sheets, shirts, girdles, the whole muddy inventory with the clothespins still attached.

"See! See!" Myrtle was shrieking. "You did it!"

"Yeah! You did it! You did it!" her offspring chimed in.

"Look at this." Myrtle was showing me the ends of the clothesline cords that had been nailed to the house. "Now you can't deny it, there's proof, you cut them!" It was plain the cords had been sliced. But not by me. I was being falsely accused.

"That wasn't me," I said. "I wasn't even here."

"No, that's right, you weren't, were you?" Myrtle's face turned cunning. "And you didn't have to be, did you? You cut them lines this morning when you left for school." She showed her teeth. "But you only cut them partway so they'd still hold when I hung the wash because you knew—oh, you thought you were smart, all right—you knew when the wind got up and started blowing, them lines was going to break. You knew that and that's how you planned it, didn't you?" She had moved in with her teeth bared, her eyes slitted. The flashlight was a garish beam between our faces.

I took a closer look at the cords. She was right, the lines had been cleanly cut but not all the way through. A few spriggly broken threads showed at the edge of each slice. My first reaction was admiration. A secret operation had been planned and carried out. Somebody had used commando tactics and a devious oriental mind had been at work. But whose? You couldn't say the minds around me. The operation had required a certain amount of imagination.

I shook my head. "You can think what you want," I said, "I didn't do it."

"And I know you did, I know you're lying."

Mouse jumped in. "I seen him, Mama, I seen him with the knife and he did it! I seen him!"

"There, see, a witness." Myrtle was vindicated. "Now what've you got to say?"

Mouse piped up again. "He oughta get a whupping, Mama, he oughta get a whupping good!"

The three girls were agreeing shrilly, Eenie, Meenie, Minie. Charlie was backed away in the dark. What was the use? Why even argue? I started back to the house.

"Where you think you're going? You come back here!"

I kept going.

"You come back here, I'm not finished with you yet!"

I didn't answer. Then I was in the house but I could still hear outside. "Charlie, you see that, stop him!" Myrtle was ordering Charlie. "Now you're going to do something about that boy, you hear? I won't have this!"

I sat on my cot on the back porch. I didn't bother with the lamp. It usually didn't work anyway. So I just sat. Was this the way people lived? I had wanted the clothesline to break, that was true, but I hadn't cut the lines. Mouse had cut the lines to pay me back for nearly throwing him to the dog. I should have thrown him to the dog. I started untying my shoes.

Charlie appeared in the doorway as a silhouette. The kitchen light was behind him. I could tell he was nervous. He was glancing back as he came toward me. "I have to do this," he said. "Stand up." He had a belt in his hand.

I felt surprised. "You're going to whip me?"

"Stand up and bend over." He was at the foot of the cot with the belt half raised. No one else was showing but I sensed they were in the kitchen listening. Charlie was waiting for me to stand or not. A small man with big ears. I was bigger than he was. Even sitting, I was nearly as tall. He'd spent his manhood in General Delivery sorting mail. He'd wanted people to respect him for knowing his job and no one ever did.

I felt sad. "You have to do this?"

"You know what you done." His voice flat.

"But it wasn't me. Myrtle says I cut that clothesline, I didn't, now that's the truth."

His face strained. "Stand up."

Myrtle was making him do it, he'd have to answer to her. He was probably miserable with himself. But he was my father, why couldn't he take my side? It wasn't fair.

"No." I fixed him as straight as I could. "I'm not going to stand. And you're not going to whip me." That was definite. I went back to untying my shoe.

The next second I didn't see it coming. The belt stung me across the shoulder, whipping my neck. I shot up and grabbed the belt. Charlie held but I jerked it from his hand. It was like I was suddenly towering and I was going to hit him. He'd hit me. I stood clinching the belt. Charlie was frozen, his eyes wide. Maybe he was afraid to move. I started whipping my leg with the belt. Myrtle was listening behind the door, she'd hear leather slapping Levi's. I whipped my leg until it hurt, my eyes locked on Charlie's—see? I threw the belt at his chest. "There, I've been whipped."

I stormed out the back door, slamming it hard. Then I was driving but I didn't know where. It was like the car was driving itself. It crossed the railroad tracks and passed the feed mill. The blacktop turned to gravel and the road took on the look of a long ghostly ribbon. The road was following a line of telephone poles with droopy wires. All around only night and dark empty fields.

I finally stopped the car somewhere at the edge of one of those fields and got out. In front of me, the stubble of an old crop. I sat on the ground in the dirt. And that was me. I'd been born in the dirt, in a cotton field. Marie and Charlie were share-cropping and one day picking cotton, Marie felt the pangs. She knew she'd been due for a couple of weeks. She smoothed the cotton in the sack she was pulling and lay down on it. A soft bed. She remembered it was easy. The other pickers gathered round and I was born. Charlie couldn't watch. Someone cut the umbilical cord with a maize knife. They washed me from a can-vas-wrapped water jug that had been left to cool in a shade. I was healthy and chubby. Two days later Marie was back in the field picking more cotton. I think about that. She worked as a field hand.

I'd worked the same, up and down the rows, stooping, picking. I could still feel the ache in my hands. But in the fields, you plodded like a dumb animal, it wasn't thinking work. Except I would look over and see the migrants working separately and think about them. What were they? Wetbacks and greasers, spics and pepper bellies. And thieves, too. They would arrive in the fall in their caravans and when things turned up missing somewhere, you could blame them. But they were also strangely appealing. They'd camp at night with their fires alongside some old muddy irrigation ditch, I'd hear them laughing. I'd wanted to know them. They were exiles and misfits with nowhere to belong except to each other. Yet that was something, they had each other, and I'd wanted to be included, maybe slip into their camp at night and join them. They'd hand me a plate of chili and watch me eat. The chili would burn my mouth but I'd eat it anyway and we'd laugh. So that was why. They were laughing people and I wanted to laugh with them and feel good. If they liked me, maybe they'd keep me and take me with them. Then wandering the land, following the crops, I might've felt I belonged somewhere, but really belonged.

I remembered those days with both a warm feeling and a sense of loss. It was too late. I was too old now to just go off with a bunch of foreigners. I knew that. It wouldn't work. But when I was younger it seemed I'd come close. And if I had, I would've had a different life. I might've learned to laugh easier and take things in stride.

An hour later I'd climbed the water tower and stood looking down. Dalton was spread beneath me and appeared smaller than I'd imagined but it was my first high overall view of the entire town and that was interesting. I was surprised the streets looked straight and the square was actually square. My house was a smudge at the edge of town. I could barely see it and only in my mind with the clothesline mess and Sybil pacing in back. That was north. A layer of night. To the east, however, at the end of the one street lighted all the way, Darlene's house was clearly visible. So was Randy Caudell's and about six others in the same area. Each was a big home with shining yard lights and wide lawns. And space. It hit me. The area was known as Dalton Estates and every house had acres of space. All the others in town looked small and cramped. I felt struck. I was seeing the stark spread of the silent town, the darkness of smothered hovels jammed together, and to one side, this singular private compound, a picture that still holds. Those few spacious houses in their own special place. Could they see themselves? An illumination in a darkened world. A fortune in the midst of blight. I imagined the silken sheets Darlene must sleep on, the delicate china she must eat from, the smoothness and ease in every way she must live. She was going to Europe with trunks full of clothes. She'd come back with foreign lands stamped in her passport. But she'd come back to go away to college, back east, she said, and I would be left the same.

I kept looking at the town. The feed mill where Billy worked was next to the tracks. Billy would join the army soon and be gone four years. Then he'd come back and work in that mill another twenty years and end up with emphysema. The definition: "A condition of the lungs in which there is a dilation of the air vesicles following atrophy of the septa, resulting in labored breathing and increased susceptibility to infection." The condition, in Billy's case, from breathing grain dust. But he'd been a good worker, they said. He steadily filled a couple hundred sacks a day. Calculated over time at a thousand sacks a week, fifty weeks a year for twenty years, that's a million sacks of grain, a nice round number. But with every sack the same, one after another, the sameness measures a life.

I could see Fayette's daddy's furniture store on the corner of the square. In another year Fayette would marry Buster in the Church of the Nazarene. If she remembered me at all, it would probably be only dimly. She'd had her guidelines. She'd say, Tell me you love me, and when I did, she'd make it a trade, a quickie for love. Though not love, she had to know.

In the middle of the square, Skinny's Shoe Repair. Ol' Skinny with the end of his belt dangling and his mouth full of tacks. Some joker would slap him on the back—Hey, Skinny!—and Skinny would swallow his tacks. But he'd been fair with me, I wouldn't forget. Nor the leather he carved with such graceful smoothness it was almost mesmerizing to watch.

Off the square, the lighted Sinclair, the only all-night spot in town, but after midnight there were never any cars pulling in and Max, the night man, would sleep. You could wake him and he'd pee over the telephone wire. His one claim to fame. Still, an amazing feat.

On the western edge of town, Thumper Joe's boxcar. Today it would be condemned for human habitation but it was a good place for Thumper and Minie, too, when she moved in. It was low-maintenance housing.

Then farther west, the lumps of the junked cars around Puddle's house, his daddy's salvage yard. His daddy, the raging pint-size drunk. And big ol' good-hearted Puddles, the saddest story of all. His drunken daddy would hit him with a lead pipe and break his neck and Puddles would live the rest of his life paralyzed from the shoulders down. I wouldn't be there when it happened and I wouldn't know about it until more than twenty years later when I found him in a house for the handicapped in Houston. He was quadriplegic and skin and bones, his body a ninety-pound skeleton. I hardly recognized him but he could talk and move his head and we had a good visit. He wanted to know what I'd been doing, he'd thought about me a lot, he said. I told him I'd been moving around, and who could've known, I'd become a writer. Well, he knew. He'd read my first book and the story wasn't bad, he said, but he couldn't help feeling I'd left the real story between the lines. I told him he was probably right. For his part, he had a computer he worked with a pointer fixed to a special headband—his unicorn, he called it—and after fifteen years, he'd gotten a college degree. It had taken him that long, but guess what, he's been a real smartass and made straight A's. His daddy had whipped him for being a smartass. So what about his daddy? Well, the little man had died several years before. That was all. Was Puddles bitter? No. Not anymore. Would he have liked to walk again and feed himself and all that? Oh, sure, you bet. But he was all right. What is, is, he said. We talked a couple of hours and I left feeling I'd finally seen the real Puddles. The old Puddles had been trapped in the wrong body, he'd had to be the ignorant overgrown blimp people expected, but that body was gone now and the real Puddles was stronger. I'm not being insensitive. He was living a tragedy but he was also freer. He was living his mind.

That was in the future. For the moment I was still on the water tower looking down at the town and the surrounding night. I was seeing my whole world and for all I knew, the sudden flat limits of the rest of my days. I wanted to go home. But not to that place with the dirt yard and the chained dog and Myrtle. I wanted to go to where somebody like me and I liked them. But where was that?

It wasn't a choice. But it was also beginning to be dawn and another day. I climbed down the water tower.

I T WAS PROM NIGHT. I might've taken Fayette but I didn't want to be with her anymore so I was working instead. A slow night at the Sinclair. At ten o'clock Max arrived to take the night shift and I started to leave. At that same moment Darlene pulled up in her big Lincoln. "Want a ride?" She was dressed in a strapless blue formal. She should've been at the prom with Randy but he wasn't with her.

"You drive." She scooted over. I slid in behind the wheel and collected myself. I'd never driven a new car before. The engine was idling and I could barely hear it. The sound was a low luxurious purr. I thought, so this was what it felt like being rich, you felt smaller. There was so much room. The seat was wide and plush. "You're sure?" I said. "I might wreck us." She wasn't worried. The shift was automatic and I pushed the indicator to D, the car eased forward and we were immediately cruising weightlessly. But where to? Darlene snuggled my arm and her breasts against my arm was all I could think. "I want to dance," she said. Which had to mean the country club. The prom dance was at the country club. Her thigh moved against mine. "But not in a crowd," she said. The scent of her perfume was filling my brain. It might've been Shalimar, the Exotic East. Her thigh, the road to Mandalay. "I want us to be alone," she said. She put her arms around my neck, and murmured in my ear, I didn't know what, she was so warm and close. "Darlene—" She was nibbling my ear. "What are you doing?"

"I'm driving you crazy."

"You're toying with me."

"I'm playing." She was kissing my neck. "But with a prefix. It's called foreplaying." She bit my ear. "Want a hickey?"

I swerved off the road and pulled to a stop. She sat back and I stared at the headlights shining the space ahead. I didn't know where I'd driven. I was lost. I rested my head on the steering wheel and closed my eyes. She'd apparently ditched Randy to be with me, but why? Randy was Mr. Everything.

I said, "I don't think I'm handling this."

"Why?"

"Darlene, look, you can be with anyone, why me?"

"Why not?"

"Just tell me."

She took a moment. "All right, I'll tell you, I'm attracted to you."

"Attracted."

"I like your buns."

"My buns."

"You've got great buns."

"That's it?"

"Well, you're also kinda basic."

"Meaning what?"

"Think of it this way, a primary construction, sort of a rudimentary model with no frills attached."

"Like plain."

"But singular, one of a kind." She leaned into me and spoke softly. "Look, you, it's simple, let's don't make it complicated. I think you're audacious, I like that."

"But you're leading me."

She reacted. "I am?"

"It's like—" I couldn't find the words. "I dunno, it's like you're about four jumps ahead of me. I don't know if I can keep up, if I can do my best with you."

"Sure you can."

"You know more words than I do."

"That's a problem? Vocabulary?"

"You're smarter than I am."

She rolled her eyes. "Now it's my brains."

"You're beautiful."

"And that's bad?"

"I don't want to be a fool."

She laughed.

"Well, I don't." I hit the steering wheel, dammit, I was frustrated, I was ruining myself. But maybe hitting the steering wheel was what I needed. My mind miraculously cleared and I was my old self again. I took a breath. "Okay, here's the deal." I faced her. "It's like this. I think you're beautiful. I think you're wonderful, sexy, everything. You're also a little scary. So I'm afraid. Okay? Now that's the bad part." I paused. She waited. "The good part—" I paused again. A couple of good pauses, the audience is hooked. "The good part is, I don't care if I'm afraid, I'm going to give it my best shot. Which may not be good enough but no more hangdog why me stuff. Tonight it's you and me and we're going to have a great time."

She raised an eyebrow. "Now I think I'm afraid."

"You wanna dance?" I drove back onto the road. I was strong. The car was power. In the driver's seat, look, the Man of Destiny. The world the for the taking. And what a life, I thought. Up, down, good, bad, it was all there. You wanted a taste, help yourself.

"But where?" Darlene asked.

I patted her knee. "It's okay, kid, it's going to be fun."

So, finally, the night to remember. That night forever. It was going to hold my heart in thrall for thirty years nearly. It was going to break my heart and I've tried to understand but given the play of happenstance, the time and place, and someone like me with someone like Darlene, I can only believe it was inevitable.

The State Park again. We were alone and dancing in the sand. We'd kicked off our shoes. The car radio was playing the slow old songs and our bodies were pressed tightly, moving together. It seemed a dream. All around, the moonlit dunes, the starry sky. "Darlene," I whispered, "Darlene—" She shushed me. "Don't say it." Not words of love, she meant, don't ruin it. So I didn't. We were cheek to cheek, our eyes closed. I could smell the cleanness in her hair. Her body was a blend with mine. Her cheek was warm and smooth. When the music became a waltz we danced in slow circles round and round. We kissed. A light kiss. Her mouth lingered and I tasted her lips, delicious, moist, tender petals. It goes without saying I wanted her badly, but strangely, the wanting was without urgency.

Darlene eased from me and stepped away. She turned on the first dune and faced me. She had loosed her gown and it fell to her feet. Her eyes held mine. She dropped her bra and slipped out of her panties. She wanted me to see. A woman, not a girl. But suddenly a woman. It was clearly her moment and her way of sealing the moment, but for me, too. She was posed above me on a high dune, her body a silhouette against the dotted sky. The picture is frozen. She raised her arms. The music rose. Her leg lifted and extended. The dunes appeared to ripple beyond her and she was dancing. A shooting star streaked the night and I was held spellbound. She was dancing gracefully, elegantly, a singularly beautiful and exotic vision. She was a naked ballerina distinctly figured in a field of stars.

Not long. We'd already spread the blanket and I started to unbutton but she wouldn't let me. She wanted to unclothe me herself, and she did, yet so slowly and teasingly, it was almost more than I could stand. Then the first embrace was a splash of pure delight. It was so simple, so natural, we laughed and made love quickly. We lay afterward and held each other as if sleeping. But I was too filled with feeling. With love.

So again. I see myself raised, gazing down at her body. She is lying with one arm above her head, the other resting beneath her breasts. Her thighs are slightly parted with one knee bent wantonly to the side. I see myself traveling the fine lines of her body, the soft curves and dips, the perfect circles of her nipples. I kiss the pout of her navel and stroll the smooth paths of her thighs. I slide her calves. Her skin is like satin, and in all, in every way, she is completely beautiful. I feel the tide of her distant moon and the lure so whole it is weakening. I want to burrow, to descend and lose myself within her. I lick the sweetness between her legs and feel her rising. A soft purr in her throat pours down and she is quickly with me, quickly humid. She takes me in and holds me tight. Yes, she says. She is savoring her hold. Oh, yes. The sounds she makes are exciting and I can feel her flowing, her body pulling. She is needing me and I am needing her more. I want my body to fill hers completely even as she straightens and shivers and clutches me closer. I can't, please, I can't, she says. But she can't stop, she doesn't want to stop. She is swept to sea, the rolling of the sea has her, and her body at once becomes very precious to me. I want to save her and protect her, the helplessness in her. I feel a deep caring and the rushing in my hips and the flashing. Darlene feels it, too, and clasps me tighter. She wants it. She wants all of me to the last drop and cries. Then I am fading and she is absorbing me. I am dissolving and in another world it seems Darlene is holding my head to her breasts. Her tears are wet on my face and she is smearing the wetness with her mouth. She is kissing my face and rocking my head.

The first gray line of dawn was just beginning to show and we were stopped in her car behind the Sinclair. My car was back there, so this was to let me out, to say goodbye. Because this was the end. She was leaving the next day for Europe. I hadn't known it would be that soon but she was skipping the graduation ceremony. That was only a formality and she wanted to be gone. But it was so sudden, so abrupt.

She touched my arm. "I'll miss you."

"I'll miss you, too." My throat tight.

She put her arms around me and we held each other miserably. Or I held her miserably. But I loved holding her. She was the world to me.

She pulled back. "I have to go."

"I don't want you to. I don't want you to leave." She made a face. "Well, I don't," I said. I wanted to cry.

We sat a moment more. She nudged me. "C'mon, I have to go, I really do."

I forced myself to move. "Okay, you have to go." It seemed all I could do to get out of the car. She slid behind the wheel and raised her face. I leaned in and gave her a last kiss and stood back. "I hope you have a good trip," I said.

"Oh, I will. It's going to be fun."

I wanted to say something clever, to be easier, but I couldn't think. I tried to sound offhand. "So, I guess this is it."

"We don't have to say goodbye."

"Maybe just so long."

She smiled. "You won't forget me?"

I tried to laugh. "Are you kidding?"

She put the car in gear and hesitated. She bit her lip and a tiny hope leaped in my chest, she wasn't going, she was going to stay. She took a long breath and let it out. Her eyes held mine as if slightly pained. But only slightly. She smiled again, a small thin smile. "Okay?"

"Okay."

She pursed her lips in a kiss goodbye and drove away. The only love in my life. And just like that. I watched until her car disappeared. She didn't look back. Then I was simply standing in the road with nowhere to go, and it seemed absolutely flat nowhere. I was alone in the dreary gray dawn, and in my mind, alone in every way.

I finally shook myself. Well, what did you expect? She'd been attracted, she said. It was more like curious maybe, so she'd allowed herself a little fling on the side but at the last moment so she wouldn't have to fool with me again. And it wouldn't count. In her world it was slumming for fun. I could pretend I had some pride. I didn't. So chalk it up, a night in the sand, a little nooky in the park. She was going her way, that's all, I'd have to do the same. She had her life, I had mine. Besides, what's a little hurt? You get sideswiped, you pick yourself up and keep going. *Now, dammit, that's what you do!* I was suddenly kicking rocks in the road.

I think I went a little crazy, I don't know how long.

Then I was calmer and drove home. It was just beginning to be daylight but the house was still asleep. I went in the back door and found a wash hanging on lines strung the length of the porch with two lines particularly above my cot. I had to squat-walk to my cot. I didn't care. If this was a hint to make me put up the clothesline again, that would be a cold day in hell first. I lay down on my cot with my thoughts. I should've told Darlene my feelings. We were dancing, I'd wanted to whisper, Darlene, I love you. But she'd shushed me, don't say it, don't ruin it. I should've told her anyway. And it wasn't goodbye either. We didn't say goodbye. So it wasn't finished. I told her I didn't want her to go. I should've said, no, you can't go, I won't let you go. I was wide awake, my feelings in turmoil. But I was also aware the wash above my head was dripping. Billy was on his cot dead asleep. The wash wasn't bothering him. I moved my head but my pillow had been dripped on in that spot, too. All right, that did it. I jerked the lines down from over my head and the wash fell in a wet tangled heap. To hell with it. I gathered a gloppy armful and heaved the mess into the backyard. Sybil was already pouncing and pieces of shredded laundry began flying in the air. It was going to look bad. Good. I sat against the side of the shed and watched the show. Sybil was like a feeding shark and pretty soon the yard was littered with remnants of skirts, rubber girdles, the works. When Myrtle saw, her face would turn about four colors of purple probably. She'd appear stricken with blotched fever, maybe even have another heart attack. I couldn't wait. Sybil was crunching clothespins like doggie biscuits.

I started hearing inside the house the beginning of another dull morning, the creaking of the board floors, the calendar kids banging the bathroom door, Myrtle in the kitchen. No sound of Charlie. A man of no note. Billy was snoring. It would take him another ten minutes, he'd roll over and smack his mouth and go back to sleep.

I was still sitting against the shed but now with Sybil beside me, slobbering, trying to nuzzle a pat. Okay, okay, I patted his head. Jesus, you get a little affection, you want more, don'tcha? You and everybody else. But you smell, you know that? You oughta take a bath. I scratched his haunch, he sat grinning with his good eye closed wistfully, the white blind one staring out at space. He was so simple, a good scratching on his scruffy ol' hide, he really loved it. So what're you going to do? You think this is living, it's not even a dog's life. I was talking to myself and I saw as if from a distance a solitary form sitting in the dirt with a dog. The wind was starting and a smattering of sand was hitting against me. The night had been magic, a night of beauty. Now the world was bleakness. The house was tacked with tarpaper. I saw my face slowly blowing away in the wind. I saw an old man still working at the Sinclair. It could happen. Or I could slip out of the picture and disappear. Sybil was chained in place. People ended up the same.

I think that's when I decided I was going to leave after another week's pay. School was a thought. I had a year to go to graduate. But school didn't matter. I had a car, I could just take off. I would think later I should've planned ahead a little. I should've saved more money to start on. But I would also think

I'd left at the right time, too. Any longer, I might've lost my sense of humor with Myrtle.

She was at the screen door staring down at the littered laundry in the yard. Her jaw had dropped and it was like she couldn't believe her eyes. She was dumbstruck. Her face turned different colors and throttled sounds came from her throat. I hoped for a stroke but she finally gained control and her eyes pointed their aim at me. Now it was going to get good, I thought, let her rant. When she spoke, though, her voice was icy calm. "I suppose you think you deserve breakfast now."

"I don't want breakfast."

"Then don't expect any, not until you learn to behave."

"Well, y'know, I get these urges sometimes."

"You're going to learn to respect me."

"You ever see yourself in the mirror?"

"What's that supposed to mean?"

"You ever see that movie about the creature from outer space?"

"All right, that does it!" Her face was purple now. It was kinda funny. "No breakfast and no other meal either, not in this house, not one more bite, you hear? Now that's what you deserve. And that's not all. I want that clothesline back up and this time it better stay up. You're going to mind me and show some respect!" She stomped back in the house, the door slammed, and I heard the click, the kitchen door locked from inside.

I told Sybil, There, y'see, that's how you burn your bridges.

I slept in my car the next few nights and showered at the school gym. If I was missed at the house, I never heard. I ate at the school cafeteria with Puddles. He'd heaped his tray with enough food for four people and we'd both dig in.

Then school was out. The last week was only going through the motions, but the end of a school year was also a marker, the end of a way of life. I had another week's pay from the Sinclair and a total of $80, not a bad wad. So I was ready to go. The future was out there somewhere and I was going to find it. I'd head west to California, the land of movie stars and Sonny Tufts, and fate would see me through. I might even hop a freighter to the South Seas. In my mind, the Exotic East with palm trees and beautiful girls all the way from Rangoon to Mandalay. I'd recited Kipling in Miss Dowd's class. But I would live an exciting life. If I had to, I was experienced, I could get a job at a service station.

I went by the house to get my clothes. The stepkids were in the yard as I drove up. They saw me coming and ran into the house. That's right, outta my way, I thought. In back, Sybil was chained as always. I unchained him. I went onto the porch and stuffed my clothes in a pillowcase. Myrtle was not in sight. I imagined her stretched out on the couch in the living room taking her daily rest from doing nothing but I didn't bother to see. Outside again, Sybil was still there. I gave him a pat on the rump, Look, you're free, the chain's off. I stood back. He shook his head and looked around. He knew something was different but not exactly what. C'mon. I walked to the corner of the house and he started to follow but stopped automatically at the spot the chain had always ended. He stretched his neck and peered into the distance as if into the great unknown. What was out there? C'mon, I said. He looked at me hopefully and grinned, then paced back to the shed and returned, but again only to the place he'd always been stopped. It was like some invisible chain was still holding him and he could go no farther. I called him, C'mon, dammit, you're free! But Sybil had never been free, he'd been a prisoner his whole life. And just then I watched him revert to his old self pacing the length of a phantom chain, stiff-legged, the hair raised on his neck. Poor ol' Sybil, I thought. And that's the last I saw of him, chained all his days, the heart had been chained right out of him.

I drove away from the house, curious faces were peeking at me from the windows, the kids' small gargoyle faces, and maybe Myrtle's, too. She probably thought she'd won. She could think what she wanted. I roared away in a cloud of smoke.

I stopped at the feed mill. Billy was filling sacks from a pouring chute, his face covered with grain dust. I told him I was leaving, just thought I'd let him know.

He wagged his head. "Never satisfied, are you? You think you can take off somewhere and things'll be different, but you're just going to go off and get in trouble because that's what you do. You better stay put where you belong." He was concentrating on his sacks, shaking them, hefting them, making sure they were filling completely. The grain dust was hanging around his head in a heavy cloud. "You oughta listen to me," he said. "I know things you don't."

I told him I was still leaving and I was trying to make it friendly but if he didn't want to say goodbye, that was up to him. He gave me a look and I could see he was hurt. He was my big brother, he'd always wanted to look after me, but I wouldn't let him. He'd never been appreciated. "You're going," he said, "all right, then go, I got work to do." Fine, if that's the way he wanted it, I left him to it. No need to waste words. But when I got to my car, he called after me, "Hey, you take care, you hear, I'm not going to worry." He was standing on the loading dock and that made me feel better, he was hating to see me leave. I raised a hand and drove away. But the feed mill, I thought, you're filling sacks, one after another, pretty soon every sack's the same. You'd have to stand the monotony. You fill one sack, you've filled 'em all. And without knowing it, you're breathing, you're filling your lungs, too.

I didn't say goodbye to Charlie. I parked in front of the post office intending to go in, but I couldn't. Charlie would've been at his General Delivery window. I'd say, Well, I'm taking off. He'd mumble, Yeh, I figured you might. He'd pretend to count stamps. I'd wait for him to look at me but he'd keep his eyes averted, his mouth clamped. *Nope, no mail today. Are you sure? I was kinda expecting something. He'd slap his hand at an empty slot, Nope, nothing.* I'd stand there waiting for something to pass between us, I wouldn't know what, he wouldn't either, and that would be it. The best, I decided, was to simply close the door.

Which is easier said than done. Charlie was my father and remains in some way a determining part of me. If he loved me, I'm not sure I knew it. If he didn't, I probably figured early on the way it was. I think of him as an absence but I wonder sometimes if my memory of him is fair. It may not be. But it's the only memory I have. Marie and Myrtle were both domineering. Is that what he wanted? I feel he lived humiliated. Then I think: *Which of us has known his brother? Which of us has looked into his father's heart?* I pass on that one.

When I pulled up, Puddles was working with his dad in the middle of the junked cars beside his house. He didn't see me and I sat watching. His dad was mad at something and obviously drunk. The two of them were trying to free an engine part from an old wrecked pickup. Puddles was prying under the hood. His dad was banging the pickup with his wrench and reeling. Then he was swinging his wrench at Puddles but Puddles dodged and the little drunken man was carried around with his own swing in a hapless tilt-a-whirl until he fell down.

Puddles saw me and came over. We said a few words and he poked at the stuffed pillowcase on the seat beside me. My clothes, I told him, I was taking off, why didn't he come with me? Well, he couldn't, he had to help with the work, his dad couldn't do much anymore. His dad was stretched out on the ground staring straight up at the sun. He might have been catatonic. Was he going to make it? Oh, sure, he was just sorta passed out. I think at that moment I may have felt a shadow. I told Puddles he really oughta come with me. I was being serious but he still said he couldn't, his dad was depending on him, so I didn't press him. I should have. Puddles was a loyal friend. If you were happy, he was happy for you. If you felt bad, he'd feel bad with you. Ask him, he'd give you the shirt off his back. And I think of the word decent. Puddles was a completely decent human being who never hurt anyone.

I pulled away and at the end of the block, glanced back. Puddles had lifted his dad and was carrying the little guy over his shoulder into their house. But for Puddles, not much to lift, a small burden, I thought. Then I didn't look back again. I was headed west and feeling good.

Now, the last turn with Tracy.

First, there was no Six Flags commercial and hadn't been, that was the subject. Or it was the spark for a deeper hurt and Tracy started in, I'd lied, I didn't love her. She was mad, then crying, then mad again. For once I didn't want the hassle and left the house. Let her calm down. One of her tantrums could last for hours.

I drove around. Another time, I might've gone to the Chateau Club and had a few drinks where the bartender and I were old conspirators. By that I mean he always knew to tell Tracy when she called that I wasn't there. The bartender was Johnny Khuel, pronounced Cool. Great name. This time though I didn't want to drink, I wanted to get back to my writing, so I cruised the streets a couple of hours, then went home.

Which was probably a mistake.

Tracy had trashed my desk and read what I'd written about Darlene, several pages, but one sentence especially caught her eye: "I remember the taste of you and the touch of you and exactly the way it was being inside you." Not great literature but that's what tipped it for Tracy. Six Flags had been bad enough, now I was fucking another woman. Not true, but Tracy knew what she'd read, right there on the printed page. I told her she had it wrong. She still had to know, who was the woman? I said, "Oh, c'mon, that's not even a woman, that's a seventeen-year-old girl." Now—don't say it, I know—I should have phrased it differently. Too late. Tracy heard the present tense and imagined a seventeen-year-old, the age she would never be again. Besides I'd written of being in love. I said that was in the past. In my heart of course it wasn't in the past and Tracy sensed that. So I was lying and fucking another woman/girl, whoever, and more, I was in love with somebody not Tracy. What was wrong with me? She was screaming. I tried to hold her. She slapped me. I grabbed her wrists and she started kicking. I finally held her wrapped against me until she stopped. She didn't have to be mad, I said. She appeared to calm. Now, that's better, I wanted her to listen, okay? Okay. She was controlled so I released her and stepped back. It always seemed a trick that she could so quickly switch like that from rage to composure. Which was real?

She sat on the edge of the bed and waited—well?

Well, how to talk when no one understands? I started lying. I was writing a story, I said, just a story. It wasn't anything that ever happened, only fiction, one hundred percent pure fiction.

She didn't pretend to believe me and I kept trying to logically prevaricate. I said it had to do with imagination, I was a creative person, right? Look at the TV stuff I produced, I was good at imagining things—and so on. Then I saw myself. I was pretending to spare her feelings. My real concern was my own feelings. I was sick of arguments and emotional tantrums, they were so damned draining, but look at me, I'd turned into a mealy-mouth hedging for the sake of peace. And that was weak. You're a man, you should stand your ground. Otherwise you're cowed into meekness. The wife hammers, pretty soon the man sits in flattened silence, the mousy husband. I had in mind, I'm sure, Myrtle and Marie. They could browbeat their men. Not me.

I stopped talking.

Tracy looked up. Finished? Yeah, I was through pussyfooting. You're not happy, all right, let's get it out, let's spell it out once and for all, what's the problem?

"One thing," same old thing, "why can't you love me?"

"Tracy, I repeat," but this time with the qualifier, "I love you as much as I can."

"How much?"

"I'm sure not as much as you'd like."

"Then what's wrong with you?"

"Why is it me?"

"Then it's me?"

"No, I'm not saying that. I'm saying why does something have to be wrong with me if you're not happy?"

"Because I don't understand." She didn't cry but she sat looking at me with teary eyes. Help me. The only child. The center of a universe. She'd been special. And spoiled. And beautiful. Men had always loved her. They had only to look at her to love her because desire was love and every man she knew desired her.

They could prove it, too. Why couldn't I? She was sitting there expressing need waiting for me to make it better. The term "emotionally unavailable" was not used then but that was probably me.

I said, "I guess I don't want to be hurt again."

I said that? I'd never known I felt that way. Hurt was what you shrugged off. You were hurt, you didn't whimper, you went on. But hurt was what happened when you loved and couldn't help it, you were left behind, the middle was left a hollow of pain. Darlene. Jimmy. And maybe it started with Marie, who knows? You can talk the lingo, repression, sublimation, you're chasing your tail in a circle. Look, this is the world, everyone gets hurt, line up and take your turn. I might've had that attitude. But not that hard-lined. Tracy was almost in tears and I wanted to sympathize. If I didn't love her enough, I still liked her a lot. I liked her more than I knew. Yet it was hopeless. She was waiting. I could give a little sympathy, she'd need more. And that was the thing, she was so damned *needy*.

"Help me," she said. The help she meant was in the bodily department. She would pull me down with her. It would be a replay of a hundred other times because as always her frustration with me aroused her sexually. That's what the fighting was for. So we could fuck mindlessly and the rest would hold off for another day. But the fucking was never enough either, even as she described it with the thousand silvery fishes swimming her body, the promised land was beyond her. And I'm not talking orgasms. She had those. She would come again and again. She was simply never answered, if that's the word. In an odd moment once, she told me, "I wanted release. I thought you would release me." I imagined a cliché, a bird in a cage. But what did she mean? Well, it was a line she'd heard in a movie and it sounded good so she thought she'd try it out, what did I think?

I told her she had it right, it sounded good. But of all the lines to pick, that one had somehow struck a chord with her. She was the girl waiting for the highwayman to return by moonlight and steal her away. I don't knock it, but romance and moonlight *every* night? Half the time the moon is behind clouds. But back to release. We all know the feeling. We're so small in the overall and there's so much within with no place to go and only one time to be—it's like being trapped, *forever prison-pent*. So what to do? I don't know. You can wait at the window for the rescue but in the poem the highwayman never returns.

Tracy looked so forlorn, I put my arms around her. I knew better. I intended comfort, she wanted more. As I said, fighting turned her on and I've never understood, how can you be mad as hell for three solid hours and suddenly switch to melting passion? Well, I say I don't understand, I do. But for me at the time, when the fighting was with Tracy, I was usually turned off. She would switch, I wouldn't, and then I wouldn't want to be prodded into faking it. Which is tough to do. A woman can say she's not in the mood, that's a time-honored reason. You're a guy, it's different, you have to pretend you can't get it up because you want it so bad you're trying too hard and thinking about it too much. The woman says, hey, it's okay, relax. This forces you into faking it more subtly.

I put my arms around Tracy and she pulled me down with her. I can't, I said. She was already breathless, massaging and kneading my body, Yes, you can. It took an effort to pull away and stand. She rolled in a groan in my empty place and buried her face in the pillow. I'm sorry, I said.

I went to write in the sunroom. My special place to be and all inside my head. A place to find meaning. I'd thought to write first of the time I'd been shot in California, now that had to be significant, I'd faced death, right? But it turned out to be only an incident, not even interesting. Then how about Jimmy? But I couldn't write about him, not then. So I wrote about Darlene, the part Tracy read.

Now I was into it again. Darlene, the girl of my dreams. Yet how much was fantasy, how much real? It didn't matter. But why didn't I ever really love another woman? Simple, I compared every woman with Darlene and they all fell short. Which meant maybe I was using the ideal of Darlene as an excuse to play it safe, to keep from being hurt again. Could be. Dump them before they dump you. But I couldn't feel I was ever that afraid. So instead of the fear of hurt again, what if I'm only the detached type? Sounds good. Except then I'd always need someone from whom to be detached. Can't win that one. So back to Darlene. She said, look, it's simple, let's don't make it complicated. So we didn't. In fact the first embrace was so simple, so natural, it was—how to say it—refreshing? A splash of pure delight? Yes. Close enough. I wrote that, "The first embrace was a splash of pure delight. It was so simple, so natural—"

I looked up. Tracy was standing in the doorway. What? She didn't move but only stared blankly, her face pale beneath her dark hair. She was standing in a long ghostly nightgown. Finally her lips moved and she said dully, "I can't stand this." It wasn't a conversation. She made a hopeless turn and walked away.

I suppose in her mind I had gone from her to another woman, even if it was only into that room, it was still a betrayal. I was fucking that girl on the page and my words of love were for someone else. So what if it was an imaginary rendezvous in some nebulous space, it was a personal space that excluded Tracy. Okay, I could understand. It wasn't very grown-up on Tracy's part but she was jealous and I didn't know what else but as long as she saw me writing in that room, she was going to see me with another woman. It was going to be one emotional trauma after another. Or I could stop writing. But I wasn't going to do that. My mind was set. I sat back and looked around. Nice room. My place to be. Except the place wasn't going to be in this spot anymore, was it? Not the way Tracy was acting. So, only one thing to do.

The next morning I rented a small apartment on the west side of town. It was going to be my writing retreat where Tracy couldn't see and wouldn't be bothered. I believe I also intended to keep the place a secret but how I imagined I could do that, I have no idea. Where were you? Out, with a client. I could say that a couple of times, but night after night, it wasn't going to fly. Besides, I had nothing to hide. "Look, it's a place I'm writing, that's all, you want to check on me, here." I gave her the address. Big mistake. For the next week she had me staked out. How she then obtained a key to the apartment is still a mystery. A locksmith? I never knew.

Incidentally, the morning after she said she couldn't stand it, Tracy was still in her nightgown and her face was still pale, but she had given it a lot of thought, she said, and she wanted to have a baby, our baby. A pretended hope in her eyes. But what else could she do? Her worth had been reflected in men, in her ability to capture men with her beauty, her sex. It had been easy. Then simply put, I believe the capture was somehow her life's measure of accomplishment. It was how she saw herself judged. But now this one man was escaping, and especially with his writing, so she was losing. And time, too, was passing. If she didn't look thirty, she would. Maybe a baby was a way to still win.

But a baby. Tracy didn't know about Jimmy. I'd never told her, and the word, baby, froze in my blood. You bring a child into this world, it's on you to protect that child and keep it safe. No, no way, I said. And I wasn't about to discuss it.

Tracy didn't push it, she hadn't really wanted a baby anyway, but in the next days it seemed a vague pressure weighed in the air around me. Out there. MorningStar was out there. Tracy was out there. I didn't want to fool with MorningStar and I didn't want to contend with Tracy. So I stayed mostly in my apartment with my writing. It was Step One, learning to write. I didn't know Step Two is never learned. But I couldn't escape entirely. Vicky kept calling, I was needed to take care of business. A couple of training films were in the works, nuts-and-bolts stuff. I told Irving he could handle them. He knew the nuts-and-bolts side better than I did anyway. But Irving couldn't make decisions. Besides, the clients expected me. So, okay, I made an appearance several times, in and out. Then two nights in a row I slept in the apartment. Without quite realizing it, I was replacing a pointless hole in my life with some sort of purpose.

I was also into replacing all the big words I had purposely located on most pages in order to appear more intelligent. Words like "solipsist," "exiguous." I had remembered Pascal in his *Précis* said when he read a book he expected to encounter an author, but with a good book, he met a natural man instead. A neat point. So no big words for me, even if I knew what they meant. And the shorter the word the better to be clear and simple. Now that's the way to write, I thought.

As if I could. But I was excited. I believed I had discovered a breakthrough on my own and with a few plain words, I would get right to the meat of meaning. And it wouldn't take long.

So I was in the apartment scribbling away. A knock on the door. What's a shorter word for oblivious? I was sort of aware but didn't answer. The next I knew the door was being strangely unlocked and opened. It was Tracy, of course, but where did she get the key? She stood framed in the doorway in a sexy dress, Hi.

Well, hello. Am I invited? Sure, come in. We were acting friend-ly except she appeared a little blurry. Her shoulder bag dropped and she wobbled picking it up, then sat on the couch with her eyes not quite focusing. Guess what, she smiled, I'm drunk. She groped in her bag and pulled out a bottle. Jack Daniel's. Got a glass? I handed her a paper cup. I wasn't set up with glasses and dishes. Where's yours? She asked. I didn't want one. She poured herself a drink and missed setting the bottle on the table. Whoops. Liquor spilled on her dress. My party dress, too, she said, she was celebrating. She downed her drink and made a face. Ugh. I'd never seen her drunk before. What's the occasion? I asked. What occasion? She laughed, then remembered, Oh, the occasion! She was getting a divorce, didn't I know? I told her she was snockered. No, she was happy and she was getting a divorce because she'd been abandoned. The word abandoned came out slurred. She raised the bottle again. Sure you won't join me? It was such a switch. She was drinking, I wasn't, and for the first time in my life it seemed I was the only sober person in a room full of drunks. It was almost a new perspective.

But the break was coming. She'd said divorce and I was glad I wouldn't have to say it first. Where had we connected anyway? Maybe in pretense. But she'd needed more attention than I could give and felt ignored. Well, I had ignored her, whoever she was. I still didn't know. And she didn't know me. We'd lived together without becoming acquainted. And like a joke, I'd even expected to be understood when I couldn't understand myself. She imagined we were dancing on the exciting edge of showbiz. I saw it as the edge of an abyss. And the list goes on. But it's the usual list. We were the modern American twosome, a cou-ple of strangers.

"So this is it?" Tracy meant the apartment, casting her eyes around the room. It was her first time inside. Until now she'd only watched from her car parked down the block. She shook her head. "And you're writing," she said. She repeated "writing," like a sound she couldn't fathom, then she was no longer smiling but suddenly morose. I knew the itinerary. With the first drinks, you're traveling levitated, look, no hands, it's not real time, then around a corner, the vehicle crashes. A darkness takes hold. You don't know it but you're in the depths, in pain. The drinking is supposed to anesthetize the pain, it only spreads the darkness, and right there is where the demon appears, sometimes a bunch of demons. Nobody's responsible, and perhaps they won't remember, but in the depths of that darkness the nicest people go bad and do terrible things. The kill is made.

I might have seen it coming. I don't think I did.

Tracy said, "So where is she?" I ignored her. But she wanted to know. I tried saying, C'mon, Tracy, don't do this, don't be this way. She wasn't registering. "She's right there, isn't she?" Pointing and shaking her finger at my writing table, her eyes glittering. It was crazy. It was also the precise moment I knew all I wanted from Tracy was to be left to myself. It came out, "Now that's enough, you got a problem, it's yours, not mine, so take it somewhere else, I don't care, leave me alone!" Something like that. But inebriates don't listen. I was yelling at myself. I exited into the bathroom. Calm down. I hated the damn fighting. Maybe she'd just leave. But she was drunk, I couldn't let her drive that way, I'd have to take her home. Okay, I'd do it. I was a good guy. She'd be sober tomorrow, we'd make it a clean break, we still liked each other, we could part friends, see each other occasionally, have dinner, maybe a nooner now and then, that's the way it should have been all along. It wasn't her fault. It was the constant togetherness.

I splashed my face with water. Now, this next part lasted perhaps a minute. It seemed longer. But the way I remember it, if

I'm not mistaken, I splashed my face, and in doing that, in bending over, the bullet missed my head. The shot sounded, the mirror shattered. I probably ducked, then I was flattened against the wall beside the door. A small hole was in the door. Another shot sounded, another hole appeared, but higher up almost missing the door. Not aiming good, I thought. Yet the first shot could have been a direct hit. I felt the blood rushed to my face, my senses alive to every hair on my head. I'd have to be quick to knock the gun away. She'd want to see the results and open the door, I'd better be ready. In my mind, she had the pistol from the garage, but how had she known where to find it? She would've ransacked the garage, the house first, and she'd planned this, maybe not the shooting through the door, she didn't know I would turn my back and walk away, and that's what did it, seeing my back leaving her and the door closing. She'd lost it. But she'd purposely brought the weapon, and a friendly drink first, to celebrate. She wasn't a drinker but she'd been abandoned and she'd carried the pistol in her bag along with the bottle. Sure you won't join me? Nicely. Why not make it pleasant? She'd rehearsed in her mind. First, a sociable drink, a little stage business, smiling, levitated. This was acting. The bottle was Jack Daniel's. I would've made it Old Charter. But she wouldn't remember. She'd already crashed. Another shot sounded, only this time no hole popped in the door and I didn't feel an impact in the wall. The bullet had gone off in another direction.

Then nothing. Silence.

That was the scariest. The waiting. The room was so abruptly quiet with not a tick of movement, not a living sound, my brain leaped, the last shot, she'd shot herself, jesus, she'd planned both me and herself. Now her body would be slumped on the couch. I jerked the door wide. At the same instant the room exploded my face with more shots. But I wasn't hit and she wasn't slumped. She was standing away in her sexy dress shooting my writing table. I believe I actually thought, Hey, man, you're killing the fucking table! Then I distinctly saw her cocked hip, her high heels, and the beautiful line of her legs as she turned with the gun pointed straight at my face, the pistol so heavy it appeared she could hardly lift it, and not the hidden pistol but a different larger one with the round rifled eye wavering—the thing kicked and the shot blasted my ears, but I had already moved and knocked the pistol from her hands.

Tracy didn't struggle, didn't collapse, didn't do anything. She was only blurry and vaguely smiling. I was beginning to shake. Hi, let's have a drink, she said. As if she'd just arrived. We were standing in the middle of the room. That was all. But she was so bleary she couldn't focus. I pulled her into my arms and held her close. Oh, Tracy, Tracy, I thought, what happened to the pretty child? She may have felt me trembling. What's the matter? she asked. It was so damned sad. We were both so damned pitiful.

I finally took her hand. C'mon, I said, let's go home.

Final details:
Tracy was passed out by the time we made it home and I put her to bed. Then I didn't have to think, my course was already set. And I think it was the right course. If I stayed with Tracy, I was going to continue to be the problem. But I was afraid to leave her alone. I called Sara to come over and she arrived with Spencer. I didn't tell them about the shooting, only that I was leaving and Tracy was pretty distraught, she'd need a friend. Sara said she'd take over and stay. Spencer, too.

In that way I was out of the house before Tracy woke. You

can say I passed on the responsibility. I moved into another apartment and this time I kept the location secret. It would take me a few weeks more to be gone entirely. Meanwhile Tracy tried to find me at MorningStar but I was never there so we only talked on the phone. Again, what was wrong with me, why was I gone? She didn't understand. I described the shooting episode. She flatly denied it. How could I make up such an insane story? It never happened. I didn't push it. And I imagine to this day her mind is still blanked on the subject. Which may be normal for someone who acted so completely out of sync and would never act that way again.

So what happened? I'll say it was partly my fault. I was certainly the wrong person at the wrong time in Tracy's life. Or it might have been anyone, but I think my particular makeup sparked some darker character in her. A darker force. I usually don't much buy that kind of theory, but neither can I much explain it otherwise.

When Tracy didn't immediately file for divorce, I did. She claimed she'd never mentioned the word divorce. She didn't want one. Then a little vanity crept in. She decided she should be the one to say she'd divorced me, not the other way around. So she filed. And that was fine with me. Then it was no contest. She wanted half, I gave her everything, the house, furniture, car, a nice chunk of cash, and I assumed all debts. And it wasn't so much I was being generous, I just didn't care. I wanted to be gone. I ended up with enough money to last me a year if I watched my pennies.

The day I left town for good, I called to tell her. She was still hurt. A woman scorned. She said I would find out someday what I had missed and she hoped I would go to hell. I asked her if that meant she wished me well. With that, her humor returned and we talked almost as friends. She was worried I didn't know what I was doing. I had thrown away everything, not incidentally a beautiful wife, and what man in his right mind would do that? She really thought I should "seek professional help." She used the jargon. I told her she might be right, I might not know what I was doing, but I was okay. We said goodbye pleasantly. The following morning I was in Portugal. The final divorce papers arrived in the mail a couple months later and I signed them. In the next year Tracy married Spencer and somehow I wasn't surprised. Spencer was the attentive type and old enough to be her father. Maybe that's what she wanted.

MorningStar went to Vicky and Irving. That is, we made a deal they would buy the business by paying me a percentage of the earnings. It turned out they didn't make the earnings and went out of business within about six months. No big loss. Vicky and Irving moved on to another film company in Houston. As for me around that time, I was in Austria, not Portugal, and halfway into my first novel. A good place to be.

The day I left Dallas, I remember, I felt suddenly freed. Anyone seeing would've raised the alarm: Stop him, he's escaping! But I was already gone. I felt even better than the day I left Dalton. The future was still out there somewhere and I was going to find it. Only this time I should've known, no matter how far the future, the past always follows.

And in that regard, I want to mention Marie again.

After my first book, Marie wrote to me through my publisher. She'd read about me in the *Dallas Times Herald*, a feature article saying I was a former Dallas resident who'd become a novelist.

Now over the years I'd seen Marie a few times but each time only briefly and it had been perhaps ten years since I'd seen her last. When her letter reached me, however, I was living in Texas again and it just happened she was in a town only a hundred miles away, so I drove by to see her.

This was in 1972 and she was married to what turned out to be her last husband. She was also the same as I remembered her when I was eleven, twelve, fourteen. That is, she was still an unhappy person given to mood swings, laughing one minute and depressed the next. And as always, as she said, her life was a mess. She'd broken a leg. Her husband was unemployed. I gave them a little money and made it a short visit.

In the next twenty years I saw Marie infrequently at yearly intervals and each time, again, only briefly. We never became close. I'd sit with her an hour and she'd talk a steady stream of negatives. I'd pretend to listen and make my exit. Then every few months she'd write to tell me her troubles. Her husband had died, she'd been terribly sick, she had migraines, her car needed repairs, and so on. Her letters were always lengthy complaints and I didn't care to receive them but I suppose I felt I should try to help when I could. If I didn't love her, she was still my mother, there was that inexplicable tie, and I felt sorry for her. But whatever I tried to do never made her happy. And I'm not sure she really wanted help, not until she was virtually hiding as a recluse and I moved her into my house, then the real help she wanted, that she thought I could handle, was her final request. Which I may not have handled. It still preys on my mind.

POSTSCRIPT

THE YEAR IS 1976 and I've written two novels. It's also early evening in midtown Manhattan and I'm at the bar in the Algonquin. Supposed to meet my agent later. Because I have one now, Sterling Lord, Madison Avenue, New York City. I always think, gee, what a terrific name and address. Henry Smith, 43rd Street, just wouldn't have the same ring to it. I'm musing to myself. When people ask, I say I'm a writer but I'm not comfortable with that label. I really think I'm somehow more a person who also happens to write. What's a writer, any-way? Gotta watch those labels. You're a human being first. Of course, you can also be a jackass. But I'm thinking, how does anyone become who they are? The everyday improbabilities are so surprising, I like pondering the quirks of fate. We want to believe in cosmic forces at work, but all the while it's a quirk. The world turns on a dime.

Anyway, I'm at the bar having a drink. I don't imbibe when I'm writing, don't want to, but I'm in between books and this is New York. My night out. Tomorrow I'll be gone to Mexico where maybe I can afford to live awhile. After two novels, and because of two novels, my livelihood is sorta hand-to-mouth, month-to-month. I don't mind. It's the way I started out. So in a way I've circled back. Yet all in all I have a good life. I'm lucky. I sip my drink with the ghosts of the old Algonquin Round Table at my shoulder, Thurber and Parker and all those old acerbic wits. But I'm not thinking about them. I'm remember-ing that night. I'm always remembering that night. Only this time I'm seeing her face more clearly. It's like a mirror image. I blink. Still, her face is reflected before me. Talk about improb-abilities, this is a heart stopper. I shut my eyes. Need to get it straight. Two drinks. So I'm not drunk, a little high maybe, but definitely not drunk. Oh, boy, I think, how many times have I imagined *across a crowded room, some enchanted evening,* the car radio playing that song, the dunes shining in the moonlight? We would meet again someday and it would be that same night again.

I opened my eyes and her face was still in the mirror behind the bar. Four places down, the same sinful beauty, the same lips, and that look—*just put that on my daddy's account, wouldja? Across the plain of the dash and the moon of the steering wheel.* But the look was slightly changed now. She was older. I sipped my drink. She was no longer the beautiful girl, but a beautiful woman, a lovely exquisite woman. Or I'll just say it, she was a knockout. Her dress obviously expensive, a single strand of pearls at her throat, *in a field of stars.* But how long, how many years? Twenty, No, twenty-four years, a lifetime. She would be forty-one but with her face still smooth and perfect. I took a long drink. She hadn't seen me yet. She was alone and sipping a glass of wine. Not Mogen David. I'd drunk most of the Mogen David. She glanced at the door as if expecting someone. *I looked up and there they were gliding by in Randy Caudell's new Ford Deluxe. She was laughing and it was like they were comfortable and careless, they were happy maybe, and they had time, my sudden thought, they had all the time in the world to go someplace and have fun and never think a thing about it.* She was so far above me but she'd said, I think you're wonderful. In the flat nowhere. Did she mean it? I should have told her my feelings. Did she know I'd written my first book for her and no one else had ever come close, even the ones I might've loved? *Our faces covered with sand, she licked her finger and made lines on my cheek and on my forehead and chin. Ha! Cochise. I licked my finger and painted lines on her face the same but I couldn't name her. She'd become a strange and wonderful primitive mask and I'd felt mesmerized. She was the face of woman down through the ages.*

I took another drink. Don't get silly, I thought. It's been a long time. Just be yourself and act natural. *But who was me in any room anywhere? I didn't have the foggiest blinkiest notion.*

I took a deep breath. Now or never. Four places down, four steps. I approached. She was facing away.

"Excuse me."

She turned. So close. So near. I felt weak. "Darlene?"

"Yes?" She waited.

"Remember me?" A small frown, she didn't recognize me. But I had a mustache, I looked different. "Bobby Jack—back in Dalton—I worked at the Sinclair, remember?"

She raised her chin. "Oh, yes—in Dalton." She smiled. "So. How are you?"

I laughed. I was excited. "I'm fine, just fine. And you?"

"I'm fine, too." She took a sip of wine and she was the same, poised, confident. The way she sipped her wine held me, the way her tongue delicately touched the glass.

I tried to sound casual. "So. What've you been doing?"

"Oh, different things."

"Well, that sounds interesting." I said that? "I mean, different things—" I was so vague to her, I'd meant so little. She glanced at her watch. I hurried, "Can I buy you a drink?"

"I'm sorry, I'm meeting someone." And she was. A man would come in, not Randy Caudell, but a handsome distinguished-looking man with silver hair and an air of command. He would kiss her cheek and they would leave together.

I felt suddenly stupid. She didn't remember but I'd never told her my true feelings and the moment was passing. "Darlene, you didn't know—" I gave it my best chuckle. "I mean, this is kinda funny. Back in Dalton, y'know, you were the most beautiful girl in the world. I was in love with you. Really. I was always in love with you." She had to think I was an idiot. I stopped. Then I couldn't help it, I said helplessly, "I still am."

Her eyes changed. I thought she was going to be alarmed, but she was only beginning to see me. She didn't move and I could tell she was remembering, if barely, hazily. I felt frozen. I stood miserably.

Then her face softened and she sighed. Her lips formed my name, "Bobby Jack—" She reached her hand gently to my cheek, her eyes filled with infinite tenderness. "Oh, Bobby Jack," she murmured, "we never left the Sinclair, did we?"

That was all. The man she was waiting for came in at that moment. He apologized for being late. Was she ready? Yes, of course. Then they had to go, they had to hurry, and I was left standing. I watched them walk away until they disappeared in the lobby. She never looked back.

She'd said "we." Was that patronizing or sympathetic? And by never leaving the Sinclair, were "we" still stuck in the past? Or just me? I didn't want to know. I only knew I'd seen my soul in her eyes and felt her melting touch on my cheek.

I sat back at the bar. Well, so, that's how it ends, I thought. I felt bad. Then I didn't. Who would've thought, from out of the blue, I'd seen Darlene again and she was still beautiful and my dream of her was the same. Not a thing had changed. If I had meant nothing to her, what mattered was what she had meant to me. The dream of love, I thought, but what else was love?

Besides, this was New York, my night out. I motioned to the bartender. "Set 'em up, drinks for the house." What the hell, easy come, easy go, shoot the works. Fortunately, there were only about four other people in the bar, I could afford it. The bartender set the drinks around. The guy on the end stool raised his drink to me and I raised mine to him, Cheers.

The thing is, you pick up the pieces, you keep going.